D0516804

ENCYCLOPEDIA OF ENVIRONMENTAL ISSUES
ENERGY AND ENERGY USE

ENCYCLOPEDIA OF ENVIRONMENTAL ISSUES
ENERGY AND ENERGY USE

Editor

Craig W. Allin

Cornell College

SALEM PRESS

A Division of EBSCO Publishing, Ipswich, Massachusetts

Cover photo:
Wind farm in field. (© Frank Krahmer/Corbis)

ISBN: 978-1-42983-674-6

Table of Contents

Contributors

Robin Attfield
Cardiff University

Anita Baker-Blocker
Ann Arbor, Michigan

Grace A. Banks
Chestnut Hill College

Raymond D. Benge, Jr.
Tarrant County College-Northeast Campus

Alvin K. Benson
Utah Valley University

Cynthia A. Bily
Macomb Community College

Victoria M. Breting-García
Houston, Texas

Bruce G. Brunton
James Madison University

Robert S. Carmichael
University of Iowa

Thomas Clarkin
University of Texas at San Antonio

Matt Deaton
University of Tennessee

Joseph Dewey
University of Pittsburgh

George J. Flynn
State University of New York at Plattsburgh

James S. Godde
Monmouth College

Hans G. Graetzer
South Dakota State University

Phillip A. Greenberg
San Francisco, California

Wendy C. Hamblet
North Carolina A&T State University

Clayton D. Harris
Middle Tennessee State University

C. Alton Hassell
Baylor University

Jennifer F. Helgeson
Grantham Research Institute on Climate Change and the Environment

Thomas E. Hemmerly
Middle Tennessee State University

Joseph W. Hinton
Portland, Oregon

Laurent Hodges
Iowa State University

Bruce E. Johansen
University of Nebraska at Omaha

Karen N. Kähler
Pasadena, California

Joseph Kantenbacher
University of California, Berkeley

Narayanan M. Komerath
Georgia Institute of Technology

Padma P. Komerath
SCV, Inc.

Josué Njock Libii
Indiana University-Purdue University Fort Wayne

Donald W. Lovejoy
Palm Beach Atlantic University

Marianne M. Madsen
University of Utah

Sergei A. Markov
Austin Peay State University

Roman Meinhold
Assumption University

M. Marian Mustoe
Eastern Oregon University

Alice Myers
Bard College at Simon's Rock

Mysore Narayanan
Miami University

Peter Neushul
California Institute of Technology

Dónal P. O'Mathúna
Dublin City University

John Pichtel
Ball State University

Victoria Price
Lamar University

James L. Robinson
University of Illinois at Urbana-Champaign

Charles W. Rogers
Southwestern Oklahoma State University

Joseph R. Rudolph, Jr.
Towson University

Elizabeth D. Schafer
Loachapoka, Alabama

Rose Secrest
Chattanooga, Tennessee

R. Baird Shuman
*University of Illinois at Urbana-
    Champaign*

Courtney A. Smith
Parks and People Foundation

Dion Stewart
Adams State College

Toby Stewart
Duluth, Georgia

Rena Christina Tabata
University of British Columbia

John R. Tate
Montclair State College

John M. Theilmann
Converse College

Donald J. Thompson
California University of Pennsylvania

Shawncey Webb
Taylor University

Winifred O. Whelan
St. Bonaventure University

William C. Wood
James Madison University

Lisa A. Wroble
Redford Township District Library

Robin L. Wulffson
*Faculty, American College of Obstetrics
    and Gynecology*

Alternative energy sources

CATEGORY: Energy and energy use

DEFINITION: Sources of energy other than the dominant fossil and mineral fuels

SIGNIFICANCE: Energy sources that offer alternatives to the burning of fossil fuels such as coal and petroleum are urgently needed to address rising demand for energy in ways that will not contribute to air pollution and climate change. The ideal alternative energy source is renewable or inexhaustible and causes no lasting environmental damage.

Both the extraction and the burning of fossil fuels have caused severe and growing damage to the environment, contributing to such problems as air pollution, the release of greenhouse gases (which retain heat and contribute to climate change), and sulfuric acid in rainfall. Nuclear energy sources are very limited in supply and expensive, require extreme amounts of processing, and produce long-lasting radioactive waste. In the long term, energy release from nuclear fusion has been proposed as a limitless supply of power, but industrial-scale production of fusion power continues to pose large and uncertain obstacles and hazards.

SOLAR POWER

The sun powers winds, ocean currents, rain, and all biomass growth on the earth's surface. Because the availability and extraction means for each of these secondary sources of solar power are diverse, each forms a different field of alternative energy technology. Where solar power is extracted and converted to energy directly, the capture can be by means of flat-plate receivers that collect at the incident intensity but can operate in diffuse light, or by means of concentrators that can achieve intensities of several hundred suns but work poorly in diffuse light.

In solar photovoltaic power (PV) technology, solar radiation is directly converted to useful power through PV cell arrays, which require semiconductor mass-production plants. PV cell technologies have evolved from using single-crystal silicon to using thinner polycrystalline silicon, gallium arsenide, thin-film amorphous silicon, cadmium telluride, and copper indium selenide. The needed materials are believed to be abundant enough to meet projected global growth. The process of purifying silicon requires large inputs of energy, however, and it generates toxic chemical waste. Regeneration of the energy required to manufacture a solar cell requires about three years of productive cell operation.

Solar cell technology continues to evolve. Broadband solar cell technologies have the potential to make cells sensitive to as much as 80 percent of the energy in the solar spectrum, up from about 60 percent. High-intensity solar cells could enable operation at several hundred times the intensity of sunlight, reducing the cell area required when used with concentrator mirrors and enabling high thermal efficiency.

Direct solar conversion is another option. Laboratory tests have shown 39 percent conversion from broadband sunlight to infrared laser beams using neodymium-chromium fiber lasers. Direct conversion of broadband sunlight to alternating-current electricity or beamed power through the use of optical antennae is projected to achieve 80 to 90 percent conversion. Such technologies offer hope for broadband solar power to be converted to narrowband power in space and then beamed to the earth by satellites.

Another way of harnessing solar power is through solar thermal technology. Solar concentrators are used with focal-point towers to achieve temperatures of thousands of kelvins and high thermal efficiency, limited by containment materials. The resulting high-temperature electrolysis of water vapor generates hydrogen and oxygen in an efficient manner, and this technology has demonstrated direct solar decomposition of carbon dioxide (CO_2) to carbon monoxide (CO) and oxygen.

WIND POWER

Winds are driven by temperature and pressure gradients, ultimately caused by solar heating. Wind energy is typically extracted through the operation of turbines. Power extraction is proportional to the cube of wind speed, but wind-generated forces are proportional to the square of wind speed. Wind turbines thus can operate safely only within a limited range of wind speed, and most of the power generation occurs during periods of moderately strong winds. Turbine efficiency is strongly dependent on turbine size and is limited by material strength. The largest wind turbines exceed 5 megawatts in capacity. Denmark, the Netherlands, and India have established large wind turbine farms on flat coastal land, and Germany and the United Kingdom have opted for large offshore wind farms. In the United States, wind farms are found in the Dakotas, Minnesota, and California, as well as on Colorado and New Mexico mountain slopes and off the coasts of Texas and Massachusetts.

Because of wind fluctuations and the cubic power relation, wind power is highly unsteady, and means must be established for storing and diverting the power generated before it is connected to a power grid. In addition, offshore and coastal wind farms must plan for severe storms. Smaller wind turbines are sometimes used for power generation on farms and even for some private homes in open areas, but these tend to be inefficient and have high installation costs per unit power. They are mainly useful for pumping irrigation water or for charging small electrical devices.

Environmentalists have raised some concerns about large wind turbines. The machinery on wind farms causes objectionable noise levels, and many assert that the wind turbine towers themselves constitute a form of visual pollution. Disturbances to wildlife, particularly deaths and injuries in bird populations, are another area of concern. In addition, the construction of wind farms often requires the building of roads through previously pristine areas to enable transportation of the turbines' large components.

Construction of an offshore wind turbine, part of a wind farm off the coast of Denmark. (©Yobidaba/Dreamstime.com)

HYDROELECTRIC POWER AND TIDAL POWER

Large dams provide height differences that enable the extraction of power from flowing water using turbines. Hydroelectric power generated by dams forms a substantial percentage of the power resources in several nations with rivers and mountains. However, the building of large dams raises numerous technical, social, and public policy issues, as damming rivers may displace human inhabitants from fertile lands and may result in the flooding of pristine ecosystems, sometimes the habitats of endangered species. Increased incidence of earthquakes has also been associated with the existence of very large dams.

In some of the world's remote communities, micro hydroelectric (or micro hydel) plants provide power, generating electricity in the 1-30 megawatt range. Very small-scale systems, known as pico hydel, extract a few kilowatts from small streams; these can provide viable energy sources for individual homes and small villages, but the extraction technology has to be refined to bring down the cost per unit of power.

Although tidal power is abundant along coastlines, the harnessing of that power has been slow to gain acceptance, in part because of the difficulties of building plants that can survive ocean storms. Tidal power is extracted in two principal ways. In one method, semipermeable barrages are built across estuaries with high tidal ranges, and the water collected in the barrages is emptied through turbines to generate power. In the second, offshore tidal streams and currents are harnessed through the use of underwater equivalents of wind turbines.

Tidal power plants typically use pistons that are driven up and down by alternating water levels or the action of waves on turbines. A rule of thumb is that a tidal range of 7 meters (23 feet) is required to produce enough hydraulic head for economical operation. One drawback is that the 12.5-hour cycle of tidal operation is out of synchronization with daily peak electricity demand times, and hence some local means of storing the power generated is desirable. In many cases, impellers or pistons are used to pump water to high levels for use when power demand is higher.

BIOMASS POWER

Biomass, which consists of any material that is derived from plant life, is composed primarily of hydrocarbons and water, so it offers several ways of usage in power generation. Combustion of biomass is considered to be carbon-neutral in regard to greenhouse gas emissions, but it may generate smoke particles and other pollution.

One large use of biomass is in the conversion of corn, sugarcane, and other grasses to ethyl alcohol (ethanol) to supplement fossil petroleum fuels. This use is controversial because the energy costs associated with producing and refining ethanol are said to be greater than the savings gained by using such fuel. It is argued that subsidies and other public policies and rising energy prices entice farmers to devote land to the production of ethanol crops, thus triggering shortages and increases in food prices, which hurt the poorest people the most. Brazil has advanced profitable and sustainable use of ethanol extracted from sugarcane to replace a substantial portion of the nation's transportation fossil-fuel use.

Jatropha plants, as well as certain algae that grow on water surfaces, offer sources of biodiesel fuel. Biodiesel from jatropha is used to power operations on several segments of India's railways, and vegetable oil from peanuts and groundnuts, and even from coconuts, has been used in test flights of aircraft ranging from strategic bombers to jetliners.

BIOGAS AND GEOTHERMAL ENERGY

Hydrocarbon gases from decaying vegetation form large underground deposits that have been exploited as sources of energy for many years. Technology similar to that used in extracting energy from these natural deposits, which are not considered a renewable energy source, can be used to tap the smaller but widely distributed emissions of methane-rich waste gases from compost pits and landfills. Creating the necessary infrastructure to capture these gases over large areas poses a difficult engineering challenge, however. In addition, care must be taken to avoid the release of methane from these deposits into the atmosphere, as methane is considered to be twenty times as harmful as carbon dioxide as a greenhouse gas.

Geothermal energy comes from heat released by radioactive decay inside the earth's core, perhaps augmented by gravitational pressure. Where such heat is released gradually through vents in the earth's surface, rather than in volcanic eruptions, it forms an abundant and steady, reliable, long-term source of thermal power. Hot springs and geothermal steam generation are used on a large scale in Iceland, and geothermal power is used in some American communities and military bases.

Narayanan M. Komerath and Padma P. Komerath

FURTHER READING

Charlier, R. H., and C. W. Finkl. *Ocean Energy: Tide and Tidal Power.* London: Springer, 2009.

Edwards, Brian K. *The Economics of Hydroelectric Power.* Northampton, Mass.: Edward Elgar, 2003.

Klass, Donald L. *Biomass for Renewable Energy, Fuels, and Chemicals.* San Diego, Calif.: Academic Press, 1998.

Pollan, Michael. *The Omnivore's Dilemma: A Natural History of Four Meals.* New York: Penguin Press, 2007.

Traynor, Ann J., and Reed J. Jensen. "Direct Solar Reduction of CO_2 to Fuel: First Prototype Results." *Industrial and Engineering Chemistry Research* 41, no. 8 (2002): 1935-1939.

Vaitheeswaran, Vijay. *Power to the People: How the Coming Energy Revolution Will Transform an Industry, Change Our Lives, and Maybe Even Save the Planet.* New York: Farrar, Straus and Giroux, 2003.

Walker, John F., and Nicholas Jenkins. *Wind Energy Technology.* New York: John Wiley & Sons, 1997.

Wenisch, A., R. Kromp, and D. Reinberger. *Science or Fiction: Is There a Future for Nuclear?* Vienna: Austrian Ecology Institute, 2007.

Alternative fuels

CATEGORY: Energy and energy use

DEFINITION: Materials or substances that can be substituted for commonly used fossil fuels

SIGNIFICANCE: The development of alternatives to fossil fuels (gasoline, diesel, natural gas, and coal) has been spurred by growing awareness of the environmental damage associated with the burning of fossil fuels, as well as by the knowledge that at some time in the future the earth's supply of fossil fuels will be exhausted.

With the exception of nuclear-powered seagoing vessels, most vehicles are powered by internal combustion engines that use either gasoline or diesel fuel. Gasoline and diesel release significant amounts of greenhouse gases into the atmosphere when burned; these gases include water vapor, carbon dioxide, ozone, nitrous oxide, and methane. These gases absorb and emit radiation in the infrared range; thus they increase the earth's temperature. In addition to the fact that the internal combustion engine burns an environment-polluting fossil fuel, it also is an inefficient method for transferring the energy stored in the fuel into propulsion. Most of the stored energy is lost in heat, which escapes through the exhaust pipe. In addition, the pistons within the engine accelerate up, stop, accelerate down, and stop with each revolution. This rapid cycle of acceleration and deceleration wastes energy. Many of the alternative fuels available are used to power internal combustion engines and thus have the same limitations as fossil fuels in this regard. Using an alternative fuel such as stored electricity does not have these limitations because it does not produce heat and it propels an electric motor, which rotates (no starting and stopping with each cycle).

Comparisons of the costs and levels of pollutant production of nonfossil fuel sources must take into account the costs associated with production of the fuels. An example is the use of corn for the production of ethanol. Raising the crop requires energy for production, such as fuel for tractors. The corn must then be fermented (yeast converts the sugar in the corn into ethanol), and the fermented product must be distilled (boiled to release the alcohol), which requires fuel to heat the still. The process increases the cost of ethanol and also produces pollution. The electricity that charges an electric vehicle may have been produced by a fossil-fuel source such as a diesel generator. Another problem with alternative fuels lies in the difficulty consumers may have in replenishing their supplies. Facilities distributing gasoline and diesel are prevalent throughout most developed nations; in contrast, sources of alternative fuels such as hydrogen and ammonia are not readily available. The ideal alternative fuel is one that is nonpolluting, cheap to produce, and easy to replenish.

BIOFUELS

Biofuels are derived from plant sources such as corn, sugarcane, and sugar beets; in some cases, they are blended with a fossil fuel, usually gasoline. Alcohol, methanol, butanol, biodiesel, biogas, and wood gas are all examples of biofuels.

Alcohol was initially used as a fuel in the Ford Model T automobile, which was first produced in 1908. The carburetor (a device that mixes fuel with air prior to entry into the engine) of the Model T could be adjusted to burn gasoline, ethanol, or a mixture. Many modern-day vehicles can run on a mixture of 10-15 percent ethanol and gasoline (E10, or gasohol, is 10 percent alcohol). The fuel known as E85 is a mixture of 85 percent ethanol and 15 percent gasoline; this fuel can be used only in flexible-fuel vehicles (FFVs). FFVs are designed to run on gasoline, E85, or any other gasoline-ethanol mixture. A disadvantage of ethanol is that it has approximately 34 percent less energy per volume than gasoline. Because ethanol has a high octane rating, ethanol-only engines may have relatively high compression ratios, which increases efficiency. In developed nations such as the United States, ethanol blends are available in many areas. Critics of ethanol as an alternative fuel note that it requires a large amount of agricultural land, which is diverted from producing crops used for food; also, the use of crops such as corn for ethanol production drives up food prices.

Methanol can be used as an alternative fuel, but automakers have not yet produced any vehicles that can run on it. Butanol is more similar to gasoline than ethanol and can be used in some engines designed for use with gasoline without modification.

Biodiesel can be manufactured from vegetable oils and animal fats, including recycled restaurant grease. It is slightly more expensive than diesel; however, it is a safe, biodegradable fuel that produces fewer pollutants than diesel. Diesel engines are more efficient than gasoline engines (44 percent versus 25-30 percent efficiency); thus they have better fuel economy than gasoline engines. Some diesel engines can run on 100 percent biodiesel with only minor modifications. Biodiesel can be combined with regular diesel in various concentrations (for example, B2 is 2 percent biodiesel, B5 is 5 percent biodiesel, and B20 is 20 percent biodiesel).

Biogas is produced by the biological breakdown of organic materials—for example, rotting vegetables, plant wastes, and manure produce biogas—and the energy produced varies depending on the source. Biogas can replace compressed natural gas for fueling internal combustion engines. Wood gas is another biofuel that can power an internal combustion engine. It is produced by the incomplete burning of sawdust, wood chips, coal, charcoal, or rubber. Depending on the source, the gas produced varies in energy content and contaminants. Contaminants in wood gas can foul an engine.

ELECTRIC VEHICLES

At the beginning of the twentieth century, automobiles powered by steam, gasoline, and electricity were available. Electric vehicles were popular into the early 1920's, but then the automotive industry became dominated by gasoline-powered vehicles. The decline in electric-powered vehicles occurred for several reasons: Road improvement allowed travel over longer distances, and the range of electric vehicles was limited; fossil fuels became cheap and plentiful; the electric starter replaced the hand crank on gasoline engines, which greatly simplified starting such engines; and mass production of automobiles by Henry Ford's company made gasoline-powered vehicles much less expensive than electric-powered vehicles ($650 versus $1,750 average price at that time). By the end of the twentieth century, a growing emphasis on environmentally friendly energy sources encouraged the reemergence of electric vehicles and the development of hybrid vehicles powered by both gasoline (or diesel) and electricity.

A hybrid vehicle contains an electric motor that can both propel the vehicle and recharge the battery. Hybrid vehicles have achieved greater popularity than electric-only vehicles, as electric-only vehicles continue to have some of the same basic problems as earlier electric cars: limited range and higher cost than gasoline-powered or hybrid vehicles. Public recharging facilities for electric vehicles remain few and far between; furthermore, recharging takes time. The latest electric and hybrid vehicles use lithium-ion bat-

Reagan Signs the Alternative Motor Fuels Act

President Ronald Reagan made the following statement before signing the Alternative Motor Fuels Act of 1988:

Well, Members of Congress and distinguished guests, good afternoon. We're here today to sign into law an investment in America's future: the Alternative Motor Fuels Act of 1988. This bill is a landmark in the quest for alternative forms of energy. And believe me, when you're my age you just love hearing about alternative sources of energy.

I'm particularly proud this afternoon because I remember more than 4 years ago, at a Cabinet meeting in January 1984, and I asked Vice President George Bush to launch a thorough investigation of alternative energy and see what he could find—not pie-in-the-sky demonstration projects but real-world possibilities and realistic options that would help keep our air clean and our nation less dependent on foreign oil.

That's what's so exciting about the bill before us today: The forms of energy encouraged by this bill are already in use. Methanol, for example, is used in the Indianapolis 500 and in other race cars because it simultaneously en-

hances performance and safety. And cars that run on methanol have the potential to reduce emissions by an amazing 50 percent and improve efficiency. For areas like southern California, that could be a Godsend. A few months ago, Vice President Bush dedicated the first methanol pump on Wilshire Boulevard in Los Angeles. And this bill gives American automobile companies a real incentive to start building cars powered by alternative fuels by adjusting the federally mandated average fuel economy ratings to reflect the gasoline saved by these vehicles.

This legislation also opens up new markets for natural gas and coal, our two most plentiful energy resources in this country. The success of these projects could improve employment and the economies in the hard-pressed oil- and gas-producing areas of the country. This bill takes advantage of existing government programs and mechanisms to assist alternative fuels. Most important, it's not intended to create massive new bureaucracies or new taxpayer subsidies.

teries rather than the lead-acid batteries used by earlier versions (and still used in gasoline and diesel vehicles). Lithium-ion batteries are much lighter than lead-acid batteries and can be molded into a variety of shapes to fit available areas. One criticism of electric vehicles, including hybrids, is that many are small and lightweight and thus less safe for passengers, in the case of collisions, than are larger gasoline-powered vehicles.

OTHER FUELS DERIVED FROM NONFOSSIL SOURCES

Ammonia has been evaluated for use as an alternative fuel. It can run in either a spark-ignited engine (that is, a gasoline engine) or a diesel engine in which the fuel-air mixture ignites upon compression in the cylinder. Modern gasoline and diesel engines can be readily converted to run on ammonia. Although ammonia is a toxic substance, it is considered no more dangerous than gasoline or liquefied petroleum gas (LPG). Ammonia can be produced by electrical energy and has half the density of gasoline or diesel; thus it can be placed in a vehicle fuel tank in sufficient quantities to allow the vehicle to travel reasonable distances. Another advantage of ammonia is that it produces no harmful emissions; upon combustion, it produces nitrogen and water.

Compressed-air engines are piston engines that use compressed air as fuel. Air-engine-powered vehicles have been produced that have a range comparable to gasoline-powered vehicles. Compressed air is much less expensive than fossil fuels. Ambient heat (normal heat in the environment) naturally warms the cold compressed air upon the air's release from the storage tank, increasing its efficiency. The only exhaust is cold air, which can be used to cool the interior of the vehicle.

Hydrogen vehicles can be powered by the combustion of hydrogen in the engine much as the typical gasoline engine operates. Fuel cell conversion is another method of using hydrogen; in this type of vehicle, the hydrogen is converted to electricity. The most efficient use of hydrogen to power motor vehicles involves the use of fuel cells and electric motors. Hydrogen reacts with oxygen inside the fuel cells, which produces electricity to power the motors. With either method no harmful emissions are produced, as the spent hydrogen produces only water. Hydrogen is much more expensive than fossil fuels, and it contains significantly less energy on a per-volume basis, meaning that the vehicle's range is reduced. Experimental

fuel cell vehicles have been produced, but such vehicles remain far too expensive for the average consumer.

Liquid nitrogen (LN_2) contains stored energy. Energy is used to liquefy air, then LN_2 is produced by evaporation. When LN_2 warms, nitrogen gas is produced; this gas can power a piston or turbine engine. Nitrogen-powered vehicles have been produced that have ranges comparable to gasoline-powered vehicles; these vehicles can be refueled in a matter of minutes. Nitrogen is an inert gas and makes up about 80 percent of air. It is virtually nonpolluting. Furthermore, it produces more energy than does compressed air.

Oxyhydrogen is a mixture of hydrogen and oxygen gases, usually in a 2:1 ratio, the same proportion as water. Oxyhydrogen can fuel internal combustion engines, and, as in hydrogen-fueled engines, no harmful emissions are produced.

Steam was a common method of propulsion for vehicles during the early twentieth century, but, like electricity, it fell into disfavor with the advent of the electric starter, cheap gasoline, and mass production of Ford automobiles. A disadvantage of steam-powered vehicles is the time required to produce the steam. A steam engine is an external combustion engine—that is, the power is produced outside rather than inside the engine. Steam engines are less energy-efficient than gasoline engines. Fuel for steam engines can be derived from fossil fuels or from nonfossil fuel sources.

ALTERNATIVE FOSSIL FUELS

Some fossil fuels are less polluting than gasoline or diesel, and some are in plentiful supply. Natural gas vehicles use compressed natural gas (CNG) or, less commonly, liquefied natural gas (LNG). Internal combustion engines can be readily converted to burn natural gas. Natural gas is 60-90 percent less polluting than gasoline or diesel and produces 30-40 percent less greenhouse gases. Furthermore, it is less expensive than gasoline. Limitations of natural gas vehicles include a lack of available fueling stations and limited space for fuel, given that natural gas must be stored in cylinders, which are commonly located in the vehicle's trunk.

Liquefied petroleum gas is suitable for fueling internal combustion engines. Like natural gas, LPG is less polluting than gasoline, with 20 percent less carbon dioxide emissions; it is also less expensive. LPG is added to a vehicle's fuel tank through the use of a specialized filling apparatus; a limitation to LPG is the lack of fueling stations.

Robin L. Wulffson

FURTHER READING

DeGunther, Rik. *Alternative Energy for Dummies*. Hoboken, N.J.: John Wiley & Sons, 2009.

Gibilisco, Stan. *Alternative Energy Demystified*. New York: McGraw-Hill, 2007.

Hordeski, Michael F. *Alternative Fuels: The Future of Hydrogen*. 2d ed. Lilburn, Ga.: Fairmont Press, 2008.

Lee, Sunggyu, James G. Speight, and Sudarshan K. Loyalka. *Handbook of Alternative Fuel Technologies*. Boca Raton, Fla.: CRC Press, 2007.

Nersesian, Roy L. *Energy for the Twenty-first Century: A Comprehensive Guide to Conventional and Alternative Sources*. New York: M. E. Sharpe, 2007.

Alternatively fueled vehicles

CATEGORIES: Energy and energy use; atmosphere and air pollution

DEFINITION: Vehicles fueled, wholly or partially, by energy derived from sources other than petroleum

SIGNIFICANCE: The development of vehicles that operate efficiently using little or no petroleum-based fuel is an important part of efforts to address the problems of declining petroleum resources and the pollution caused by emissions from petroleum-based fuels.

Almost all of the fuel used for transportation in the United States is derived from petroleum. In California, a huge consumer of fuel to run its millions of vehicles, a mere one-fourth of 1 percent of those vehicles used alternative fuel sources in 2010. As the world's oil fields become depleted and petroleum reserves shrink, and as awareness grows regarding the harm to the environment caused by the burning of fossil fuels, the pressure to develop alternative fuels and vehicles that can operate using them has become intense. Since the late twentieth century, significant progress has been made in this area: Between 1970 and 2010, advances in automotive technologies decreased toxic vehicle emissions by an estimated 90 percent. These advances included the development of vehicles powered by non-petroleum-based fuels.

Auto manufacturers long resisted producing vehicles that would not be dependent on petroleum-based energy sources; for many years, they rejected alternative technologies in favor of the entrenched gasoline-burning internal combustion engine. Significant gasoline shortages in 1973 and 1979, however, clearly demonstrated the need for mass production of vehicles that could be powered by renewable resources. Whereas automobile companies and the petroleum industry had previously discouraged technologies related to the development of practical electric vehicles, many such corporations came to recognize the need to explore and encourage the production of alternative fuel sources.

HYBRID AND ELECTRIC VEHICLES

By the late twentieth century, automobile manufacturers, first in Japan but later in the United States and Europe, turned their attention to producing reasonably priced, fuel-efficient, nonpolluting vehicles. The most popular of such vehicles are hybrid vehicles; by 2010, nearly twenty versions of such vehicles were available commercially.

Hybrids such as Toyota's Prius and Honda's Insight are powered by gasoline-fueled internal combustion engines in combination with electric motors. These motors, which receive their electricity from batteries, provide power for the automobiles, but when they run down, small internal combustion engines take over. The batteries in hybrid vehicles are recharged by the friction created every time the brakes are applied. The ranges of such vehicles—that is, the distances that they can be driven between refuelings—are comparable to those of conventional vehicles.

Plug-in electric vehicles have a much more limited range than do hybrids; most can be driven only about 160 kilometers (100 miles) before they require recharging. Such vehicles are useful for service within limited areas, where they can be driven for short periods and recharged when not in use. Recharging a plug-in electric vehicle's batteries fully can take four to eight hours. Anticipated improvements in electric vehicle technology include drastic shortening of the time required to recharge batteries and enhancement of battery life to extend the vehicles' range.

OTHER FUELS FOR INTERNAL COMBUSTION ENGINES

The conventional internal combustion engines found in most vehicles can often be run on non-petroleum fuels or on mixtures of petroleum-based and other fuels. One frequently used alternative fuel is ethanol, an alcohol derived from plants that can be mixed with conventional gasoline. Such mixtures usually consist of 5 percent ethanol and 95 percent conventional gasoline, however, so the gasoline savings are negligible.

Another nonpetroleum fuel is hydrogen, which can be used to fuel slightly modified existing vehicles. As of 2010, more than one hundred buses fueled by hydrogen were operating in the United States, Canada, Mexico, Brazil, Japan, Egypt, Iceland, and India. Hydrogen has the advantage of producing water as its sole emission, so it does not contribute to air pollution. The major problem with using hydrogen is that it is not readily available to consumers. Proponents of hydrogen as a motor vehicle fuel assert that successful solution of the problem of distribution might revolutionize how vehicles are fueled.

Although hydrogen is among the most plentiful elements in the universe, it is not available merely for the taking. Because it bonds with other elements, such as oxygen, it is a carrier of energy rather than a source of energy like petroleum or coal. To power a vehicle, hydrogen must pass through onboard fuel cells in which a chemical reaction reduces water into its component parts, hydrogen and oxygen. This hydrogen, available in a free state, is converted to electricity and used to fuel the vehicle. When hydrogen is used in its gaseous state, leakage is a problem. Hydrogen can be liquefied and can also exist in powder form. Its most efficient use in fueling vehicles is usually in its gaseous or liquefied form.

Liquefied natural gas, which is less expensive to produce than gasoline, is used to fuel some fleets of taxicabs and other commercial vehicles. Liquefied petroleum gas, or propane, is also used to provide the power for many commercial fleets. It is less expensive and less polluting than regular gasoline.

R. Baird Shuman

FURTHER READING

Chan, C. C., and K. T. Chau. *Modern Electric Vehicle Technology.* New York: Oxford University Press, 2001.

Ehsani, Mehrdad, et al. *Modern Electric, Hybrid Electric, and Fuel Cell Vehicles: Fundamentals, Theory, and Design.* Boca Raton, Fla: CRC Press, 2005.

Erjavec, Jack, and Jeff Arias. *Hybrid, Electric, and Fuel-Cell Vehicles.* Clifton Park, N.J.: Thomson Delmar Learning, 2007.

Halderman, James D., and Tony Martin. *Hybrid and Alternative Fuel Vehicles.* Upper Saddle River, N.J.: Pearson/Prentice Hall, 2009.

Hanselman, Duane C. *Brushless Permanent-Magnet Motor Design.* New York: McGraw-Hill, 1994.

King, Nicole Bezic, ed. *Renewable Energy Resources.* North Mankato, Minn.: Smart Apple Media, 2004.

Lee, Sunggyu, James G. Speight, and Sudarshan K. Loyalka. *Handbook of Alternative Fuel Technologies.* Boca Raton, Fla.: CRC Press, 2007.

Atomic Energy Commission

CATEGORIES: Organizations and agencies; nuclear power and radiation; energy and energy use

IDENTIFICATION: Agency established by the U.S. Congress to promote and monitor the use of nuclear energy

DATES: 1946-1974

SIGNIFICANCE: Because the Atomic Energy Commission was responsible for both the promotion of nuclear power and the safety regulation of nuclear facilities, many critics asserted that the commission was not as diligent as it should be in its regulatory duties.

In 1946, the U.S. Congress passed the Atomic Energy Act, which created the Atomic Energy Commission (AEC) to promote, monitor, and control the development and use of nuclear energy for civilian and military use. Not only was a buildup of nuclear weapons for defense expected, but also the development of nuclear science for peaceful uses. For security reasons, all nuclear production facilities and reactors were owned by the U.S. government, but the information from research was to be controlled by the AEC. The Manhattan Project facilities, where scientists had developed the first atomic bombs during World War II, were taken over by the AEC. In 1954, Congress passed the Atomic Energy Act Amendments, which made possible the development of commercial nuclear power. The AEC was assigned the responsibility of promoting commercial nuclear power at the same time it was charged with developing safety regulations and controls for nuclear power plants.

The work of the AEC encompassed all areas of nuclear science. The AEC studied the production of nuclear weapons, improved and increased nuclear facilities, and oversaw the development of new weapons, such as the thermonuclear device, a fusion bomb, and nuclear propulsion for warships, especially submarines. The study of nuclear reactors led to improved energy-producing reactors and a new type of reactor, the breeder reactor, that produced new fuel while producing energy. Commercial production of nuclear energy became a reality. Regional research centers were established—at the Argonne National Laboratory near Chicago; at Oak Ridge, Tennessee; at Brookhaven, New York; and at the University of California Radiation Laboratory in Berkeley—where scientists could work on projects in nuclear or radiation science. The AEC also contracted with industrial and university researchers to conduct nuclear-related studies in all areas of scientific research, including medical diagnosis using nuclear techniques, disease treatment by radiation, and treatment for radiation exposure. Other areas of study included the effects of radiation, production of new isotopes, uses of new isotopes, and radiation safety. Reactors to produce energy for satellites were developed and sent into space.

Many observers were critical of the AEC's double role as promoter of nuclear power and monitor of radiation safety, saying that this was a conflict of interest. Many asserted that the AEC was promoting nuclear energy at the expense of regulation and that the safety regulations for reactors especially, but also for materials production, location of plants, and environmental protection, were inadequate.

The AEC was abolished in 1974, and its former two roles were split. The promotion of nuclear science in the United States was assigned to the Energy Research and Development Administration; these duties later became the responsibility of the Department of Energy. Responsibility for the safety monitoring of nuclear facilities went to the Nuclear Regulatory Commission.

C. Alton Hassell

FURTHER READING

Cooke, Stephanie. *In Mortal Hands: A Cautionary History of the Nuclear Age.* New York: Bloomsbury, 2009.

Hewlett, Richard G., and Oscar E. Anderson. *A History of the United States Atomic Energy Commission.* 1962. Reprint. Berkeley: University of California Press, 1990.

Walker, J. Samuel. *A Short History of Nuclear Regulation, 1946-1999.* Washington, D.C.: U.S. Nuclear Regulatory Commission, 2000.

Biomass conversion

CATEGORY: Energy and energy use

DEFINITION: Process of converting biological organic material, such as plant material and animal waste, into fuels

SIGNIFICANCE: The conversion of biomass into fuels provides alternatives to the use of fossil fuels and thus can contribute to the reduction of air pollution. Biomass conversion also serves to reduce the amount of wastes that must be disposed of in other ways.

Plants and algae use solar energy and transform carbon dioxide (CO_2) from the atmosphere into their biomass (also called primary biomass). Human beings have converted biomass into energy for centuries. For example, burning biomass in the form of wood is the oldest form of such conversion. Biomass can also be converted into other energy sources or fuels—for example, through fermentation to alcohols (ethanol or butanol) or biogas and through gasification to a substitute for natural gas. In addition, biomass such as plant oil can be transformed by the chemical reaction of transesterification into biodiesel, a diesel fuel substitute. The processing of primary biomass by organisms creates secondary biomass sources, such as animal manure and other wastes. Several countries around the world use incinerators to convert this kind of biomass into electricity. Biomass is produced naturally (for example, in forests) and agriculturally (for example, agricultural residues and dung).

The processes used to convert biomass into fuels can have both positive and negative environmental impacts, but the positive influences on the environment outweigh the negative ones. It is widely recognized that the use of fossil fuels is the leading cause of global climate change due to carbon dioxide release. Biomass conversion does not result in net CO_2 emissions because it releases only the amount of CO_2 absorbed in the biomass during plant growth. Biomass conversion into energy is thus a favorable option for reducing CO_2 emissions.

Biomass conversion also offers a means of reducing wastes, such as agricultural residues and human wastes. A great number of wastes result from the cultivation of crops such as corn, and these wastes can be turn into ethanol, which is used as a transportation fuel. Conversion of biomass from landfills produces biogas, which is two-thirds methane. Methane is a very powerful greenhouse gas, and thus a contributor to global warming, but it is also a very good fuel. It can be burned in electrical generators to produce electricity, and it can be used as a fuel for vehicles. To prevent the methane produced by landfills from being released into the atmosphere, some municipalities have installed "gas wells" in landfills to tap the methane for use as fuel.

Biogas can also be generated from wastewater and from animal waste. In 2006 the city of San Francisco contemplated a plan to extend its recycling program to include conversion of dog feces into methane to produce electricity and to heat homes; given the city's dog population of 120,000, this initiative was seen to have the potential to generate significant amounts of fuel while reducing waste. The plan was never initiated, however, as the city opted to focus on other recycling programs.

Sergei A. Markov

FURTHER READING

Bourne, Joel K. "Green Dreams." *National Geographic*, October, 2007, 38-59.
Hall, David O., and Joanna I. House. "Biomass: A Modern and Environmentally Acceptable Fuel." *Solar Energy Materials and Solar Cells* 38 (1995): 521-542.
Wright, Richard T. *Environmental Science: Toward a Sustainable Future*. 10th ed. Upper Saddle River, N.J.: Prentice Hall, 2008.

Biopiracy and bioprospecting

CATEGORY: Resources and resource management
DEFINITION: Extraction of biological resources from areas of biodiversity
SIGNIFICANCE: The practice of extracting biological resources from regions of the world known for their great biological diversity, often carried out by scientists working for corporations or educational institutions, is the subject of ongoing debate. Many environmentalists and indigenous peoples see such resource extraction as a form of exploitation.

With the signing of the United Nations Convention on Biological Diversity at the Earth Summit in Rio de Janeiro, Brazil, in 1992, participatory nations agreed to no longer consider biological resources the "common heritage of mankind" but conceded the rights to distribute such resources to the individual nations that housed them. Around the same time, the terms "biopiracy" and "bioprospecting" began to be used to describe the acquisition of these newly protected resources. The two terms refer to essentially the same thing, the extraction of biological resources from areas of biodiversity, but they have decidedly different tones, the former having been coined by opponents of such activity and the latter being preferred by the practitioners of this type of resource extraction.

Biological resources include whole organisms such as crops or livestock, chemical compounds that can be purified from specific organisms that produce them, and even the genetic material taken from organisms that can then be used to produce desired proteins, usually in conjunction with some form of genetic engineering. These resources hold value in that they can be used to improve agricultural yields, perform certain industrial processes, or serve various pharmaceutical applications. The debate over the appropriate acquisition of these resources led to the split in the terms used to describe the same activity. "Biopiracy" brings to mind a swashbuckler who pillages resources without regard to the victims; "bioprospecting," in contrast, conveys the image of a gold miner staking out a claim and then working it, with no guarantee of ultimate success.

BIOPROSPECTING

The image of the gold-rush prospector is perhaps most appropriate for one particular type of resource collection: the biodiversity-driven, or random-collection, approach. Scientists taking this approach sample large amounts of organisms for a desired chemical activity or genetic attribute without prior knowledge of precisely where to look. The screened organisms are typically plants, microorganisms, insects, or marine invertebrates. This is called the biodiversity-driven approach because mass sampling is best done in areas with wide ranges of different organisms living in close proximity.

Just as modern mining methods include scientific means for discovering deposits of minerals, however, bioprospecting often makes use of prior knowledge to narrow the pool of organisms being tested. This knowledge falls into three main categories: chemotaxonomic, ecological, and ethnobotanical/ethnopharmacological. The use of chemotaxonomic knowledge involves the sampling of organisms that belong to the same taxonomic class as an organism that is already known to have a desired property. An example would be screening a number of bacteria from the class Actinobacteria, the taxonomic group known to be responsible for the production of streptomycin, for antibiotic properties. Ecological knowledge is knowledge that can be gained from field observations of the interactions between particular organisms. Certain plants and animals, for example, produce chemical compounds called secondary metabolites that they use to defend themselves against predator attack. A scientist taking an ecological approach to bioprospecting may detect such interactions and choose species for further testing based on these observations.

The use of ethnobotanical/ethnopharmacological knowledge is the most controversial approach, as it seeks to capitalize on the medical practices of indigenous peoples who inhabit the areas of interest. Ethnobotanical knowledge focuses on plants that have traditionally been used for healing purposes by indigenous peoples, whereas ethnopharmacological knowledge is broader, encompassing all traditional drugs as well as their biological activities. Using such knowledge, scientists can screen specific organisms for desired properties with a much higher degree of success than is seen with randomly sampled collections.

Biopiracy

Much of the world's biodiversity lies in the tropical regions, often in developing countries that have historically experienced oppression by wealthier nations. It is not surprising, therefore, that indigenous peoples in these regions tend to be wary of the academic institutions and multinational corporations that engage in what these entities may view as simple bioprospecting. Often, indigenous peoples have concerns regarding the entire practice of treating biodiversity as a biological resource, including the patenting of living organisms and profiting from biological materials that for many years previously were exchanged freely among those who reaped the benefits. Even if these concerns are allayed, questions often remain about who should be compensated for traditional knowledge that leads to a "discovery," as well as what would constitute a fair level of compensation.

Although no entity has been prosecuted officially for biopiracy under the Convention on Biological Diversity, many allegations of biopiracy have been made, and a number of planned bioprospecting projects

have been abandoned after information about them became public and protests ensued. It may be partially because of such controversies that bioprospecting activities actually decreased in the decades following the convention's signing, as many companies turned away from using natural resources and instead developed synthetic processes, such as combinatorial chemistry to produce lead compounds that could be screened for a desired activity.

James S. Godde

Further Reading

Godde, James S. "Genetic Resources." In *Encyclopedia of Global Resources,* edited by Craig W. Allin. Pasadena, Calif.: Salem Press, 2010.

Hamilton, Chris. "Biodiversity, Biopiracy, and Benefits: What Allegations of Biopiracy Tell Us About Intellectual Property." *Developing World Bioethics* 6 (2006): 158-173.

Soejarto, D. D., et al. "Ethnobotany/Ethnopharmacology and Mass Bioprospecting: Issues on Intellectual Property and Benefit-Sharing." *Journal of Ethnopharmacology* 100, nos. 1-2 (August, 2005): 15-22.

Tan, G., C. Gyllenhaal, and D. D. Soejarto. "Biodiversity as a Source of Anticancer Drugs." *Current Drug Targets* 7, no. 3 (March, 2006): 265-277.

Tedlock, Barbara. "Indigenous Heritage and Biopiracy in the Age of Intellectual Property Rights." *Explore: The Journal of Science and Healing* 2, no. 3 (May, 2006): 256-259.

Breeder reactors

CATEGORIES: Energy and energy use; nuclear power and radiation

DEFINITION: Nuclear reactors designed to create more fuel than they use in the production of energy

SIGNIFICANCE: Properly managed and maintained breeder reactors produce useful energy, generate less waste than conventional light-water fission reactors, and reduce greenhouse gas emissions by reducing the use of fossil fuels.

As opposed to normal nuclear fission reactors that use uranium 235 as their energy source, breeder reactors can make use of the much more abundant uranium 238 or thorium 232. Whereas a typical fission reactor uses only about 1 percent of the natural uranium 235 that starts its fuel cycle, a breeder reactor consumes a much larger percentage of the initial fissionable material. In addition, if the price of uranium is more than two hundred dollars per kilogram, it is cost-efficient to reprocess the fuel so that almost all of the original fissionable material produces useful energy. Breeder reactors are designed to produce from 1 percent to more than 20 percent more fuel than they consume. The time required for a breeder reactor to generate enough material to fuel a second nuclear reactor is referred to as the doubling time; the typical doubling time targeted in power plant design is ten years.

Scientists have proposed two main types of breeder reactors: fast-breeder reactors and thermal breeder reactors. The fast-breeder reactor uses fast neutrons given off by fission reactions to breed more fuel from nonfissionable isotopes. The most common fast-breeding reaction produces fissionable plutonium 239 from nonfissionable uranium 238. The liquid metal fast-breeder reactor (LMFBR) breeds plutonium 239 and uses liquid metal, typically sodium, for cooling and for heat transfer to water to generate steam that turns a turbine to produce electricity. The thermal breeder reactor uses thorium 232 to produce fissile uranium 233 after neutron capture and beta decay.

Unlike fossil-fuel-powered plants, breeder reactors do not generate carbon dioxide or other greenhouse gas pollutants. Environmental concerns related to any type of breeder reactor include nuclear accidents that could emit radiation into the atmosphere and the difficulty of safely disposing of radioactive waste byproducts. In addition, for plutonium-based breeders a major concern is the possibility of the diversion of bred plutonium for nuclear weapon production. This concern can be addressed through the intermixing of actinide impurities with the plutonium; such impurities make little difference to reactor operation, but they make it extremely difficult for anyone to use the bred plutonium to manufacture a nuclear weapon.

France has been the most prominent nation in the implementation of breeder reactors. The Superphénix breeder reactor built on the Caspian Sea was used for power generation and desalination of seawater from 1985 to 1996. India has plans to build a large fleet of breeder reactors, including a large prototype LMFBR that uses a plutonium-uranium oxide mixture in the fuel rods. Russia, China, and Japan are also developing breeders. The Russian BN-600 fast-breeder reactor has experienced several sodium leaks and fires. If the sodium coolant in the central part of an LMFBR core were to overheat and bubble, core melting could accelerate in the event of an accident and release radioactive material into the environment. A strong reactor containment building and a reactor core designed so that the fuel rod bundles are interspersed within a depleted uranium blanket that surrounds the core could greatly decrease this effect.

Alvin K. Benson

FURTHER READING

Bodansky, David. *Nuclear Energy: Principles, Practices, and Prospects.* 2d ed. New York: Springer, 2004.

Mosey, David. *Reactor Accidents: Institutional Failure in the Nuclear Industry.* Sidcup, England: Nuclear Engineering International, 2006.

Muller, Richard A. *Physics for Future Presidents: The Science Behind the Headlines.* New York: W. W. Norton, 2008.

Brundtland Commission

CATEGORIES: Organizations and agencies; resources and resource management

IDENTIFICATION: Body formed by the United Nations to propose long-term environmental strategies for achieving sustainable development through international cooperation

DATE: Established in 1983

SIGNIFICANCE: The work of the Brundtland Commission raised global awareness of the concept of sustainable development and thus led to the Earth Summit in 1992, which produced the Rio Declaration on Environment and Development as well as conventions on biological diversity and on climate change.

The World Commission on Environment and Development—commonly known as the Brundtland Commission, for its chair, Gro Harlem Brundtland—was established because of growing worldwide recognition of the impacts of human development on the environment. Publication of the commission's 1987 report, titled *Our Common Future* (often referred to as the Brundtland Report), propelled issues of sustainable development to the forefront of international policy debates and decision making.

The Brundtland Commission's Report

The report of the Brundtland Commission, published as Our Common Future, *includes the following summary statement of the status of the relationship between nature and humanity near the end of the twentieth century.*

Over the course of this century, the relationship between the human world and the planet that sustains it has undergone a profound change.

When the century began, neither human numbers nor technology had the power radically to alter planetary systems. As the century closes, not only do vastly increased human numbers and their activities have that power, but major, unintended changes are occurring in the atmosphere, in soils, in water, among plants and animals, and in the relationships among all of these. The rate of change is outstripping the ability of scientific disciplines and our current capabilities to assess and advise.

Our Common Future defines "sustainable development" as "development that meets the needs of the present without compromising the ability of future generations to meet their own needs." The report emphasizes that such development is sustainable socially and environmentally as well as economically, and it urges support for efforts to inaugurate sustainable systems of agriculture, industry, and energy generation that satisfy these requirements. A central theme of the report is the importance of maintaining sustainable levels of population. The report also explicitly states that living creatures have intrinsic value as well as instrumental value (a biocentric stance); the international community, however, replaced this biocentric approach with an anthropocentric one in the Rio Declaration on Environment and Development, which was produced by the 1992 Earth Summit.

Robin Attfield

Carbon footprint

CATEGORIES: Resources and resource management; energy and energy use

DEFINITION: Total amount of greenhouse gases produced to directly and indirectly support a certain human activity or a representative lifestyle, usually expressed in equivalent tons of carbon dioxide

SIGNIFICANCE: The use of carbon footprint estimates allows individuals, organizations, and nations to understand their relative contribution to emissions of greenhouse gases, which have been linked to global warming. In turn, these estimates are used in the purchase of carbon offsets and in gauging progress toward goals set under international agreements such as the Kyoto Protocol.

The concept of the carbon footprint provides a useful way for individuals and organizations to understand their impact in contributing to global warming. The calculation of a carbon footprint has been extended to include assessment of the greenhouse gas contributions made by the production and shipment of individual products. The general concept is that once the magnitude of a carbon footprint is known, a strategy can be devised to reduce that footprint. Examples of reduction methods include technological developments, carbon capture, and improved process and product management. Additionally, carbon offsetting through the development of alternative projects, such as solar or wind power, is a common way to reduce carbon footprints.

The concept and name of the carbon footprint originate from the concept of the ecological footprint. The carbon footprint is related to both the ecological footprint and the overarching life-cycle assessment (LCA) approach. A carbon footprint is composed of two elements: the primary, or direct, footprint and the secondary, or indirect, footprint. The primary footprint is the amount of direct carbon dioxide (CO_2) emissions stemming from the burning of fuels—that is, for domestic energy consumption and transportation. The secondary footprint is the amount of indirect CO_2 emissions caused over the whole life cycle of products, including the manufacture and eventual breakdown of the products.

Calculation of a carbon footprint generally begins with CO_2 emissions based on fuel consumption. Greenhouse gases other than CO_2 are typically translated to CO_2 equivalents through conversion rates, based on mass. Common greenhouse gases include methane, nitrous oxide, and chlorofluorocarbons (CFCs). To allow comparisons among the varied effects of different gases on the environment, scientists have developed methods of determining the greenhouse potency (global warming potential) of gases relative to that of carbon dioxide.

The calculation of carbon footprints for products

is becoming mainstream in people's understanding of products and lifestyle adjustments to reduce greenhouse gas emissions. These carbon footprint analyses are also useful in guiding regulation. For example, the U.S. Environmental Protection Agency has calculated carbon footprints for paper, plastic, glass, cans, computers, and tires, among other materials. Researchers in Australia, Korea, and the United States have addressed the carbon footprints of paved roads. The United Kingdom Carbon Trust has worked with manufacturers on assessing foods, shirts, and detergents.

The ready availability of carbon footprint calculators on the Internet has led many individuals to analyze their own carbon footprints. These calculators ask questions concerning lifestyle (such as how many times a year an individual takes airline flights) to arrive at an approximate carbon footprint.

On an international scale, the 1997 Kyoto Protocol defines targets and timetables for reductions in greenhouse gas emissions. An understanding of carbon footprints is necessary to the implementation of the flexible mechanisms defined under this international agreement (certified emission reduction, joint implementation, and emissions trading), which require nations to determine necessary levels of reduction and to maintain benchmarking activities.

Jennifer F. Helgeson

FURTHER READING

Brown, Marilyn A., Frank Southworth, and Andrea Sarzynski. *Shrinking the Carbon Footprint of Metropolitan America.* Washington, D.C.: Brookings Institution Press, 2008.

Sim, Stuart. *The Carbon Footprint Wars: What Might Happen If We Retreat from Globalization?* Edinburgh: Edinburgh University Press, 2009.

Weber, Christopher L., and H. Scott Matthews. "Quantifying the Global and Distributional Aspects of American Household Carbon Footprint." *Ecological Economics* 66 (June, 2008): 379-391.

Wiedmann, Thomas, and Jan Minx. "A Definition of 'Carbon Footprint.'" In *Ecological Economics Research Trends*, edited by Carolyn C. Pertsova. Hauppauge, N.Y.: Nova Science, 2007.

Chalk River nuclear reactor explosion

CATEGORIES: Disasters; nuclear power and radiation

THE EVENT: The world's first serious nuclear reactor accident

DATE: December 12, 1952

SIGNIFICANCE: After an experimental nuclear reactor at Chalk River, Ontario, overheated, resulting in a hydrogen-oxygen explosion and release of more than one million gallons of radioactive water, a pipeline had to be constructed to divert the radioactive water and avoid contamination of the Ottawa River.

The experimental NRX reactor, run by the National Research Council of Canada, began operation at Chalk River, Ontario, in 1947. It was operating at low power on December 12, 1952, when a technician mistakenly opened four air valves in the system used to insert the control rods that slowed the rate of reaction. This action caused the control rods to move out of the reactor core, increasing the reaction rate and the amount of heat produced in the core. In the effort to return these control rods to their proper position, miscommunication resulted in the removal of additional control rods, causing the power generated in the reactor core to double every two seconds.

When the operator realized that the power was rapidly increasing, he "scrammed" the reactor, a process that forced the control rods into place, thus halting the nuclear reaction. However, the earlier error of opening the air valves kept some of the control rods from being pushed into place, and the temperature in the reactor continued to increase. To stop the reaction, operators dumped water rich in deuterium (heavy water) from the reactor core. Without this water, which slows the neutrons to a point where they can induce fission in the uranium core, the reaction ceased and the core began to cool. However, more than one million gallons of highly radioactive water flooded the basement of the reactor building. The reactor dome, a 4-ton lid on the reactor vessel, rose upward to release pressure from a hydrogen-oxygen explosion, and more radioactive water escaped, flooding the main floor of the building. The reactor operators were forced to evacuate the building, and eventually the entire reactor site, as radioactivity rose above safe levels.

The small size of the experimental NRX reactor minimized the radiation release. Since the Chalk River site was remote, the exposure of the general population to radioactivity was minimal. Nonetheless, a pipeline had to be constructed to divert the radioactive water and avoid contamination of the Ottawa River. The high levels of radioactivity made decontamination and cleanup of the NRX reactor difficult. In some parts of the reactor, workers participating in the cleanup effort could spend only minutes at work before accumulating the maximum permissible annual radiation dose for reactor workers. About three hundred military personnel from the United States and Canada, including future U.S. president Jimmy Carter, volunteered to participate in the cleanup of the NRX reactor. A 1982 study of the health of more than seven hundred workers who participated in the cleanup showed no increase in their death rate from cancer when compared to the general population.

George J. Flynn

FURTHER READING

Bodansky, David. "Nuclear Reactor Accidents." In *Nuclear Energy: Principles, Practices, and Prospects.* 2d ed. New York: Springer, 2004.

Krenz, Kim. *Deep Waters: The Ottawa River and Canada's Nuclear Adventure.* Montreal: McGill-Queen's University Press, 2004.

Chelyabinsk nuclear waste explosion

CATEGORIES: Disasters; nuclear power and radiation

THE EVENT: Nuclear explosion at a weapons production facility in the Chelyabinsk province of the Soviet Union

DATE: September 29, 1957

SIGNIFICANCE: The nuclear explosion that took place at Mayak, a weapons production facility in Russia's Chelyabinsk province (then part of the Soviet Union), exposed 270,000 people to high levels of radiation.

The Mayak industrial complex began producing weapons-grade plutonium in 1948. For years after production began, workers dumped the complex's radioactive waste into the nearby Techa River. A waste storage facility was constructed in 1953 after people living near the Techa suffered from radiation poison-

ing. On September 29, 1957, one waste tank at the facility exploded. Although the exact cause of the explosion remains unknown, it is known that a cooling system failure contributed to the disaster.

A radioactive cloud consisting of between 70 and 90 tons of waste released an estimated 20 million curies of radiation into the environment. Of the waste material that was released, 90 percent fell back on the blast site and 10 percent drifted through the atmosphere, contaminating 2,000 square kilometers (772 square miles) of territory and exposing 270,000 people to radiation. Eyewitnesses later recalled seeing red dust settle everywhere, and the waters of the Techa River turned black for two weeks. Soon thereafter, plants died and leaves fell off the trees in the area. In less than two years, all the pine trees in a 28-square-kilometer (11-square-mile) area around the Mayak complex were dead.

The Soviet government closed all the stores in the area and shipped in food for the local population. Some ten thousand people were evacuated from the area, and the government burned houses and demolished entire towns to ensure that the residents could not return. However, many smaller communities continued to use local water sources, and later anecdotal accounts indicated that not all the contaminated crops in the region were destroyed. A dairy farm near the Techa River was allowed to operate until 1959.

The Chelyabinsk accident was kept secret, and for almost twenty years few people outside the region knew the extent of the disaster. The U.S. Central Intelligence Agency (CIA) learned of the incident but did not make the information public. Zhores Medvedev, a Soviet émigré, published the first account of the accident in 1976.

Evaluating the impact of the explosion proved difficult for two reasons: The Soviet government consistently denied the magnitude of the event, and the region was heavily polluted by other sources, especially the dumping of waste into the Techa River. In 1989 a U.S. official who visited the Mayak complex declared it to be the "most polluted spot on earth." By 1992 nearly one thousand area residents had been diagnosed with chronic radiation sickness. Rates for cancer were higher near Mayak than anywhere else in the Soviet Union, and the general health of the population, especially children, was poor by any standard.

Cleanup efforts were hampered by the secrecy that surrounded the event for nearly three decades, limited funds, and the high levels of contamination. Lake

Karachay, located near Mayak, was so radioactive that a person standing on its shore for more than one hour would be exposed to a lethal dose of radioactivity. In the early twenty-first century the area remained a pressing environmental problem.

Thomas Clarkin

FURTHER READING

Garb, Paula, and Galina Komarova. "Victims of 'Friendly Fire' at Russia's Nuclear Weapons Sites." In *Violent Environments,* edited by Nancy Lee Peluso and Michael Watts. Ithaca, N.Y.: Cornell University Press, 2001.

Hoffman, David E. *The Dead Hand: The Untold Story of the Cold War Arms Race and Its Dangerous Legacy.* New York: Doubleday, 2009.

Makhijani, Arjun, Howard Hu, and Katherine Yih, eds. *Nuclear Wastelands: A Global Guide to Nuclear Weapons Production and Its Health and Environmental Effects.* 1995. Reprint. Cambridge, Mass.: MIT Press, 2000.

Chernobyl nuclear accident

CATEGORIES: Disasters; nuclear power and radiation

THE EVENT: Explosion of a nuclear power reactor at the Chernobyl power plant in the Soviet Union

DATE: April 26, 1986

SIGNIFICANCE: The accident at the Chernobyl nuclear power plant drastically changed the lives of thousands of residents in the northern part of Ukraine and the southern portion of Belarus. It also raised questions about the future of the plant itself; the ecological, human health, economic, and political repercussions of the incident; and the future of nuclear power programs throughout the world.

On April 26, 1986, nuclear power reactor number 4 exploded at the nuclear plant located about 15 kilometers (9 miles) from the small town of Chernobyl in the republic of Ukraine. As the core of the reactor began to melt, an explosion occurred that blew the top off the reactor and sent a wide trail of radioactive material across large parts of what was then the Soviet Union as well as much of Eastern and Western Europe. More than 116,000 people were evacuated within a 30-kilometer (19-mile) radius.

In addition to the political, social, and economic aftermath of the explosion, the consequences of human inability to prevent widespread damage were evident in the environment within five years of the Chernobyl disaster. A major release of radioactive materials into the atmosphere occurred during the first ten days following the explosion. Radioactive plumes reached many European countries within a few days, increasing radiation levels to between ten and one hundred times normal levels. Over time the contaminated lithosphere created a new biogeographical province characterized by irregular and complicated patterns of radioactivity in Belarus, Ukraine, and Russia, the countries most affected. In spite of some success in efforts to slow the flow of certain soluble radionuclides into the Black and Baltic seas, as well as into the Pripet, Dnieper, and Sozh rivers (all of which contribute water to the Kiev water reservoir), much contamination occurred that only time can resolve.

CONTAMINATION EFFECTS

The effects of the radioactive contamination on vegetation have varied depending on the species. Damage to coniferous forests was more than ten times greater than that to oak forests and grass communities, and more than one hundred times greater than the damage to lichen communities. Ten years after the explosion, pine forests still had high levels of radionuclides in the uppermost layer of the forest floor, while birch forests had considerably lower levels. Large numbers of highly contaminated trees were felled, and restrictions were placed on cutting and using the wood in industry and for fuel. Likewise, the degrees of radiation damage and the doses absorbed varied among plant communities. In addition to killing or damaging plant life, the radiation disturbed the functioning of plant reproductive systems, resulting in sterility or decreases in both seed production and fertility. Other effects involved changes in plant chlorophyll, necessary for removing carbon dioxide from the air.

Among animals, lower life-forms have been found to have higher radiosensitivity levels; that is, mammals are less sensitive to radioactivity than are birds, reptiles, and insects. The severity of damage also depends on whether it is external or internal. The impact of environmental contamination may be less severe for animals than for plants because of the ability of animals to move from place to place and make selective contact with the environment. Irradiation can have a wide range of effects among animal species, including

Chernobyl, Ukraine, 1986

death, reproductive disturbances, decrease in the viability of progeny, and abnormalities in development and morphology.

The contamination of aquatic ecosystems by Chernobyl radiation has been considerable. The contamination of freshwater ecosystems has fallen with time, but continuing contamination has been evidenced by factors such as a transfer of radionuclides from bottom sediments and erosion of contaminated soil into water sources. Some restrictions have been placed on fishing in contaminated aquatic ecosystems.

The consequences of the Chernobyl accident for agriculture have been severe. Drastic changes in land-use and farming practices have been necessary as a result of contamination. As with other life-forms affected by radiation, the degree of contamination varies; in the case of agriculturally related contamination, damage depends on such things as the type of soil and the biological peculiarities of different plant species. Since Ukraine produces 20 percent of the grain, 60 percent of the industrial sugar beets, 45 percent of the sunflower seeds, 25 percent of the potatoes, and about 33 percent of all the vegetables used in the former Soviet Union, the problem of soil contamination is serious. Furthermore, the problems extend beyond the borders of Ukraine: The effects on the reindeer herds of Scandinavia and on sheep breeding in mountainous regions of the British Isles have been serious as well.

The scale of the contamination of the environment by the Chernobyl accident was so enormous that the task of protecting the population has not been entirely successful. The long-term health effects of environmental contamination are caused only in part by external radiation. Scientists studying the problem believe that nearly 60 to 70 percent of future health problems in affected areas will be caused by the consumption of contaminated agricultural products.

If international standards were applied for the use of agricultural land in the affected areas, nearly 1 million hectares (2.5 million acres) would be declared lost for one century, and about 2 million hectares (5 million acres) would be lost for ten to twenty years. In terms of the economy, continuing to use heavily contaminated land for food production at the expense of human health cannot be justified rationally because whatever is salvaged in the agricultural economy will be lost in future health costs.

Victoria Price

Further Reading

Alexievich, Svetlana. *Voices from Chernobyl: The Oral History of a Nuclear Disaster.* Translated by Keith Gessen. New York: Picador, 2006.

Bailey, C. C. *The Aftermath of Chernobyl.* Dubuque, Iowa: Kendall Hunt, 1993.

Marples, David R. *Chernobyl and Nuclear Power in the USSR.* New York: St. Martin's Press, 1986.

_____. *The Social Impact of the Chernobyl Disaster.* New York: St. Martin's Press, 1988.

Medvedev, Zhores A. *The Legacy of Chernobyl.* New York: W. W. Norton, 1990.

Savchenko, V. K. *The Ecology of the Chernobyl Catastrophe.* New York: Informa Healthcare, 1995.

Yaroshinskaya, Alla. *Chernobyl: The Forbidden Truth.* Lincoln, Nebr.: Bison Books, 1995.

Coal

CATEGORY: Energy and energy use

DEFINITION: Combustible sedimentary rock composed primarily of carbon and variable quantities of other elements, such as sulfur, hydrogen, oxygen, and nitrogen

SIGNIFICANCE: Coal mining and the burning of coal as a fuel both have adverse effects on the environment. The burning of coal has been found to be the largest contributor to human-caused increases of carbon dioxide, a greenhouse gas, in the earth's atmosphere.

Coal normally occurs in rock strata in layers or veins called coal beds or seams. The earth's Carboniferous period, some 300 million years ago, provided the special conditions for widespread coal formation. Coal formed as layers of plant matter accumulated at the bottoms of bodies of water, protected from biodegradation and oxidation, most often by mud or acidic water. Eventually, the plant matter buried by sediments changed over time and through geological action to create the solid known as coal.

Classifications and Uses

Types of coal are classified based on the pressures and temperatures to which their precursors were subjected, known as their degree of metamorphism. From lowest to highest degree of metamorphism, the types of coal are lignite, subbituminous, bituminous, and anthracite. Darkness of color and hardness both increase with rank. Accordingly, the harder coals, anthracite and bituminous, are also known as black coals, and the softer coals, subbituminous and lignite, are known as brown coals.

Coal is most commonly used as a fuel for the production of electricity and heat. Coal-fired generation accounts for roughly 40 percent of electricity throughout the world. In some countries, this figure is significantly higher: Poland relies on coal-fired plants for more than 94 percent of its electricity, South Africa for 92 percent, China for 77 percent, and Australia for 76 percent. When coal is used to generate electricity with a standard steam turbine, the coal is pulverized (crushed or ground into powder form) and then burned in a furnace equipped with a boiler. The furnace heat causes the boiler water to convert into steam, and the steam powers spin turbines that turn generators, creating electricity.

Another important use of coal is in the form of coke. In the production of coke, low-ash, low-sulfur bituminous coal is baked such that the fixed carbon and residual ash become fused. Coke is used as a fuel and as a reducing agent in the process of smelting iron ore in blast furnaces.

Mining

The majority of coal is strip-mined. In this process, large industrial machines strip off soil and coal, scarring the land. In some nations, laws have been passed that require mining companies to restore the land after mining operations have ended, but such reclamation projects often leave much to be desired. It has been estimated that up to one-fourth of the 3.2 million hectares (8 million acres) that are above coal mines have subsided—that is, the ground on the surfaces above the mines has caved in. Coal mining has also sometimes resulted in water drainage patterns that make land unfit for farming and uninhabitable for wildlife.

The act of mining coal also presents health risks. Even in the twenty-first century coal mining remains one of the most dangerous occupations, killing more than one hundred people per year in the United States. Further, coal miners are subject to long-term inhalation of coal dust and other mineral dusts, and so are susceptible to emphysema and other respiratory conditions such as coal workers' pneumoconiosis, commonly known as black lung, a chronic, nonfatal disease that causes extreme discomfort.

CONTROVERSIES

Because of its global abundance and relatively low cost, coal is a mainstay for both developed and developing nations, which use it for power generation and steel production throughout the world. The burning of coal, however, contributes significantly to carbon dioxide (CO_2) emissions, which are linked to global warming, and to the generation of sulfur and nitrogen oxides, which are elements in acid rain. It also releases heavy metals (including mercury, selenium, and arsenic) that are harmful to the environment and human health, and it generates waste products (fly ash, bottom ash, boiler slag, flue gas desulfurization

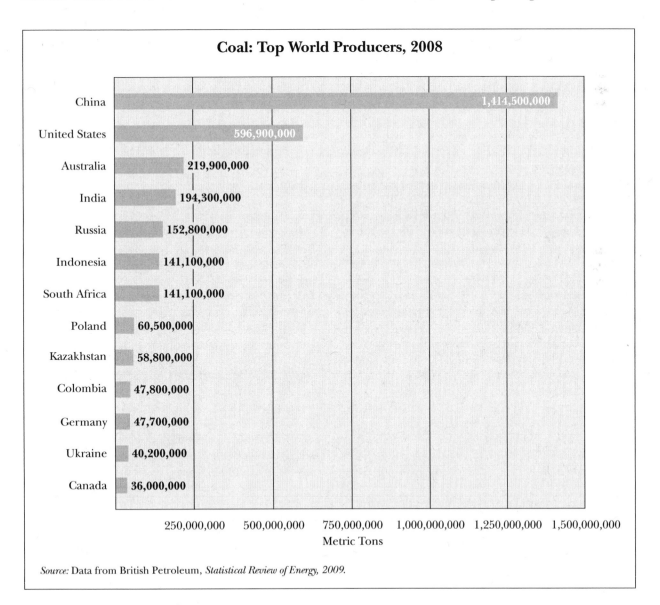

Coal: Top World Producers, 2008

Country	Metric Tons
China	1,414,500,000
United States	596,900,000
Australia	219,900,000
India	194,300,000
Russia	152,800,000
Indonesia	141,100,000
South Africa	141,100,000
Poland	60,500,000
Kazakhstan	58,800,000
Colombia	47,800,000
Germany	47,700,000
Ukraine	40,200,000
Canada	36,000,000

Source: Data from British Petroleum, *Statistical Review of Energy, 2009.*

gypsum) that pose disposal problems. Other environmental problems related to the mining and use of coal include disturbances of groundwater and water-table levels, contamination of land and waterways and destruction of property caused by spills of fly ash, disturbances to water use on flows of rivers, and dust generation.

The pollutants generated from coal burning affect not only the environment but also human health. Sulfur dioxide is associated with respiratory diseases such as asthma, bronchitis, and emphysema. Nitrogen oxides similarly are known to irritate the lungs, cause bronchitis and pneumonia, and lower the body's resistance to respiratory infections. Particulates from coal burning, when inhaled, can damage the respiratory system, causing acute and chronic respiratory illnesses.

Given that the continuing use of coal to meet the world's energy needs will exacerbate both the problem of global climate change and other negative environmental impacts, scientists recognize that there is a growing need for technologies that can better manage the emissions generated by coal burning. Carbon capture and sequestration or storage (CCS), also known as carbon dioxide air capture, is a technology in which the CO_2 generated by coal burning is captured or eliminated before it can be released into the air. CCS, however, has not yet demonstrated its efficacy and safety on an industrial scale at competitive cost.

Rena Christina Tabata

FURTHER READING

Freese, Barbara. *Coal: A Human History.* Cambridge, Mass.: Perseus, 2003.

Goodell, Jeff. *Big Coal: The Dirty Secret Behind America's Energy Future.* New York: Houghton Mifflin, 2006.

Thomas, Larry, Annedd Bach, and Michaelchurch Escley. *Coal Geology.* New York: John Wiley & Sons, 2002.

Coal-fired power plants

CATEGORIES: Energy and energy use; atmosphere and air pollution

DEFINITION: Power-generating plants that burn coal to produce electricity

SIGNIFICANCE: The dirtiest of fossil fuels, coal is the most widely used source of electricity generation

worldwide. Between 2002 and 2008, worldwide consumption of coal rose by 30 percent, two-thirds of which went into power generation.

Coal is the most widely used source of electricity generation worldwide. In 2009, 44 percent of electricity generated in the United States came from coal, 24 percent from natural gas, 20 percent from nuclear power, and 7 percent from hydroelectric sources (the remaining 5 percent came from sources such as solar, wind, and geothermal energy). Coal is the most plentiful fossil fuel; it is estimated that 90 percent of the earth's remaining fossil-fuel reserves are in the form of coal. Coal is also the most dangerous fossil fuel from the point of view of climate scientists, as most coals produce roughly 70 percent more carbon dioxide (a greenhouse gas linked with global warming) per unit of energy generated than natural gas and about 30 percent more than oil.

Coal poses environmental problems other than carbon emissions as well. The mining of coal produces methane, and its combustion produces sulfur dioxide and nitrous oxide in addition to carbon dioxide. The transport of coal also usually requires more energy than the transport of any other fossil fuel.

THE ROLE OF CHINA

During the 1980's China replaced the Soviet Union as the world's largest coal producer. China controls 43 percent of the world's remaining coal reserves and uses coal to generate more than 80 percent of its electrical energy, spewing out some 19 million tons of sulfur dioxide per year. By 2005 China was using more coal for electrical generation than the United States, the European Union, and Japan combined.

From 2004 to 2009 China increased its coal consumption an average of 14 percent per year, adding one to two coal-fired electricity plants per week to meet the demands of its booming economy, which was involved in human history's largest-scale industrialization. Many of the plants built in China during this period use old technology that lacks protections against pollution; it is expected that they will operate for an average of seventy-five years.

CARBON SEQUESTRATION

In 2007 James E. Hansen, an expert in atmospheric physics and director of the Goddard Institute for Space Studies at the National Aeronautics and Space Administration (NASA), proposed that a moratorium be placed on construction of new coal-fired power plants until technology allowing the capture and sequestration of the carbon dioxide produced by such plants is more widely available and economically feasible. About a quarter of power plants' carbon dioxide emissions will remain in the air more than five hundred years, long after new technology is refined and deployed. Hansen has estimated that all power plants without adequate sequestration will be obsolete and slated for closure (or at least retrofitting) before 2050.

By the beginning of 2008 the European Commission was weighing whether to require new power stations to include facilities that will retrofit to store greenhouse gas emissions through carbon capture and storage (CCS) technology when it is available, the first legal move of this type in the world, and a large step toward making CCS a commercial reality. The requirement as written does not include a date on which actual CCS would be required. Installation of CCS technology, now still in its infancy, could reduce global carbon dioxide emissions by one-third by 2050, if widely deployed. By 2010 Norway, Great Britain, China, and the United States were planning CCS pilot plants.

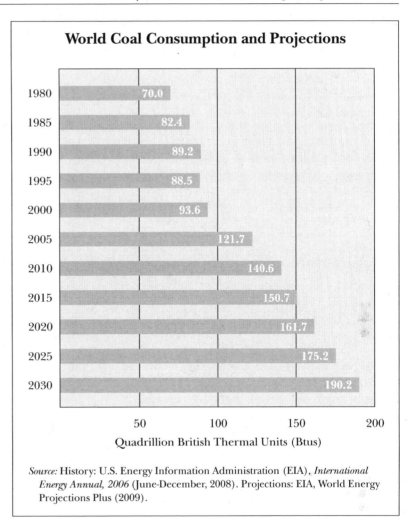

Source: History: U.S. Energy Information Administration (EIA), *International Energy Annual, 2006* (June-December, 2008). Projections: EIA, World Energy Projections Plus (2009).

OPPOSITION TO NEW PLANTS

In 2007 opposition to the building of new coal-fired plants accelerated in the United States. In one instance, when the mayor of Missoula, Montana, won city council support to buy electricity from a new coal-fired plant starting in 2011 to save the city money, he was inundated by hundreds of e-mails and phone calls from protesting constituents. Between 2006 and 2008 plans for eighty-three coal-fired power plants in the United States were voluntarily withdrawn or denied permits by state regulators.

Cancellations or delays of coal-fired power plants continued into 2009, when NV Energy delayed a plant in eastern Nevada until such time as "clean coal" technology is available, and Southern Montana Electric Generation and Cooperative halted work on a plant near Great Falls in favor of building wind turbines and another plant that will burn natural gas. Michigan's governor, Jennifer Granholm, told regulators not to approve any of five new proposed coal-fired plants in her state until all feasible and prudent alternatives had been considered. Peabody Energy dropped plans for a coal-fired energy plant in western Kentucky in favor of a plant that would convert coal to natural gas. In early March, 2009, Alliant Energy dropped plans to build a very large coal-fired power plant in central Iowa that would have provided enough energy to supply 500,000 homes. Several of these actions were challenged by coal-power advocates.

Bruce E. Johansen

FURTHER READING

Brown, Lester. *Plan B: Rescuing a Planet Under Stress and a Civilization in Trouble.* New York: W. W. Nor-2ton, 2003.

Goodell, Jeff. *Big Coal: The Dirty Secret Behind America's Energy Future.* New York: Houghton Mifflin, 2006.

Palmer, Margaret A., et al. "Mountaintop Mining Consequences." *Science* 327 (January 8, 2010):148-149.

Romm, Joseph J. *Hell and High Water: Global Warming—The Solution and the Politics—And What We Should Do.* New York: William Morrow, 2007.

Cogeneration

CATEGORY: Energy and energy use

DEFINITION: Power generation that produces useful electricity and heat simultaneously

SIGNIFICANCE: Since the mid-twentieth century cogeneration power systems have become increasingly attractive for the on-site industrial production of energy because of their cost-effectiveness and their efficiency.

Cogeneration is an energy recycling process. The cogeneration process puts to work the heat produced by the generation of electricity, energy which when produced off-site at conventional power stations is routinely lost, vented into the atmosphere largely through cooling towers. In conventional energy production, public utilities produce electricity at power plants and transmit thermal energy through miles of insulated piping to distant industrial and commercial complexes, most often factories, a process that routinely works at a tremendous inefficiency, roughly 25 percent (that is, nearly 75 percent of the energy is lost). Factories that rely on that energy must thus pay high rates for electricity that reflect the inefficiency of the system. In contrast, when a factory opts for a cogeneration plant on-site, a primary fuel source (most often natural gas, wood, or fossil fuel) is used to generate electricity, in this case a secondary fuel, and the heat that is naturally and simultaneously produced in that process is retained and used on-site, most prominently in space heating (and cooling) and in heating water. In utilizing the heat that is a by-product of electricity production, cogeneration (also known as CHP, for "combined heat and power") offers a nearly 90 percent efficiency. Because it uses significantly lower amounts of fuel to produce usable energy, cogeneration production is often cited for its potential to save industry jobs.

Cogeneration, although attractive in an era of energy conservation, is hardly new—in fact, the original commercial electrical power plant designed by Thomas Edison more than a century ago was a cogeneration plant, largely for practical reasons: No network grid existed to move energy across distances. As power networks became established and government regulations sought to protect public utilities from unlicensed competition, public utilities gradually became the dominant providers of energy in return for government control of pricing and rates. When fuel prices were relatively stable and low, industries had little incentive to develop cogeneration technology. Since the major energy crisis of the mid-1970's, however, industries have increasingly looked toward cogeneration. In addition, a process that increases energy efficiency and recycles heat offers an environmentally friendly alternative to traditional power generation.

Given that the cogeneration process involves the burning of fossil fuels, it has the potential to contribute to air and water pollution, but most established environmental groups, most prominently the Sierra Club, have long backed cogeneration as part of any responsible comprehensive domestic energy agenda. Cogeneration is far better established in Europe than in the United States; in 2010 only about 10 percent of U.S. electricity needs were being met through cogeneration facilities, but the figure was rising. The kinds of facilities that most often use cogeneration are those in various process industries (breweries, food-processing plants, paper mills, brick and cement factories, textile plants, mineral refineries); some commercial and public buildings (hospitals, hotels, large universities, airports, military facilities) also use cogeneration. Given its potential to secure at least some short-term constraints on carbon dioxide emissions and its ability to maintain power supplies despite whatever interruption might affect the larger power grid, cogeneration has emerged as a significant element of environmentally conscious energy production.

Joseph Dewey

FURTHER READING

Flin, David. *Cogeneration: A User's Guide.* Stevenage, Hertfordshire, England: Institution of Engineering and Technology, 2009.

Jonnes, Jill. *Empires of Light: Edison, Tesla, Westinghouse, and the Race to Electrify the World*. New York: Random House, 2003.

Kolanowski, Bernard F. *Small-Scale Cogeneration Handbook*. Lilburn, Ga.: Fairmont Press, 2008.

Kutz, Myer. *Environmentally Conscious Alternative Energy Production*. Hoboken, N.J.: John Wiley & Sons, 2007.

Compact fluorescent lightbulbs

CATEGORY: Energy and energy use

DEFINITION: Lightbulbs that consume less energy and radiate a different light spectrum than incandescent bulbs and are designed to replace them

SIGNIFICANCE: Compact fluorescent lightbulbs can have positive impacts on the environment in that they last longer than traditional incandescent lightbulbs and use significantly less energy than incandescents, so they create less waste and aid in energy conservation. Because compact fluorescent bulbs contain mercury, however, care must be taken in their disposal to avoid doing environmental harm.

Compact fluorescent lightbulbs (CFLs) were first introduced as an energy-saving alternative to traditional incandescent lightbulbs during the mid-1990's. They use less energy and have longer life spans than incandescent lightbulbs, which they are designed to replace. CFLs can use up to 75 percent less energy and last up to ten times longer than incandescents. CFLs can be used in most of the same lighting fixtures as incandescent bulbs, but different types of CFLs have been created for compatibility with various types of lighting fixtures, including those that use dimmer switches, three-way lamps, and outdoor fixtures.

Several kinds of fixtures and circumstances can reduce the overall efficiency of CFLs; enclosed light fixtures, for example, can create high temperatures that can shorten CFLs' life, and CFLs cannot withstand extremely low temperatures. Additionally, CFLs should not be used in fixtures that vibrate, including ceiling fans and garage door openers. The efficiency of CFLs is greatly reduced when they are turned on and off frequently, as most CFLs take at least three minutes to warm up and emit their maximum light.

CFLs and incandescent lightbulbs use different methods to produce light, which accounts for the different amounts of energy they use. An incandescent bulb produces light by running an electrical current through a wire to heat a filament. A CFL produces light by using electricity to ignite a gas within the bulb to produce invisible ultraviolet light, which then produces visible light by exciting a fluorescent white coating (phosphor) inside the bulb. A ballast regulates the electrical current within the bulb. After the gas within the CFL is ignited, the amount of electricity needed to keep the bulb lighted is significantly less than that used to heat the filament in an incandescent bulb.

State and local governments in the United States have set rules regulating the disposal and recycling of broken and intact CFLs because these bulbs, like all fluorescent bulbs, contain small amounts of mercury; on average, each CFL contains about 4 milligrams (0.00014 ounce) of mercury. When a CFL is intact no amount of mercury is released, but mercury may be released from a broken CFL. The U.S. Environmental

Compact fluorescent lightbulbs save energy in comparison with traditional incandescent bulbs and are designed to be used in the same kinds of light fixtures as incandescents. (©Bert Folsom/Dreamstime.com)

Protection Agency advises that the following special precautions should be taken when a CFL breaks, to avoid the possibility of mercury exposure. All people and animals should leave the room in which the bulb was broken, and the room should be allowed to air out for at least fifteen minutes. Disposable materials should then be used to clean up the remnants of the bulb, and all the cleanup materials should be disposed of immediately, along with the broken bulb and its remnants, in a glass jar or plastic bag that can then be sealed. The jar or bag should then be disposed of according to guidelines for disposal of toxic materials set by the local government.

Courtney A. Smith

FURTHER READING

Chiras, Daniel D. "Foundations of a Sustainable Energy System: Conservation and Renewable Energy." In *Environmental Science*. 8th ed. Sudbury, Mass.: Jones and Bartlett, 2010.

Goldblatt, David L. *Sustainable Energy Consumption and Society: Personal, Technological, or Social Change?* Norwell, Mass.: Springer, 2005.

Krigger, John, and Chris Dorsi. *The Homeowner's Handbook to Energy Efficiency: A Guide to Big and Small Improvements.* Helena, Mont.: Saturn Resource Management, 2008.

Corporate average fuel economy standards

CATEGORIES: Energy and energy use; resources and resource management

DEFINITION: Federal standards designed to improve automobile fuel efficiency in the United States

SIGNIFICANCE: Vehicle fuel economy standards were imposed in the United States during the 1970's in an effort to reduce fuel consumption, but increased driving and use of larger vehicles led to higher per-capita consumption over the next three decades. During the early twenty-first century, however, rising gasoline prices revived interest in improving the standards.

In response to the energy crisis of the 1970's, the U.S. Congress enacted legislation intended to reduce American dependence on oil imports. The 1975 corporate average fuel economy (CAFE) standards mandated fuel-efficiency levels for automobile manufacturers. Each manufacturer's annual automobile output had to meet the assigned average for that model year. If a fleet exceeded the CAFE standards, the manufacturer faced a substantial fine. To ensure that manufacturers did not import fuel-efficient foreign cars to offset low averages in their domestic output, the legislation required that import and domestic fleets be evaluated separately.

The 1978 standard for passenger cars was 18 miles per gallon (mpg). Averages gradually increased over the years (with the exception of a rollback during the late 1980's, prompted by a petition from automakers). By the 1990's the passenger car standard had reached 27.5 mpg, while the standard for light trucks (which included vans and sport utility vehicles, or SUVs) was 20.7 mpg. Between 1996 and 2001, provisions in the Department of Transportation's appropriations bills prohibited changes in the standards.

During the late 1990's many environmentalists pressed for more stringent CAFE standards. They argued that improved fuel economy would reduce the introduction of greenhouse gases and other harmful automobile by-products into the atmosphere. In addition, it would serve to protect U.S. wilderness areas where the threat of oil drilling remained a possibility. Proponents of more stringent standards also pointed to the increased use of minivans and SUVs. When CAFE standards first were imposed, light-truck-class vehicles were used predominantly for business and agricultural purposes, and lower standards were set for light trucks in order to protect small businesses and farmers. SUVs, vans, and trucks weighing between 8,500 and 10,000 pounds were not subject to any fuel economy standards at all. During the 1990's, minivans and SUVs proliferated as means of personal transportation, meaning more fuel-hungry vehicles on the road and a rise in per-capita fuel consumption.

Critics argued that CAFE standards had no impact on foreign oil imports, which continued to rise after the regulations were enacted. After a period of concern during the Persian Gulf War in 1991, most consumers regarded the continuing decline in gasoline prices that marked the mid-1990's as evidence that the issue was not critical. CAFE opponents also contended that the standards hurt the U.S. automobile industry and the country's economy in general. They claimed that the costs of manufacturing vehicles with increased fuel efficiency were passed on to consumers in the form of higher vehicle prices that unfairly affected not only individuals but also small businesses. More important, critics asserted, manufacturers achieved better performance by building smaller cars from lighter materials—vehicles that provided less protection to passengers in the event of accidents. This argument gained ground in 1991 when the U.S. Department of Transportation released a study indicating that higher CAFE standards were directly related to increases in traffic injuries and fatalities. (Later studies, however, suggested that the quality of a vehicle's engineering plays a greater role than its mass in determining how it fares in an accident.)

Environmentalists countered that higher vehicle costs were offset by savings in fuel expenses. As for the increase in traffic deaths, they maintained, automobile exhaust causes environmental damage that also results in deaths. They pointed to global warming and its consequences as proof that CAFE standards were necessary. However, as long as gasoline prices remained low, these arguments made little headway with most politicians and automobile manufacturers.

In 2003, with gas prices on the rise, new light-truck standards were issued: 21.0 mpg for model year (MY) 2005, 21.6 mpg for MY 2006, and 22.2 mpg for MY 2007. By 2007, per-capita fuel consumption in the United States had exceeded pre-1975 levels. That year, lawmakers increased CAFE standards to a combined level of efficiency for new cars and light trucks of 35 mpg by 2020. The legislation also subjected vehicles weighing between 8,500 and 10,000 pounds to CAFE standards for the first time, effective in 2011. In 2009, following a spike in gas prices the previous year, President Barack Obama's administration accelerated the timetable, calling for a fleetwide average of 35.5 mpg (39 mpg for cars, 30 mpg for trucks) by 2016 in conjunction with a 30 percent reduction in tailpipe greenhouse gas emissions.

Thomas Clarkin
Updated by Karen N. Kähler

Further Reading

An, Feng, et al. *Passenger Vehicle Greenhouse Gas and Fuel Economy Standards: A Global Update.* Washington, D.C.: International Council on Clean Transportation, 2007.

National Research Council. *Effectiveness and Impact of Corporate Average Fuel Economy (CAFE) Standards.* Washington, D.C.: National Academies Press, 2002.

Nivola, Pietro S. *The Long and Winding Road: Automotive Fuel Economy and American Politics.* Washington, D.C.: Brookings Institution Press, 2009.

Department of Energy, U.S.

CATEGORIES: Organizations and agencies; energy and energy use

IDENTIFICATION: Cabinet-level division of the executive branch of the U.S. government that oversees energy matters

DATE: Created on August 4, 1977

SIGNIFICANCE: In addition to maintaining standards for the regulation of production and distribution of energy within the United States, the U.S. Department of Energy oversees and supports energy-related research, promotes energy conservation, and supports public education and information dissemination about energy.

The U.S. Department of Energy (DOE) began operations October 1, 1977, having been created by legislation signed into law by President Jimmy Carter on August 4, 1977. That legislation merged a number of existing federal agencies into a single cabinet department answering to the president. This action was taken during a time of energy shortages in the United States; it was believed that a single governmental body would be more effective than a variety of independent agencies in implementing a national energy policy.

During the early twentieth century, the U.S. government was little involved in making policy concerning energy use other than its role in implementing daylight saving time during the world wars. After World War II, the Atomic Energy Commission (AEC) was established to oversee nuclear energy technology. In 1974 the AEC was dissolved, and two new agencies, the Nuclear Regulatory Commission (NRC) and the Energy Research and Development Administration (ERDA) were created by the Energy Reorganization Act. ERDA, along with other agencies, became the Department of Energy in 1977. By the twenty-first century DOE included dozens of offices, agencies, and administrations.

Through its various offices and agencies, DOE seeks to provide a framework for a comprehensive en-

U.S. Department of Energy

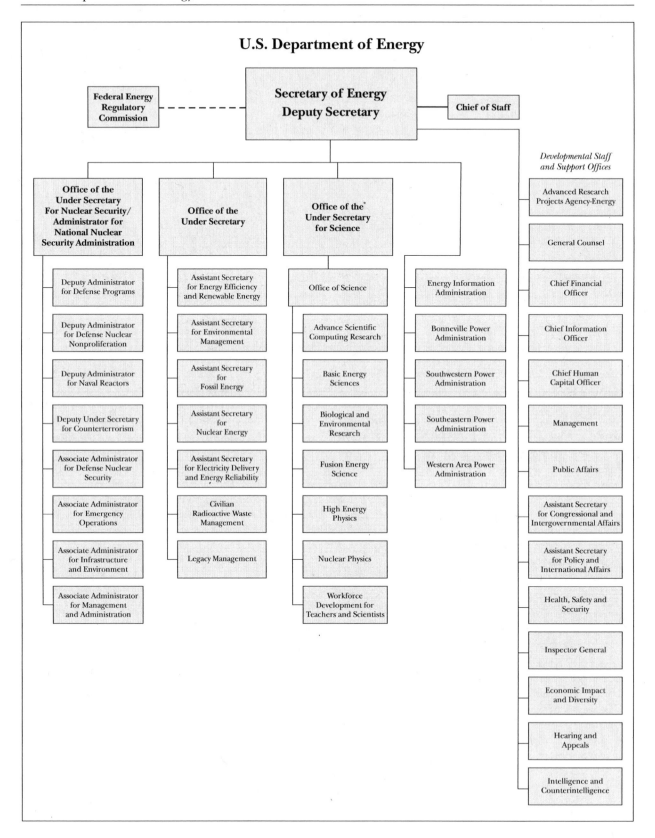

ergy policy for the United States. The department is responsible for the regulation of various parts of the energy industry within the United States. Another important function of DOE is the management of energy information; through its Energy Information Administration, DOE collects and distributes statistics about energy usage and U.S. energy reserves. The related Office of Scientific and Technical Information disseminates current energy research information.

DOE is also heavily involved in scientific and technological research. The DOE Office of Science, with its several program offices, is one of the nation's largest supporters of research in the physical sciences. The Office of Science also supports environmental and biological research. The research supported by DOE is conducted in various government laboratories throughout the United States and in university and corporate labs funded through DOE grants. DOE strongly supports research in innovative and developing fields of energy production and usage.

In addition to energy regulation and research, DOE is heavily involved in hydroelectric power. Four power administrations within DOE oversee the production and sale of electricity produced in federal hydroelectric power plants. DOE also works nationwide to support the modernization of the nation's electric grid to make electric energy more efficient and more reliable.

Nuclear Energy and Weapons

DOE works closely with the NRC to oversee the nation's nuclear energy industry. DOE's Nuclear Energy Office manages research programs for both fission and fusion energy systems. Naval nuclear reactors are managed directly by DOE, but the department shares responsibility with the NRC for management and regulation of civilian reactors. Through its Office of Civilian Radioactive Waste Management, DOE is responsible for both civilian and military radioactive waste storage and disposal.

The National Nuclear Security Administration (NNSA), an agency within DOE, oversees military nuclear technology. This includes military nuclear reactors, such as naval nuclear propulsion systems, as well as the nation's nuclear arsenal. American nuclear weapons are technically on loan to the Department of Defense from DOE. The NNSA assumes responsibility

for the manufacture, maintenance, transport, and safekeeping of these nuclear weapons. DOE also works to limit the proliferation of nuclear weapons through controls on the export of technology that could be used in the production of such weapons.

Environmental and Conservation Efforts

DOE works with other federal agencies, such as the Environmental Protection Agency (EPA), to research technologies that may reduce the environmental impacts of energy production and use. Much of this research is conducted through DOE's Office of Energy Efficiency and Renewable Energy (EERE), which supports research into renewable energy technologies such as wind, solar, hydroelectric, and geothermal. EERE is involved in research into high-risk, high-value energy technologies that private industry is unwilling to investigate until they can be proven economically viable. DOE also works with local and state governments to provide information on energy efficiency and clean energy technology.

In addition to its role in developing new sources of clean energy, DOE works to promote energy conservation and supports research into more efficient energy production, transmission, and consumption. As part of this work, DOE is involved, along with the EPA, in supporting the Energy Star program, which promotes efficiency in a wide variety of home and office products. The Weatherization Assistance Program, administered by EERE, assists low-income home owners with weatherproofing their homes and making them more energy-efficient. EERE also provides information to the public regarding energy-efficient construction.

Raymond D. Benge, Jr.

Further Reading

Consumer's Union of the United States. "Energy Star Has Lost Some Luster." *Consumer Reports*, October, 2008, 24-26.

Dietz, Thomas, and Paul C. Stern, eds. *Public Participation in Environmental Assessment and Decision Making.* Washington, D.C.: National Academies Press, 2008.

Holl, Jack. *The United States Department of Energy: A History.* Washington, D.C.: Government Printing Office, 1982.

Ducktown, Tennessee

CATEGORIES: Places; land and land use; resources and resource management

IDENTIFICATION: Town in southeastern Tennessee

SIGNIFICANCE: Copper mining operations that began in Ducktown, Tennessee, during the late nineteenth century led to the eradication of plant life and subsequent soil erosion in the region. The transformation of forestland into an artificial desert demonstrated the hazards of extracting natural resources without consideration for its effect on the surrounding area.

In 1843 a gold rush led prospectors to the southeastern corner of Tennessee, where, instead of gold, they found copper. This discovery led to the founding of several mining companies in 1850. The Copper Basin, an area of approximately 19,400 hectares (48,000 acres) surrounding the area where the city of Ducktown is located, was the only place in the eastern United States to produce significant amounts of copper, and by 1902 Tennessee was the sixth-largest copper-producing state in the nation.

After the copper ore was mined, it was put through a process called roasting to separate the copper from the rest of the ore, which included zinc, iron, and sulfur. Firewood was harvested from the surrounding forests and placed in heaps in roofed sheds with open sides. The ore was piled onto the heaps of firewood, which were then lit. These heaps, which covered vast areas of ground, were then allowed to roast for three months.

The smoke arising from the ores during the roasting was highly sulfuric. In addition to hindering vision, the smoke contained sulfuric gas, sulfuric dust, and sulfuric acid that descended onto the earth. The extent of the pollution was first acknowledged around 1895, when individual citizens filed lawsuits for damage to vegetation. The state of Georgia filed similar lawsuits in 1904 and 1905. The heap method was soon abandoned. Instead, raw ore was smelted in furnaces without being roasted first.

The ore-processing companies also built taller smokestacks to take advantage of higher air currents that would disperse the smoke, but that only spread the sulfuric vapors over a larger area. It was not until 1911 that the problem of sulfuric pollution was controlled to some extent by a process that captured the smoke for the valuable sulfuric acid that could be derived from it. By that time, the years of sulfuric pollution and systematic deforestation had turned the Ducktown area into the only desert east of the Mississippi River. Erosion washed away the topsoil, leaving a bare, rocky terrain that, at its greatest extent, covered about 130 square kilometers (50 square miles). Copper mining continued until 1986, when it became impossible for local producers to compete with the price of imported copper.

During the 1930's copper mining companies worked with the Tennessee Valley Authority (TVA) to reforest the area. More than fourteen million trees were planted over the next several decades, and grasses were also planted. Little resulted from the plantings until the 1970's, when improved methods of fertilization and soil churning increased the plants' chances of survival. By the 1990's only about 405 hectares (1,000 acres) of land appeared to be bare, with large gullies and widely spaced trees. The restoration of the forest was not totally accepted by local residents, however, who believed that a small portion of the desert should be saved as an example of severe environmental degradation.

Rose Secrest

FURTHER READING

Davis, Donald Edward. *Where There Are Mountains: An Environmental History of the Southern Appalachians.* Athens: University of Georgia Press, 2000.

Pipkin, Bernard W., et al. *Geology and the Environment.* 5th ed. Belmont, Calif.: Thomson Brooks/Cole, 2008.

Earth resources satellites

CATEGORY: Resources and resource management

DEFINITION: Unmanned scientific satellites that collect information about the earth and its resources and relay it to land-based scientific stations

SIGNIFICANCE: Earth resources satellites provide scientists with systematic, repetitive measurements of the surface conditions of the earth, including atmospheric and oceanic conditions. The data the satellites collect help scientists understand phenomena such as climate change and how events such as deforestation, coastal erosion, and pollution affect the earth as a whole.

The first earth resources satellite was launched on July 23, 1972, from Vandenberg Air Force Base in California. Earth Resources Technology Satellite 1, which became better known as Landsat 1, was placed in an orbit in which it passed over the North and South Poles to provide scientists with information about those areas. Since that first launch, earth resources satellites have provided scientists with a wealth of data about the earth. They accurately measure and transmit values for atmospheric water vapor, cloud cover, ocean currents and temperatures, ozone distribution, surface altitude and temperatures, wave height, wind speed and direction, and a variety of other atmospheric, geological, and oceanic information. By tracking the fluctuations in these measurements, scientists can study how various events affect the earth's surface and climate. They can also use this information to observe and monitor the earth's limited resources, document the spread of pollution and changes in climate, and better understand how the earth's limited resources can be used and conserved in the best ways possible.

Earth resources satellites also document events such as earthquakes, fires, floods, oil spills, and volcanic eruptions, giving scientists a clearer picture of how these events interact across the planet. For example, scientists came to a better understanding of the El Niño weather phenomenon by using satellite-gathered data to track the ocean's surface currents, temperatures, and winds through several El Niño cycles. During the 1991 Persian Gulf War, images from these satellites were used to document and monitor the damage caused to Kuwait's oil fields during the Iraqi occupation.

Information gathered by earth resources satellites may also be used to locate mineral deposits and monitor the condition of forests, fisheries, and farms. Agricultural uses include finding underutilized areas of both sea and land and determining whether plots of land can be irrigated to produce new farming areas or whether aquaculture could be a fitting use for particular areas in the sea. Satellite-gathered information has also been used to pinpoint the origins of crop diseases and to monitor the spread of such diseases.

HISTORY

During the 1960's weather satellites and photographs from high-flying aircraft provided scientists with some information about the earth's surface. These information sources were relatively inefficient, however; the black-and-white images from weather satellites did not provide significant detail, and it was impossible to take enough aerial photographs to provide sufficient information (it was estimated that some thirty thousand photographs would need to be taken to cover the United States alone). William T. Pecora, who worked for the U.S. Geological Survey, became interested in developing a type of orbiting platform that would carry scientific recording devices and provide better information. This type of equipment was already being developed for space exploration and for possible military applications, and he saw its potential for providing detailed maps of the earth. At the same time, Archibald B. Park, who worked in

Workers inspect the Landsat 7 earth resources satellite before it is launched into orbit. (NASA)

the U.S. Department of Agriculture, was interested in the same type of information; he believed that if the world's crops and forests could be mapped and surveyed, farmers and ecologists could use the information to help them better manage land resources.

For about ten years, what became the Landsat program was managed by a private-sector company (the Earth Observation Satellite Company, a partnership between Hughes Aircraft Company and the RCA Corporation), but throughout most of the history of these satellites, the U.S. government has managed Landsat through a joint program of the National Aeronautics and Space Administration (NASA) and the U.S. Geological Survey. Other countries also have earth resources satellites circling the globe, either through their own national programs or joint ventures; these include Australia, Brazil, China, Canada, Japan, and various European nations.

The first five U.S.-based earth resources satellites were launched in 1972, 1975, 1978, 1982, and 1984. The sixth satellite, launched in 1993, failed to achieve orbit, but a seventh, known as Landsat 7, was successfully launched in 1999. All of the satellites have carried various types of cameras, including infrared cameras. The older models collected photographic images of the earth's surface; the later models (1982, 1984, and 1999) also carried additional sensors and a scanning radiometer capable of providing scientists with high-resolution images of the earth's surface.

Marianne M. Madsen

FURTHER READING

Bukata, Robert P. *Satellite Monitoring of Inland and Coastal Water Quality: Retrospection, Introspection, Future Directions.* Boca Raton, Fla.: CRC Press, 2005.

China Remote Sensing Satellite Ground Station. *The Majestic Earth: A Selection of Earth Resources Satellite Images.* Hong Kong: Science Press, 1996.

Chuvieco, Emilio, ed. *Earth Observation of Global Change: The Role of Satellite Remote Sensing in Monitoring the Global Environment.* New York: Springer, 2008.

Kramer, Herbert J. *Observation of the Earth and Its Environment: Survey of Missions and Sensors.* New York: Springer, 2002.

Mack, Pamela E. *Viewing the Earth: The Social Construction of the Landsat Satellite System.* Cambridge, Mass.: MIT Press, 1990.

Maul, G. A. *Introduction to Satellite Oceanography.*
Dordrecht, Netherlands: Martinus Nijhoff, 1985.

Short, Nicholas M. *Mission to Earth: Landsat Views the World.* Washington, D.C.: National Aeronautics and Space Administration, 1976.

Earth-sheltered construction

CATEGORIES: Energy and energy use; resources and resource management

DEFINITION: Construction of homes or other buildings mostly underground

SIGNIFICANCE: Compared with traditional aboveground structures, earth-sheltered buildings have several environment-related advantages, in particular the fact that they require significantly lower amounts of energy for heating and cooling.

Human beings have been using earth-sheltered construction techniques since they first began creating shelters for themselves as protection against the elements. In the past earth-sheltered buildings were often carved into hillsides or constructed from turf, but modern versions are usually made of concrete. Earth-sheltered homes have been found in all cultures and all parts of the world, from Iceland to China to the American Southwest.

During the 1970's "back to the land" movement, building earth-sheltered homes became popular with many people who wanted to live in harmony with nature. Malcolm Wells, often referred to as the "father of earth-sheltered construction," was an architect who believed that underground architecture was a promising and overlooked way to build without destroying the land, a "silent, green alternative to the asphalt society." Wells credited his interest in such building to an underground housing exhibit he saw at the 1964 New York World's Fair and to a trip he took to Taliesin West, the Arizona home of architect Frank Lloyd Wright, where an underground theater stayed cool despite soaring outdoor temperatures.

An earth-sheltered building is best located on a well-drained hillside; correct excavation and preparation of the building site are critical. It is not recommended that earth-sheltered buildings be constructed in areas of permafrost, areas with high water tables, or areas with high underground radon concentrations.

Two basic types of earth-sheltered buildings are common: underground and bermed. In underground construction, the structure is created and then covered with earth (at a depth of anywhere from 15 centimeters to 2.7 meters, or 6 inches to 9 feet). In a bermed building, the structure is banked with earth surrounding one or more outside walls. Both types generally have earth-covered roofs. The choice between underground or bermed construction depends on the vegetation, climate, soil, and drainage of the building site area.

An earth-sheltered home may cost 10 to 20 percent more to construct than a typical aboveground dwelling, but often low maintenance costs and energy savings offset these higher costs somewhat. The earth surrounding an earth-sheltered building serves as insulation, so that the interior maintains a constant temperature. Proponents of earth-sheltered construction have estimated that families living in earth-sheltered homes can save up to 80 percent in heating and air-conditioning costs in comparison with these costs for a traditional aboveground house. The insulation of the earth on earth-sheltered homes also keeps water lines from freezing, makes these buildings safer than traditional houses during storms, and provides soundproofing. Proponents of earth-sheltered construction also note that the outer parts of these structures are nearly maintenance-free (they require no painting, for instance) and that, compared with aboveground buildings, earth-sheltered structures have fewer problems with break-ins (as earth-sheltered buildings have fewer entrance points) and with damage from fire (as they are usually built of concrete).

Problems can arise in earth-sheltered buildings if they are not properly constructed. Potential problems include poor air circulation, flooding, condensation, and water seepage. Earth-sheltered homes may also not have very good resale value, as the numbers of people seeking out such homes remain somewhat limited.

Marianne M. Madsen

An earth-sheltered house. (©iStockphoto.com)

FURTHER READING

Roy, Rob. *Earth-Sheltered Houses: How to Build an Affordable Underground Home.* Gabriola Island, B.C.: New Society, 2006.

Underground Space Center, University of Minnesota. *Earth Sheltered Housing Design: Guidelines, Examples, and References.* New York: Van Nostrand Reinhold, 1979.

Wells, Malcolm. *The Earth-Sheltered House: An Architect's Sketchbook.* Rev. ed. White River Junction, Vt.: Chelsea Green, 2009.

Electric vehicles

CATEGORY: Energy and energy use

DEFINITION: Vehicles that use electricity to provide some or all of their power for propulsion

SIGNIFICANCE: The replacement of fossil-fuel-powered vehicles with electric vehicles offers several benefits to the environment. Electric vehicles do not contribute to air pollution with tailpipe emissions, and overall they use less energy than gasoline-powered vehicles because of their higher efficiencies.

Nearly every major automaker in the world has an active program to develop, manufacture, and sell electric vehicles. Electric vehicles include automobiles, trucks, buses, and motorbikes. The vehicles may be divided into types based on their power sources; they include battery electric vehicles, hybrid electric vehicles, and fuel cell-powered vehicles. Electric vehicles deliver instant torque, smooth acceleration, quiet operation, and lower maintenance costs than their internal combustion-powered counterparts.

A battery electric vehicle uses a rechargeable battery to power a motor controller that in turn powers one or more electric motors to propel the vehicle at different speeds depending on the position of the accelerator pedal. Neither a transmission nor an internal combustion engine is needed. A hybrid electric vehicle uses two different energy sources, an onboard internal combustion engine linked to an electric motor or generator to drive the vehicle and to recharge the batteries. Hybrid electric vehicles operate almost twice as efficiently as traditional internal combustion vehicles. In a fuel cell-powered vehicle, a fuel cell, rather than batteries, provides the electric energy. Hydrogen is the fuel used most often in such fuel cells, but other fuels—such as methanol, natural gas, and petroleum—may be used.

The replacement of significant numbers of gasoline-powered vehicles with electric vehicles would result in large reductions in the vehicle emissions that contribute approximately two-thirds of all air pollution in most cities. The amount of reduction in a given area would depend on the local power plants used to generate the electricity for battery charging and the plants that produce hydrogen for fuel cell vehicles. In areas where power is generated using solar, wind, hydro, nuclear, or carbon-capture technologies, overall pollution would be decreased much more than in areas that depend on fossil-fuel power plants, particularly those relying on coal. Battery electric vehicles themselves produce no greenhouse gas emissions in their operation, and if their batteries are charged from an electrical grid that is powered by clean sources, the battery-charging process also produces no greenhouse gases. It has been estimated that electric vehicles can reduce greenhouse gas emissions by about 20 percent compared with gasoline-powered internal combustion vehicles in areas where coal-burning plants supply all the electrical power. In areas that use cleaner electrical-grid technologies, such as Arizona and California, greenhouse emissions could be reduced by more than 70 percent.

The limitations of electric vehicles include the cost and availability of batteries with high energy densities, short charge time, and long life. Lithium-ion batteries have demonstrated the energy densities necessary to deliver driving ranges of approximately 250 kilometers (155 miles) at speeds of up to 130 kilometers (80 miles) per hour, with recharge times of less than four hours with charging systems using 208-volt, 40-amp power supplies. The overall efficiency of electric vehicles is affected by battery charging and discharging efficiencies, which depend on the efficiency of the local electricity-generating grid. On average, battery electric vehicles have been shown to be three times more efficient than internal combustion vehicles.

The aims of future advancements in battery and charger technologies are to achieve charging times that are roughly equivalent to the amount of time it takes to fill the gas tank of a gasoline-powered vehicle and to produce such charging at a lower cost per kilometer than filling a gas tank. Also, increases in production of lithium-ion or comparable batteries are expected to reduce the prices of the batteries significantly in the future, which should reduce the cost of electric vehicles.

Alvin K. Benson

FURTHER READING

Caputo, Richard. *Hitting the Wall: A Vision of a Secure Energy Future.* San Rafael, Calif.: Morgan & Claypool, 2009.

Erjavec, Jack. *Hybrid, Electric, and Fuel-Cell Vehicles.* Clifton Park, N.J.: Thomson Delmar Learning, 2007.

Fuhs, Allen E. *Hybrid Vehicles and the Future of Personal Transportation.* Boca Raton, Fla.: CRC Press, 2008.

Electronic waste

CATEGORIES: Waste and waste management; pollutants and toxins

DEFINITION: Electronic equipment or parts of equipment discarded when broken or obsolete

SIGNIFICANCE: As consumers replace outdated or broken electronic equipment or appliances, the old items are discarded, and many end up in landfills. These discarded electronic devices often contain hazardous materials that can leach into the environment.

Electronic waste, or e-waste, is generated when consumers discard broken or obsolete electronic equipment or parts of such equipment. Industrial waste that is produced during the manufacture of electronic equipment is also sometimes referred to as e-waste. Electronic waste raises environmental concerns because many electronic devices contain numerous heavy elements, such as lead and mercury, and other toxic elements, such as cadmium and arsenic. Additionally, some devices, such as smoke detectors, can include radioactive elements. Some electronic devices also contain plastics that have been treated with fire-retardant chemicals, many of which can be toxic when released into the environment.

Unlike the disposal of many other consumer products containing hazardous materials, the disposal of electronic devices did not receive regulatory attention until the early twenty-first century. When these devices were first introduced, they existed in limited quantity and were expensive. If such a device began to malfunction or stopped working, it would be re-

paired. By the late twentieth century, however, electronic devices such as computers, microwave ovens, televisions, and cell phones had become common and comparatively inexpensive. The cost of repairing a broken device was often comparable to the cost of simply replacing it.

The pace of technology, too, was such that newer devices often had more desirable features than older ones, and many consumers elected to replace broken electronics rather than repair them. Some manufacturers began to construct electronic devices that were nonserviceable—that is, they could not be repaired—so consumers would have to buy new ones when the old ones no longer worked. Manufacturers began to make some devices in which batteries could not be changed when they died; some sold devices to consumers with the knowledge that the devices would not function with later generations of the technology. Such planned obsolescence exacerbated the problem of electronic waste.

At first, most electronic waste simply ended up in landfills. However, by the 1990's, public awareness of the environmental hazards posed by electronic waste began to rise. Grassroots movements put pressure on governments and industry to curb the landfilling of electronic waste. By 2010, twenty U.S. states had passed laws designed to reduce electronic waste, generally by establishing recycling centers devoted to electronics or by requiring retailers or manufacturers to implement take-back programs for used electronics.

The EPA's Goal for Electronic Waste

The U.S. Environmental Protection Agency has stated that its overall goal in regard to electronic waste is "to promote greater electronics product stewardship":

Product stewardship means that all who make, distribute, use, and dispose of products share responsibility for reducing the environmental impact of those products. EPA intends to work towards this goal in three ways:

1. Foster a life-cycle approach to product stewardship, including environmentally conscious design, manufacturing, and toxics reduction for new electronic products.

2. Increase reuse and recycling of used electronics.

3. Ensure that management of old electronics is safe and environmentally sound.

Electronic waste is difficult and expensive to recycle. Many electronic devices have materials in them that are valuable if recovered—such as lead, copper, and small amounts of gold, platinum, and silver—but recovering these materials is a labor-intensive process. For this reason, much of the electronic waste collected for recycling in the United States is shipped to developing countries, where unskilled and poorly paid laborers break apart the devices to get to the commercially useful materials. Often this work is done without the kind of oversight and regulation required by the environmental laws of industrialized nations, creating environmental hazards in those developing countries.

International efforts to limit the environmental damage done by electronic waste have led some developing countries to limit imports of e-waste or to regulate its disposal, leaving developed nations with fewer options for disposing of their e-waste. Manufacturers and governments have sought ways to raise revenues to address the expensive process of recycling electronic waste. To handle the cost of electronic waste disposal, some companies charge fees to accept old electronics. California has legislated disposal fees that consumers must pay when they purchase new electronic devices.

Raymond D. Benge, Jr.

FURTHER READING

Consumer Reports. "Where to Recycle Electronics, Free." June, 2009, 11.

Hester, Ronald E., and Roy M. Harrison, eds. *Electronic Waste Management.* Cambridge, England: RSC, 2009.

Jozefowicz, Chris. "Waste Woes." *Current Health,* January 2, 2010, 24-27.

United Nations Environment Programme. *Recycling: From E-Waste to Resources.* Berlin: Oktoberdruck, 2009.

Energy conservation

CATEGORIES: Energy and energy use; resources and resource management

DEFINITION: Avoidance of wasteful use of energy through decreased consumption or improved efficiency of technology or services

SIGNIFICANCE: The generation of energy often involves the use of nonrenewable resources, such as fossil fuels, the burning of which contributes to environmental degradation. Energy conservation helps to reduce the negative environmental impacts of energy generation and preserves nonrenewable resources for the future.

Many common daily practices require some use of energy resources, including fuels used to generate electricity, fuels burned for heat, and fuels burned to power vehicles. As populations around the world continue to grow and developing countries become increasingly industrialized, the amounts of energy used are also increasing. Environmentalists assert that energy conservation is a necessary approach to addressing the problems of limited natural resources, global pollution, and climate change. Conserving energy can involve both changing behaviors to reduce the amount of energy used and changing technologies or services to alternatives that require less energy to begin with.

NONRENEWABLE AND RENEWABLE RESOURCES

Energy can be derived from renewable resources, which can easily replenish or renew themselves over time, or from nonrenewable resources, the supplies of which are limited and cannot be replenished. The majority of the energy used in the world comes from such nonrenewable resources as petroleum, natural gas, coal, and uranium. These sources are fixed in supply, and burning them contributes to the presence of greenhouse gases in the atmosphere, which has been linked to global climate change. Increased awareness that the supplies of nonrenewable energy sources are limited and that their use has negative environmental impacts has led governments, environmental advocates, and others to promote a movement toward energy conservation and energy efficiency, including increasing the use of renewable and nonpolluting resources. Governments, energy utility companies, and others offer financial incentives for the reduction of energy consumption in the forms of rebates and tax credits.

The use of energy derived from renewable resources, such as hydropower, solar power, wind power, and geothermal power, does not generally contribute to global pollution and climate change. The burning of some kinds of fuels derived from renewable sources, such as biomass, can contribute to pollution, however. Among the drawbacks to the use of some

Top Energy-Consuming Countries, 2005

	TOTAL (QUADRILLION BTUS)	PER CAPITA (MILLION BTUS)
Canada	14.3	436.2
China	67.1	51.4
France	11.4	181.5
Germany	14.5	176.0
India	16.2	14.8
Japan	22.6	177.0
Russia	30.3	212.2
U.K.	10.0	165.7
U.S.	100.7	340.0
World	462.8	71.8

Source: Data from U.S. Energy Information Administration, *International Energy Annual, 2005.*

Note: Values are in British thermal units (Btus). Totals are in quadrillions; hence U.S. consumption of 100.7 is 100,700,000,000,000,000. Per capita consumption is in millions; hence U.S. per capita consumption of 340.0 is 340,000,000.

kinds of renewable energy sources are habitat destruction and noise pollution; in addition, these sources can be subject to variability in the amount of power they can generate.

BEHAVIORAL CHANGES AND ENERGY RETROFITS

Individuals, particularly in industrialized nations, can take many different steps to reduce the amounts of energy they use both in their homes and in their workplaces. In addition to the positive environmental impacts of energy conservation, the practice can help home owners and building managers to reduce utility costs. One simple way to practice energy conservation is by reducing the use of household appliances and other devices that run on electricity or that heat water or air using gas; these include chargers for electronic devices, dishwashers, washing machines and dryers, and water heaters. Behaviors such as turning off lights, unplugging appliances when not in use, taking shorter showers, and reducing the use of air-conditioning or heating can have dramatic effects in energy savings.

Modifying homes and other buildings with energy-efficiency retrofits can also help to conserve energy. Such retrofits include improved insulation and the installation of energy-efficient windows and doors to reduce the amount of energy needed for heating and cooling. The use of water heaters can be reduced with the installation of low-flow showerheads and faucets as well as high-efficiency dishwashers and washing machines.

Courtney A. Smith

FURTHER READING

Chiras, Daniel D. "Foundations of a Sustainable Energy System: Conservation and Renewable Energy." In *Environmental Science.* 8th ed. Sudbury, Mass.: Jones and Bartlett, 2010.

Elliott, David. *Energy, Society, and Environment.* 2d ed. New York: Routledge, 2003.

Horn, Miriam, and Fredd Krupp. *Earth: The Sequel—The Race to Reinvent Energy and Stop Global Warming.* New York: W. W. Norton, 2009.

Krigger, John, and Chris Dorsi. *The Homeowner's Handbook to Energy Efficiency: A Guide to Big and Small Improvements.* Helena, Mont.: Saturn Resource Management, 2008.

Sawhill, John C., and Richard Cotton, eds. *Energy Conservation: Successes and Failures.* Washington, D.C.: Brookings Institution Press, 1986.

Energy-efficiency labeling

CATEGORY: Energy and energy use

DEFINITION: Consumer product labeling systems that provide information on the amounts of energy used or conserved by particular products

SIGNIFICANCE: Energy-efficiency labeling enables consumers to take energy consumption into account when they make purchases, allowing them to see how an energy-efficient option might be more expensive in the short run but less expensive in the long run because of reduced energy consumption over time.

Energy rating systems were created in an effort to encourage the conservation of energy and thereby minimize the pollution created and resources consumed when fuel is burned for power. Primary energy sources include coal, petroleum and petroleum products, natural gas, water, uranium, wind, sunlight, and geothermal energy. Coal, petroleum and petroleum products, and natural gas are fossil fuels, which are considered nonrenewable energy sources because what is consumed takes millions of years to replace. Fossil fuels are burned to power motor vehicles, heat homes, and generate electrical power.

In the United States, every major home appliance sold carries an EnergyGuide label. A requirement of the Federal Trade Commission, this label shows how much it will cost the consumer to use the appliance for one year. The estimated cost is based on an average cost per kilowatt-hour in the appliance retailer's local area. (Electrical power is measured and billed by kilowatt-hours. A watt-hour is a unit of energy supplied steadily through an electric circuit for 1 hour; 1 kilowatt-hour is equal to 1,000 watt-hours.) One purpose of EnergyGuide labeling is to encourage manufacturers to make products that use the lowest amounts of electricity possible or that use electricity as efficiently as possible. EnergyGuide and similar labels allow consumers to compare the operation costs of appliances, so that they can make informed choices; although a particularly energy-efficient appliance may cost more than one that is less efficient, consumers may be more likely to buy the product that saves energy because of its lower operating costs over time. Using less electricity not only saves the consumer money but also helps to reduce pollution and slow the depletion of natural resources.

Logo of the Energy Star program, one of the most widely known energy-efficiency labeling programs in the United States. (Courtesy, EPA)

Energy-efficiency labeling that appears on electronic equipment shows how energy-efficient computers and other devices consume less electricity, even when turned off, than standard equipment. (When plugged into electrical outlets, many electronic devices and other appliances draw standby power even when turned off. Audiovisual equipment in standby mode accounts for about 60 percent of a home's "leaking electricity.") Energy-efficiency labeling systems identify equipment that goes into "sleep" mode, or draws less energy, when not in use.

Energy-efficiency ratings systems have expanded to encompass many kinds of equipment used in homes, including air conditioners and windows. Newly built homes are often rated on their overall energy efficiency. The amount of energy needed to heat or cool a building depends in large part on how well insulated the building is; the windows and the quality of their installation can also be a big factor, as poorly installed or poor-quality windows can allow heated or cooled air to escape or allow hot or cold outside air to enter the building. Many of the products used to improve the energy efficiency of existing buildings, such as windows and insulation, receive energy-efficiency ratings.

In 1992, the year of the United Nations Earth Summit, a number of energy-efficiency labeling programs were launched in an effort to lower the amount of electrical power consumed and the amount of pollution generated by electricity plants that burn fossil fuels. These programs include Energy Star, TCO certification, and the EU Energy Label. In the United States, the Environmental Protection Agency and the Department of Energy jointly established the Energy Star program, and Energy Star labeling subsequently became an international standard employed in Canada, the European Union, Australia, New Zealand, Japan, and Taiwan. It helps consumers make energy-efficient choices in household appliances, new homes, and home-improvement projects. The program claims to have saved consumers in the United States $17 billion on their utility bills and 30 million cars' worth of greenhouse gas emissions in 2009 alone.

The Swedish Confederation of Professional Employees, a national trade union center, created TCO certification. This standard, which applies to computer monitors and other office equipment marketed in the European Union, takes into account ergonomics, emissions, and recyclability as well as energy consumption. The European Union itself launched the EU Energy Label, which covers a wide range of energy-consuming devices, from lightbulbs to major home appliances and automobiles. In 1998, China established its Certification Center for Energy Conservation Products, which issues a voluntary energy-efficiency endorsement label for major home appliances and consumer electronics.

Lisa A. Wroble
Updated by Karen N. Kähler

FURTHER READING

International Energy Agency and Organisation for Economic Co-operation and Development. *Cool Appliances: Policy Strategies for Energy-Efficient Homes.* Paris: OECD, 2003.

_____. *Energy Labels and Standards: Energy Efficiency Policy Profiles.* Paris: OECD, 2000.

McLean-Conner, Penni. *Energy Efficiency: Principles and Practices.* Tulsa, Okla.: PennWell, 2009.

U.S. Environmental Protection Agency. *Energy Star and Other Climate Protection Programs: 2008 Annual Report.* Washington, D.C.: Author, 2009.

Wiel, Stephen, and James E. McMahon. *Energy-Efficiency Labels and Standards: A Guidebook for Appliances, Equipment, and Lighting.* 2d ed. Washington, D.C.: Collaborative Labeling and Appliance Standards Program, 2005.

Williams, Wendy. *Eco-Labelling Technology: For You and the Planet.* Stockholm: TCO Development, 2008.

Energy policy

CATEGORY: Energy and energy use

DEFINITION: High-level governmental plan of action pertaining to issues of energy supply, demand, and utilization

SIGNIFICANCE: Until the 1970's the United States made no concerted effort to develop a comprehensive national energy policy. After the 1973 oil crisis created a new view of energy as a distinct and important policy arena, successive presidential administrations undertook various initiatives, and Congress enacted several broad laws addressing aspects of energy production and consumption. No enduring, coherent national policy has resulted, however.

Energy production and consumption are strongly linked to a nation's environmental quality, economic well-being, and security. Energy use is one of the greatest sources of environmental degradation. Acid rain, along with most other ecosystem and health-related air pollution, originates with power plant and vehicle fossil-fuel combustion, as do carbon dioxide emissions, which are the most important contributors to global warming. Energy extraction, transportation, and utilization facilities create land-use and conservation impacts and also use and pollute water. Nuclear power plants generate thousands of tons of long-lived radioactive wastes.

Historically, economic growth has been accompanied by rising energy use. Beginning during the mid-1970's, however, experience in the industrialized nations demonstrated that the two factors were not necessarily tightly coupled and that using energy more efficiently could significantly slow energy growth rates while still permitting vigorous economic expansion. For less developed nations, the connection remains firmer until the transition has been made to an industrialized economy.

The national security implications of energy have become increasingly important as more countries have been forced to look beyond their borders for necessary energy supplies. U.S. reliance on imported oil was first underscored by the 1973 oil embargo imposed by the Organization of Petroleum Exporting Countries (OPEC) in response to U.S. support for Israel in the 1973 Arab-Israeli War. It was soon highlighted twice more: by the 1979-1980 "second oil shock" precipitated by the Iranian revolution and unexpected collapse of Iran's substantial oil production, and by the 1990 Iraqi invasion of Kuwait—a major oil producer—and perceived threat to the vast oil fields of Saudi Arabia, which led to the Persian Gulf War. In the early twenty-first century, the wars in Afghanistan and Iraq affected the production and price of oil.

EARLY HISTORY

Before the 1970's no serious effort had been undertaken in the United States to craft a national energy policy. The principal reason was that despite transient imbalances, cheap and abundant energy supplies were readily available. Unrelated policy initiatives focused on individual fuels and industries, driven largely by the different characteristics of each and by a desire to keep energy prices low and supplies ample.

Coal was the dominant fuel in the United States

through the 1940's, having eclipsed fuelwood during the mid-1880's. Because the coal industry was large, dispersed, and competitive, there was little incentive for federal regulation. However, coal's share of total American energy consumption began to decline as oil and gas production rose after World War I.

Oil's share of total energy increased particularly rapidly. By 1950 petroleum overtook coal as the largest U.S. energy source. A complex system of tax subsidies, import quotas, and other mechanisms arose to protect the domestic oil industry. Natural gas use also increased sharply after World War II as a consequence of gradual improvements in pipeline technology, wartime pipeline construction subsidies, and a rise in demand during the war. In 1938, the Federal Power Commission was given authority to regulate aspects of interstate commerce in gas; states had exercised some regulatory authority since the late nineteenth century. Federal price regulation continued to be a thorny issue up through the mid-1980's, when most gas prices were finally deregulated.

During the early 1950's the federal government began to push strongly for the development of commercial nuclear power and provided large research, development, and demonstration (RD&D) subsidies in a unique effort to stimulate the nuclear industry. No other fuel or technology received such promotional assistance from government. Nuclear power is also unique in that most state regulation is preempted by federal law. Despite government subsidies, the development of nuclear power stalled in the marketplace during the 1970's for reasons related to costs, safety concerns, public resistance, and an intractable radioactive waste disposal problem. The U.S. Nuclear Regulatory Commission issued no construction permits for new nuclear power plants between 1973 and the end of the century. The first reactor construction application of the twenty-first century was not submitted until 2007.

Meanwhile, the electric utility industry continued to grow, with electricity consumption rising by more than 1,100 percent during the latter half of the twentieth century. This led to an increase in total fuel consumption, because when fuels are burned to generate electricity (as opposed to being used directly, such as when natural gas is used for home heating), two of every three units of fuel are unavoidably lost as waste heat during the conversion process. The monopoly market power of electric utilities was recognized early, and both federal and state regulation was imposed.

During the 1990's political pressure mounted to deregulate the utility industry and open up electricity generation to competition. By 2000 twenty-four U.S. states had passed deregulation laws; over the next decade, however, deregulation-related problems with price and supply led eight of these states to postpone, suspend, or repeal deregulation.

Prior to the 1970's technologies and initiatives aimed at increasing the efficiency of energy utilization (often popularly referred to as "energy conservation") and developing renewable energy sources such as solar, wind, geothermal, and biomass energy received little attention and no significant federal funding. Conservation and renewables began to receive more attention and funding in the wake of the 1973 energy crisis.

1973 Oil Embargo

The 1973 oil embargo drove up oil prices in the United States and, combined with other complex factors, created localized shortages. Suddenly energy, never before regarded as a distinct federal policy arena, was thrust to the top rank of the policy agenda in the United States. The elements of national policy remained deeply embedded in the unique industries, arrangements, and regulatory regimes that had co-evolved with the three fossil fuels (oil, natural gas, and coal), nuclear power, hydroelectricity, and electric utilities, but for the first time there was also strong interest in promoting technologies to utilize renewable energy sources and increase the efficiency of energy use through a combination of federal regulation, research funds, tax subsidies, and public education. Federal RD&D funds for these alternative energy sources rose sharply during the 1970's in response to concerns regarding the energy crisis.

Between 1973 and 1983 several comprehensive, groundbreaking energy policy studies were produced by groups in the private, nonprofit, and government sectors. These served to focus government and public attention on the importance of the issue. Not surprisingly, the sudden rise in concern about energy came during the same period that the modern environmental movement arose. Beginning during the late 1960's, a growing recognition of the connection between energy and environmental issues was accompanied by frequent conflicts between energy and environmental policy goals. For example, the National Environmental Policy Act of 1969 affected many energy projects and industries, while new laws regarding

Carter's Energy Address to the Nation

Our Nation's energy problem is very serious—and it's getting worse. We're wasting too much energy, we're buying far too much oil from foreign countries, and we are not producing enough oil, gas, or coal in the United States.

In order to control energy price, production, and distribution, the Federal bureaucracy and redtape have become so complicated, it is almost unbelievable. Energy prices are high, and they're going higher, no matter what we do.

The use of coal and solar energy, which are in plentiful supply, is lagging far behind our great potential. The recent accident at the Three Mile Island nuclear power plant in Pennsylvania has demonstrated dramatically that we have other energy problems. . . .

Federal Government price controls now hold down our own production, and they encourage waste and increasing dependence on foreign oil. Present law requires that these Federal Government controls on oil be removed by September 1981, and the law gives me the authority at the end of next month to carry out this decontrol process.

In order to minimize sudden economic shock, I've decided that phased decontrol of oil prices will begin on June 1 and continue at a fairly uniform rate over the next 28 months. The immediate effect of this action will be to increase production of oil and gas in our own country.

As Government controls end, prices will go up on oil which has already been discovered, and unless we tax the oil companies, they will reap huge and undeserved windfall profits. We must, therefore, impose a windfall profits tax on the oil companies to capture part of this money for the American people. This tax money will go into an energy security fund and will be used to protect low income families from energy price increases, to build a more efficient mass transportation system, and to put American genius to work solving our long-range energy problems. . . .

We are dangerously dependent on uncertain and expensive sources of foreign oil. Since the 1973 embargo, oil production in the United States has actually dropped. Our imports have been growing. Just a few foreign countries control the amount of oil that's produced and the price that we must pay. . . .

This growing dependence has left us dangerously exposed to sudden price rises and interruptions in supply. In 1973 and 1974, shipment of oil was embargoed, and the price quadrupled almost overnight. In the last few months, the upheaval in Iran again cut world supplies of oil, and the OPEC cartel prices leaped up again. . . .

There is no single answer. We must produce more. We must conserve more. And now we must join together in a great national effort to use American technology to give us energy security in the years ahead.

The most effective action we can take to encourage both conservation and production here at home is to stop rewarding those who import foreign oil and to stop encouraging waste by holding the price of American oil down far below its replacement or its true value.

This is a painful step, and I'll give it to you straight: Each of us will have to use less oil and pay more for it. But this is a necessary step.

coal mining and the 1970 amendments to the Clean Air Act tended to discourage coal combustion. During the early 1970's a wide assortment of new energy-related initiatives were adopted, but many—such as oil price controls, efforts to jump-start a domestic synthetic fuels industry, and a nuclear breeder reactor program—were soon abandoned.

Funding for energy RD&D peaked in 1980, only to drop dramatically during President Ronald Reagan's administration (1981-1989), which opposed support for them. Market forces were trusted to resolve imbalances in energy supply and demand, and in those Cold War years weapons development and construction were prioritized over energy research. Energy RD&D spending was increased during President George H. W. Bush's administration (1989-1993), and renewables and energy efficiency received particular attention in the early years of President Bill Clinton's administration (1993-2001). Cost-sharing RD&D programs involving public-private partnerships became more common, and in 1999 government spending on energy research reached a twenty-six-year low. Midway through George W. Bush's presidency (2001-2009) the total government RD&D investment in energy was only 2 percent, compared to 10 percent in 1980. The year 2007 saw an increase in funding for basic energy sciences. In 2009, during the first year of President Barack Obama's administration, funding was provided for the Advanced Research Projects Agency-Energy (ARPA-E), created for potential paradigm-shifting research. The 2011 national budget decreased research funding for fossil-fuel and nuclear energy projects while increasing RD&D moneys for projects concerned with energy efficiency, renewables, and the country's electricity distribution grid. With that fiscal year, energy became the third-largest recipient of federal RD&D funding, behind defense and health.

FEDERAL ADMINISTRATIVE STRUCTURE

Until the 1970's responsibilities for energy matters were scattered among various federal agencies, and there was little coordination from either a regulatory or a policy perspective. After the 1973 oil embargo, efforts were made to improve the situation, but there was no encompassing centralization of function until the Department of Energy (DOE) was established in 1977. The creation of this federal department reflected the elevation of energy at the national policy level and marked the first time that energy had been afforded cabinet-rank status. Even then, several regulatory commissions remained independent, and some other federal departments retained important responsibilities.

At the state level, public-service commissions exercised long-established jurisdiction over electric utility rates, and other state agencies controlled land-use decisions that could affect power plant construction. Many states established energy agencies, and some began to formulate explicit energy policies and fund energy research.

Following the 1973 oil embargo several administrations drafted national energy plans. The first, Project Independence, was launched during President Richard Nixon's administration (1969-1974). It proposed national energy self-sufficiency by the 1980's—a goal soon recognized as politically attractive but unrealistic. President Jimmy Carter's administration (1977-1981) produced the 1977 National Energy Plan, which emphasized short-term strategies to reduce oil imports, reduce total energy demand through increased energy efficiency, raise coal production, and increase the use of renewable energy. Carter's proposals regarding renewable energy sources and increased efficiency marked the first time that the federal government had proposed a serious, tangible commitment to these alternatives.

During the Reagan administration no comprehensive energy policy document was produced, although the administration strongly favored fossil and nuclear fuels and opposed funding for energy efficiency and renewables. George H. W. Bush's administration put forth a 1991 National Energy Strategy that emphasized oil, gas, and nuclear power production but offered little support for energy efficiency and renewables. The response of the environmental community was sharply critical, but many of the proposals were included in legislation enacted the following year. The Clinton administration followed with energy plans in 1994 and 1998, as well as the Partnership for a New Generation of Vehicles, launched in 1993, and the Climate Change Technology Initiative, begun in 1998. However, an opposition-led Congress was generally unreceptive, the administration did not place high priority on its energy proposals, and no major new legislation or initiatives were adopted during the Clinton years.

FEDERAL LEGISLATION

Federal legislation sometimes marks national recognition of the importance of a hitherto ignored policy area. Prior to the 1970's, energy legislation was directed at individual fuels and energy sectors. During the 1970's, however, Congress began adopting broad-scope energy laws that, for the first time, addressed disparate energy matters in single pieces of legislation. Some contained new research and regulatory initiatives and addressed issues or technologies that had never before received serious federal attention or support. Among the most important were the Energy Reorganization Act of 1974, which established the short-lived Energy Research and Development Administration (superseded in 1977 by the DOE) and companion legislation that funded a program of energy RD&D that included a renewables and efficiency component. The 1975 Energy Policy and Conservation Act mandated automotive fuel-efficiency standards, authorized a variety of energy-efficiency programs and standards, and established the Strategic Petroleum Reserve as a hedge against future supply disruptions. The 1976 Energy Conservation and Production Act funded state conservation programs and authorized a federal program to weatherize low-income housing.

President Carter signed several pieces of legislation constituting the National Energy Act of 1978. These included the National Energy Conservation Policy Act, which expanded weatherization programs, authorized utility residential conservation programs and an energy grants program for schools and hospitals, and also authorized efficiency standards for household appliances. The 1978 Public Utilities Regulatory Policies Act (PURPA) paved the way for the tremendous expansion of nonutility, independent electric power producers that occurred during the deregulation of the 1990's. The 1978 Powerplant and Industrial Fuel Use Act (PIFUA) barred the use of oil or natural gas fuel in new electric generating plants or major industrial facilities (this act was repealed in

1987). To set an example for alternative energy use, President Carter had solar panels placed on the White House, but they were removed during Reagan's administration. Carter's energy policies are widely regarded as effective in reducing oil consumption and encouraging greater use of alternative sources of energy.

No major energy legislation was passed during the Reagan administration. Congress enacted the 1992 National Energy Policy Act at the end of the following Bush administration. The most wide-ranging legislation adopted since the late 1970's, the law included provisions to help independent power producers, notably by opening access to utilities' transmission systems to nonutility electricity generators. Other important changes included easing licensing requirements for new nuclear power plants and restricting public access to the process, initiatives intended to foster energy-efficiency improvements and renewable energy resources, and a variety of measures related to alternative fuels, energy-related taxes, coal development, and other matters. No major energy legislation was enacted during the Clinton administration.

The first significant energy legislation of the twenty-first century was the Energy Policy Act of 2005, which provided tax incentives for clean energy as well as subsidies and mandates for ethanol use. Other major energy legislation passed during the George W. Bush era includes the Energy Independence and Security Act of 2007, an omnibus energy policy law intended to increase energy efficiency and the availability of renewable energy. Its provisions included raising standards for vehicle fuel efficiency, establishing energy-efficiency standards for lighting and commercial and residential appliances, and encouraging the energy efficiency of commercial, residential, and federal buildings. Some oil and gas tax incentives were repealed to offset the cost of the revised fuel economy standards. The economic stimulus bill of fall 2008 included federal tax incentives for energy efficiency and renewables.

A similar stimulus bill was passed in the winter of 2009 after Obama took office. Another piece of energy-related legislation that year was the Supplemental Appropriations Act, which included the so-called Cash for Clunkers program, which was intended to encourage U.S. residents to trade in less fuel-efficient vehicles for newer, cleaner-operating, more efficient models. The Obama administration also accelerated the timetable for implementing the new vehicle fuel-

efficiency standards set by the previous administration and added the goal of reducing tailpipe greenhouse gas emissions. In 2010 attempts to pass comprehensive energy and climate change legislation foundered for lack of bipartisan support.

U.S. Consumption Trends

As oil prices rose and fell after the events of 1973 and 1979 and other issues began to capture the public's attention, energy began to drop down the list of pressing policy concerns. The 1990 Iraqi invasion of Kuwait and the subsequent Persian Gulf War briefly raised oil prices, as well as the visibility of energy policy and energy security. Subsequently, however, friction among OPEC cartel members and increased oil production by non-OPEC countries resulted in unexpectedly abundant oil supplies and low oil prices mid-decade. After a few years' recovery, average real gasoline prices in the United States fell to record low levels in 1998. In response, public and governmental attention again shifted elsewhere. Periodic peaks such as the record-breaking high oil prices of 2008 did not shake petroleum from its place as the nation's dominant energy source. In 2009 petroleum accounted for approximately 35 percent of the total energy consumed in the United States and 94 percent of the transportation sector's total energy use. Transportation consumed 71 percent of all petroleum used in the nation.

U.S. oil production peaked in 1970; since 1993 imports have exceeded production. In 2009 the United States produced 5.31 million barrels of crude oil per day; by contrast, the nation's imports were 9.06 million barrels per day. Crude oil imports peaked in 2005 at 10.13 million barrels per day. Although non-OPEC countries have supplied more than half of U.S. imports since 1992, OPEC oil still accounted for almost 41 percent of those imports in 2009.

Total U.S. energy consumption remained remarkably stable between 1973 and 1990 in response to substantial increases in the efficiency of energy use. A key measure of energy efficiency, energy intensity (the amount of energy used per dollar of gross domestic product), declined by 28 percent during the period but leveled off after 1986, largely in response to falling energy prices. Energy consumption between 1992 and 2000 rose to record levels in each successive year as lower energy prices and vigorous economic growth led industries and consumers to give less consideration to energy efficiency in planning and purchases.

With the exceptions of 2001 and 2006, consumption continued to rise in the early twenty-first century, reaching an all-time high in 2007. Record high oil prices in 2008—double what they had been in 2007—caused a subsequent consumption decline before they subsided. In 2010 energy consumption in the United States was twice what it was in 1963 and 40 percent greater than it was during the low point in 1975 that followed the oil crisis.

For decades, energy experts have expressed concern about the economic, environmental, and national security implications of energy supply and consumption patterns in the United States. Since the 1990's environment-related concerns have been exacerbated by the growing international recognition of the probable impacts of global climate change. The ability of most of the world's governments to meet carbon emission targets set forth in the international climate agreements first made in the 1990's hinged on changes in energy technologies and consumption patterns that have yet to be implemented to a sufficient extent.

CONTINUING PROBLEMS

The United States still faces several fundamental energy policy problems. A heavy reliance on imported oil has continued for decades. No real effort has been made to stem rising transportation-sector oil consumption caused by increased total annual miles driven and the widespread use of sport utility vehicles, minivans, and light trucks as personal transportation, a trend that took hold during the 1990's when gasoline was cheap. It was not until model year 2005 that improved fuel-efficiency standards were required for light trucks, and heavier SUVs and vans were not subject to any fuel-efficiency standards before model year 2011.

Large quantities of coal are still used to produce electricity. Attempts to establish meaningful policies to curb fossil-fuel use and accompanying greenhouse gas emissions meet with legislative gridlock; meanwhile, the United States remains one of the world's top emitters of such gases. (Long the largest emitter, the United States was surpassed by China in 2006.) Another problem is the long-standing failure of the United States to include the substantial externalized social and environmental costs of energy extraction, utilization, and security in the price of energy.

Some observers argue that such problems are not serious and that aggressive responses to them would be premature and economically devastating. Environmentalists contend that the economic, social, and environmental costs of continuing the status quo will be far more serious than the economic costs of taking steps to mitigate these problems.

Several comprehensive studies by government and nonprofit groups have concluded that an aggressive national commitment to energy efficiency and renewable energy sources could, over time, result in the displacement of significant fractions of fossil and nuclear fuels and a sharp reduction in energy-consumption growth rates, with no severe economic penalty and sizable environmental benefits. For example, analyses by the DOE and others have found that energy savings in the United States resulting from appliance and equipment standards alone totaled approximately 1.2 quadrillion British thermal units in 2000, equivalent to about 1.3 percent of the nation's overall electricity use. This energy savings represented a $9 billion reduction in consumer energy bills. According to a 2002 report from the National Academy of Sciences, vehicle fuel economy standards saved the country 2.8 million barrels of oil per day in 2000, or 15 percent of oil consumption for that year.

Among the innovative energy policies favored by environmental advocates are the imposition of meaningful taxes on carbon fuels, including additional gasoline taxes, and the abolition of large and long-standing tax and research subsidies for the fossil-fuel and nuclear industries. Another strategy would involve removing market barriers and providing ample, stable RD&D funds and tax incentives for projects concerning energy efficiency and renewable energy, including alternative transportation fuels. Environmentalists also support stringent fuel economy standards for all vehicles; tighter energy-efficiency standards for appliances, motors, and buildings; and management of the deregulation of the electric utility industry in such a way that renewable energy and energy-efficiency investments, markets, and potential are protected. Environmentalists acknowledge that the strong political opposition to many of these measures makes it unlikely that effective change will be adopted without committed federal leadership and a shift in national sentiments about the importance of energy.

ENERGY POLICIES AROUND THE WORLD

Like the United States, most industrialized nations developed explicit energy policies after the oil price and supply dislocation that occurred in 1973. In every country, energy receives more or less policy attention depending on the availability and cost of domestic and imported fuels, competition from other pressing policy and social concerns, and the degree of industrial development.

For many years, European nations pursued markedly different energy strategies, but during the 1990's the increasing economic integration of Europe led to efforts to forge a common European Union (EU) energy policy. In 2008 EU leaders adopted a far-reaching comprehensive reform of European energy policy to ensure reliable energy supplies while reducing greenhouse gas emissions and becoming a world leader in low-carbon and renewable energy technologies. Japan developed its reliance on nuclear power because no significant domestic fossil-fuel resources were available to power the tremendous postwar growth of the Japanese economy. The country remains completely dependent on imports for its oil needs, and this lack of resources has led Japan to become a world leader in energy efficiency. Continued high consumption of coal in China, the United States, India, South Africa, Japan, and Russia has raised concerns about associated greenhouse gas emissions. China, while more focused on securing energy resources for the future than on curbing greenhouse gas emissions, has the distinction of being the world's top producer of renewable energy.

Most developing countries face pressing social and economic problems that eclipse energy and environmental considerations, even though the latter often aggravate the former. For example, the cost of imported energy—usually oil—constitutes a significant drain on foreign exchange for many developing nations. At the same time, scarce capital and technical expertise make it difficult for these nations to develop alternative energy resources, technologies, and infrastructure without foreign investment and assistance.

Phillip A. Greenberg
Updated by Karen N. Kähler

FURTHER READING

Chiras, Daniel D. "Foundations of a Sustainable Energy System: Conservation and Renewable Energy." In *Environmental Science*. 8th ed. Sudbury, Mass.: Jones and Bartlett, 2010.

Davis, David Howard. *American Environmental Politics*. Belmont, Calif.: Wadsworth, 1998.

Elliott, David. *Energy, Society, and Environment*. 2d ed. New York: Routledge, 2003.

Gerrard, Michael. *Global Climate Change and U.S. Law*. Chicago: American Bar Association, 2007.

Horowitz, Daniel. *Jimmy Carter and the Energy Crisis of the 1970s: A Brief History with Documents*. Boston: Bedford/St. Martin's Press, 2005.

Kash, Don E., and Robert W. Rycroft. *U.S. Energy Policy: Crisis and Complacency*. Norman: University of Oklahoma Press, 1984.

McCartney, Laton. *The Teapot Dome Scandal: How Big Oil Bought the Hardy White House and Tried to Steal the Country*. New York: Random House, 2009.

Sandalow, David. *Freedom from Oil: How the Next President Can End the United States' Oil Addiction*. Columbus, Ohio: McGraw-Hill Professional, 2008.

Temples, James R. "The Politics of Nuclear Power: A Subgovernment in Transition." *Political Science Quarterly* 95, no. 2 (Summer, 1980): 239-260.

Energy Policy and Conservation Act

CATEGORIES: Treaties, laws, and court cases; energy and energy use; resources and resource management

THE LAW: U.S. federal law intended to address American demands for energy while simultaneously promoting conservation of energy resources

DATE: Enacted on December 22, 1975

SIGNIFICANCE: The Energy Policy and Conservation Act was the first serious attempt by the federal government to address energy independence. Many of the programs the act established, including the Strategic Petroleum Reserve, corporate average fuel economy standards for automobiles, and efficiency standards for appliances, remain focal points for debate in the twenty-first century.

The first call for the United States to set aside a supply of petroleum for emergencies came in 1944, from Secretary of the Interior Harold Ickes. Over the next three decades, the need was reconsidered, but no action was taken until an embargo by members of the Organization of Petroleum Exporting Countries (OPEC) limited the supply of oil coming to the United States in 1973. The result was a dramatic increase in the prices of oil and of gasoline, long lines and rationing at gas stations, declining stock prices, calls to reduce energy consumption immediately, and even, in some cities, bans on outdoor Christmas lights. This energy crisis spurred the federal government to take action to ensure that the United States could face future embargoes, or other emergencies, without panic.

The most important part of the Energy Policy and Conservation Act of 1975 (EPCA) was the establishment of the Strategic Petroleum Reserve (SPR), a supply of petroleum stored in salt domes in the Gulf of Mexico. Planned eventually to be a supply of 1 billion barrels (42 billion gallons), the full capacity of the SPR is 727 million barrels (30.5 billion gallons), roughly the amount in the SPR inventory as of 2010. Oil can be removed from the SPR only by order of the president of the United States. Because of limits imposed by the technology that draws the petroleum from the reserve, only about 4.4 million barrels (184.8 million gallons) can be drawn each day in an emergency—about one-fourth of the average daily petroleum consumption of the United States. The SPR has been tapped only rarely since its founding, including during the first Gulf War in 1991-1992 and after Hurricanes Rita and Katrina, when oil processing was slowed.

The far-reaching EPCA addressed energy use and conservation in other ways as well. It called on the Department of Energy to create efficiency standards for home and commercial appliances such as air conditioners, refrigerators, dishwashers, water heaters, and clothes washers and dryers. It created the first corporate average fuel economy (CAFE) standards for auto manufacturers, calling for a doubling in the fuel efficiency of cars and light trucks to 27.5 miles per gallon by 1985. To move the country away from reliance on oil and natural gas, the act encouraged power-generating plants to shift to burning coal. It directed the Federal Trade Commission to encourage the recycling of oil and the safe disposal of used oil and oil products, and it created a complex set of price and import controls for petroleum. Finally, the EPCA included requirements for increased energy conservation in federal buildings and established the State Energy Conservation Program, which helped to fund energy offices and energy management plans for individual states.

Cynthia A. Bily

FURTHER READING

Bamberger, Robert, and Robert L. Pirog. *Strategic Petroleum Reserve.* Hauppauge, N.Y.: Nova Science, 2006.

Gerrard, Michael. *Global Climate Change and U.S. Law.* Chicago: American Bar Association, 2007.

Sandalow, David. *Freedom from Oil: How the Next President Can End the United States' Oil Addiction.* Columbus, Ohio: McGraw-Hill Professional, 2008.

Ethanol

CATEGORY: Energy and energy use

DEFINITION: Fermented distillate of plant life that can be a biofuel when blended with gasoline into gasohol

SIGNIFICANCE: Although ethanol has long been the key ingredient in drinking alcohol and remains an important solvent in the chemical industry, it is of primary interest in the developed world as a fuel source of value in reducing both dependence on imported oil and environmentally destructive carbon emissions emanating from internal combustion engines.

The process for fermenting biomatter into a transportation fuel was developed long ago. As early as 1860 German engineering had produced an engine designed to run on ethanol, or ethyl alcohol, and the first assembly-line automobile produced in the United States (Henry Ford's Model T) was powered by a motor based on that design. Moving a technology from the drawing board to mass deployment, however, does not depend on feasibility alone; other important factors are market conditions and, sometimes, political climate. Both have been decisive in shaping ethanol's history as a transportation fuel.

REVIVING A KNOWN TECHNOLOGY

In the mid-nineteenth century ethanol production and sales constituted a lively business concern in both the United States and Europe, as a supply of nondrinking alcohol was kept in most households for home lighting and cooking purposes. Ethanol still fulfills those roles in parts of the developing world; however, in modern American homes it is most often found in the form of rubbing alcohol. The decline of ethanol began with the high tax on the industrial use of alcohol that the U.S. Congress enacted during the Civil War, but most of the damage was done by the discovery of oil in the United States, the emergence of kerosene as a preferred source of household fuel, and the subsequently discovered advantages of gasoline over ethanol as a motoring fuel.

The ethanol industry's revival in the transportation field began with the Arab embargo on oil shipments to countries that supported Israel in the Yom Kippur War of October, 1973. Panic buying ensued, the Organization of Petroleum Exporting Countries (OPEC) seized the moment to gain control over oil production from the multinational Western oil corporations that had controlled it for half a century, and the embargo raised serious questions as to the reliability of importing oil from Arab producers. When the outbreak of warfare between Iraq and Iran in the fall of 1979 intensified those fears and pushed the price of imported oil to more than $36 per barrel, one response of the U.S. Congress was the Energy Security Act of 1980, in which funds were appropriated to assist the fledgling ethanol industry that had emerged in the United States after 1973. The collapse of oil prices during the early 1980's, however, soon made ethanol production less attractive, as did the early experience of consumers with E90 gasohol (a mixture of 10 percent ethanol and 90 percent gasoline) during this era. A natural solvent, the gasohol cleaned out fuel lines, resulting in the clogging of enough fuel pumps in older cars to earn it a bad reputation.

The Politics of Promoting Ethanol

From 1990 onward, growing concerns about the need to find green sources of energy, the availability-of-oil issue raised anew by Iraq's 1990 invasion of Kuwait, and the soaring price of oil following the 2003 occupation of Iraq by the United States combined to produce and sustain a renewed interest in ethanol as a transportation fuel throughout the oil-importing world. Politics also played a role. Ethanol does not replace gasoline, and hence its use in low volumes is endorsed by petroleum corporations. Moreover, in low-volume gasohol mixtures such as E90, its burning can be accommodated by existing internal combustion engines. Consequently, the development of the ethanol industry has been supported by an automobile industry under government pressure to become more environmentally friendly. Meanwhile, agriculture-producing U.S. states have lobbied heavily in support of all federal legislation designed to boost ethanol production.

Nevertheless, and despite the subsidies provided by the states and the federal government, and the growing number of ethanol-producing plants in Europe, ethanol has not significantly reduced petroleum imports on either continent. Some critics argue

---

Biofuel Energy Balances

The following table lists several crops that have been considered as viable biofuel sources and several types of ethanol, as well as each substance's energy input/output ratio (that is, the amount of energy released by burning biomass or ethanol, for each equivalent unit of energy expended to create the substance).

Biomass/Biofuel	Energy Output per Unit Input
Switchgrass	14.52
Wheat	12.88
Oilseed rape (with straw)	9.21
Cellulosic ethanol	1.98
Corn ethanol	~1.13-1.34

Source: Data from the British Institute of Science in Society.

---

that it may not have made any impact because the processes of planting and harvesting the corn and other grains used as ethanol's feedstock in the developed world are themselves oil-energy-intensive. Environmental costs must also be weighed against the advantage of reduced carbon emissions that gasohol has over gasoline and diesel fuel. The pesticide "cocktail" that U.S. farmers use to protect the feedstock can harm both wildlife and groundwater, and burning gasohol in internal combustion engines can produce twice as much ground ozone as ordinary gasoline.

Uncertainty over the advantages of ethanol as a transportation fuel has thus dampened the rush to embrace it in the Western world, and Brazil remains the only country that has essentially ended its dependence on imported oil in the transportation sector. Brazil, however, uses sugarcane harvested by low-cost manual laborers and has guaranteed a growing market for ethanol by requiring the manufacture after 2007 of only flexible-fuel vehicles (FFVs) capable of burning mixtures containing as much as 85 percent ethanol. Such legislation is extremely unlikely to be enacted in the developed world, where automotive manufacturers and petroleum corporations can be expected to engage in powerful lobbying efforts against it. Consequently, ethanol production in the West continues to be measured in millions of gallons produced per year (412 million gallons in all of Europe in 2006, for example), while petroleum imports continue to be recorded in billions of barrels of oil per year.

Joseph R. Rudolph, Jr.

FURTHER READING

Blume, David. *Alcohol Can Be a Gas! Fueling an Ethanol Revolution for the Twenty-first Century.* Santa Cruz, Calif.: International Institute for Ecological Agriculture, 2007.

Boudreaux, Terry. *Ethanol and Biodiesel: What You Need to Know.* McLean, Va.: Hart Energy, 2007.

Freudenberger, Richard. *Alcohol Fuel: A Guide to Making and Using Ethanol as a Renewable Fuel.* Gabriola Island, B.C.: New Society, 2009.

Goettemoeller, Jeffrey. *Sustainable Ethanol: Biofuels, Biorefineries, Cellulosic Biomass, Flex-Fuel Vehicles, and Sustainable Farming for Energy Independence.* Maryville, Mo.: Prairie Oak, 2007.

Forest management

CATEGORIES: Forests and plants; resources and resource management

DEFINITION: Policy making and supervision related to the ways in which various resources contained in forestlands are used and protected

SIGNIFICANCE: The world's forests provide lumber for homes, fuelwood for cooking and heating, and raw materials for making such products as paper, latex rubber, dyes, and essential oils. Forests are also home to millions of plants and animal species and are vital in regulating climate, purifying the air, and controlling water runoff. Issues surrounding the management of these important resources are the subject of ongoing discussion.

Thousands of years ago, before humans began clearing the forests for croplands and settlements, forests and woodlands covered almost 6.1 billion hectares (15 billion acres) of the earth. By the end of the twentieth century, approximately 16 percent of the forests had been cleared and converted to pasture, agricultural land, cities, and nonproductive land. The remaining 4.6 billion hectares (11.4 billion acres) of forests covered approximately 30 percent of the earth's land surface.

Clearing forests has severe environmental consequences. It reduces the overall productivity of the land, and nutrients and biomass stored in trees and leaf litter are lost. Soil once covered with plants, leaves, and snags becomes prone to erosion and drying. When forests are cleared, habitats are destroyed and biodiversity is greatly diminished. Destruction of forests causes water to drain off the land instead of being released into the atmosphere by transpiration or percolation into groundwater. This can cause major changes in the hydraulic cycle and ultimately in the earth's climate. Forests also remove a large amount of carbon dioxide from the air; thus the clearing of forests causes more carbon dioxide to remain in the air, upsetting the delicate balance of atmospheric gases.

RAIN FOREST DESTRUCTION

The destruction of tropical rain forests is of great concern. These forests provide habitats for at least 50 percent (some estimates are as high as 90 percent) of the total stock of animal, plant, and insect species on earth. They supply one-half of the world's annual harvest of hardwood and hundreds of food products, such as chocolate, spices, nuts, coffee, and tropical fruits. Tropical rain forests also provide the main ingredients in 25 percent of the world's prescription and nonprescription drugs, as well as 75 percent of the three thousand plants identified as containing chemicals that fight cancer. Many industrial materials, such as natural latex rubber, resins, dyes, and essential oils, are also harvested from tropical forests.

Tropical forests are often cleared by individuals, groups, or companies with the intent of producing pastureland for large cattle ranches, establishing logging operations, constructing large plantations, growing drug crops such as marijuana or coca plants, developing mining operations, or building dams to provide power for mining and smelting operations. In 1985 the United Nations Food and Agriculture Organization's Committee on Forest Development in the Tropics developed the Tropical Forestry Action Plan to combat these practices. Fifty nations in Asia, Africa, and Latin America adopted the plan, which sought to develop sustainable forest methods and protect precious ecosystems. The Tropical Forestry Action Plan was later replaced by the Tropical Forestry Action Programme.

Several management techniques have been successfully applied to tropical forests. Sustainable logging practices and reforestation programs have been established on lands that allow timber cutting, with complete bans of logging on virgin lands. Certain regions have set up extractive reserves to protect land for the native peoples who live in the forests and gather latex rubber and nuts from mature trees. Sections of some tropical forests have been set aside as na-

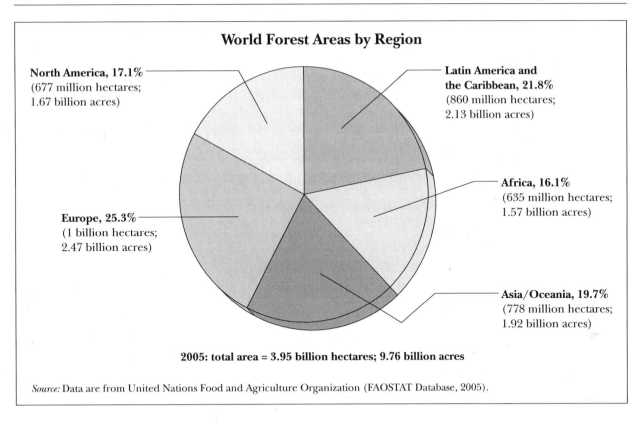

World Forest Areas by Region

North America, 17.1%
(677 million hectares;
1.67 billion acres)

Latin America and
the Caribbean, 21.8%
(860 million hectares;
2.13 billion acres)

Africa, 16.1%
(635 million hectares;
1.57 billion acres)

Europe, 25.3%
(1 billion hectares;
2.47 billion acres)

Asia/Oceania, 19.7%
(778 million hectares;
1.92 billion acres)

2005: total area = 3.95 billion hectares; 9.76 billion acres

Source: Data are from United Nations Food and Agriculture Organization (FAOSTAT Database, 2005).

tional reserves, which attract tourists while preserving trees and biodiversity. Developing countries have also been encouraged to protect their tropical forests by using a combination of debt-for-nature swaps and conservation easements. In debt-for-nature swaps, nations act as custodians of their tropical forests in exchange for foreign aid or relief from debt. Conservation easements involve tropical countries protecting specific habitats in exchange for compensation from other countries or from private organizations.

Another management technique involves putting large areas of forestlands under the control of indigenous peoples who use swidden or milpa agriculture. These traditional, productive forms of slash-and-burn agriculture follow multiple-year cycles. Each year a forest plot approximately 1 hectare (2.5 acres) in size is cleared to allow the sun to penetrate to the ground. Leaf litter, branches, and fallen trunks are burned and leave a rich layer of ashes. Fast-growing crops such as bananas and papayas are planted and provide shade for root crops, which are planted to anchor the soil. Finally, crops such as corn and rice are planted. Crops mature in a staggered sequence, thus providing a continuous supply of food. The natives' use of

mixed perennial polyculture helps prevent insect infestations, which can destroy monoculture crops. After one or two years the forest begins to take over the agricultural plot. The native farmers continue to pick the perennial crops but essentially allow the forest to reclaim the plot for the next ten to fifteen years before clearing and planting the area again.

U.S. FORESTS AND MANAGEMENT

Forests cover approximately one-third of the land area of the continental United States; American forests constitute 10 percent of the forests in the world. Only about 22 percent of the commercial forest area in the United States lies within national forests. The rest is managed primarily by private companies that grow trees for commercial logging. The land managed by the U.S. Forest Service provides inexpensive grazing lands for more than three million cattle and sheep every year, supports multimillion-dollar mining operations, and consists of a network of roads eight times longer than the U.S. interstate highway system. Almost 50 percent of American national forestland is open for commercial logging, and nearly 14 percent of the timber harvested in the United

States each year comes from national forestlands. Total wood production in the United States has caused the loss of more than 95 percent of the old-growth forests in the lower forty-eight states. This loss includes not only high-quality wood but also a rich diversity of species not found in early-growth forests.

National forests in the United States are required by law to be managed in accordance with principles of sustainable yield. The U.S. Congress has mandated that forests be managed for a combination of uses, including grazing, logging, mining, recreation, and protection of watersheds and wildlife. Healthy forests also require protection from pathogens and insects. Sustainable forestry, which emphasizes biological diversity, provides the best management. Other management techniques include removing only infected trees and vegetation, cutting infected areas and removing debris, treating trees with antibiotics, developing disease-resistant species of trees, using insecticides and fungicides, and developing integrated pest management plans.

Two basic systems are used to manage trees: even-aged and uneven-aged. Even-aged management involves maintaining trees in a given stand that are about the same age and size. Trees are harvested at the same time, then seeds are planted to provide for a new even-aged stand. This method, which tends toward the cultivation of a single species or monoculture of trees, emphasizes the mass production of fast-growing, low-quality wood (such as pine) to give a faster economic return on investment. Even-aged management requires close supervision and the application of both fertilizers and pesticides to protect the monoculture species from disease and insects.

Uneven-aged management maintains trees at many ages and sizes to permit a natural regeneration process. This method helps sustain biological diversity, provides for long-term production of high-quality timber, allows for an adequate economic return, and promotes a multiple-use approach to forest management. Uneven-aged management also relies on selective cutting of mature trees and reserves clear-cutting for small patches of tree species that respond favorably to such logging methods.

HARVESTING METHODS

The use of a particular tree-harvesting method depends on the tree species involved, the site, and whether even-aged or uneven-aged management is being applied. Selective cutting is used on intermediate-aged or mature trees in uneven-aged forests. Carefully selected trees are cut in a prescribed stand to provide for a continuous and attractive forest cover that preserves the forest ecology.

Shelterwood cutting involves removing all the mature trees in an area over a period of ten years. The first harvest removes dying, defective, or diseased trees. This allows more sunlight to reach the healthiest trees in the forest, which will then cast seeds and shelter new seedlings. When the seedlings have turned into young trees, a second cutting removes many of the mature trees, leaving enough mature trees to provide protection for the younger trees. When the young trees become well established, a third cutting harvests the remaining mature trees, leaving an even-aged stand of young trees from the best seed trees to mature. When done correctly, this method leaves a natural-looking forest and helps both to reduce soil erosion and to preserve wildlife habitat.

Seed-tree cutting harvests almost every tree at one site with the exception of a few high-quality, seed-producing, and wind-resistant trees, which function as seed sources to generate new crops. This method allows a variety of species to grow at one time and aids in erosion control and wildlife conservation.

Clear-cutting removes all the trees in a single cutting. The clear-cut may involve a strip, an entire stand, or patches of trees. The area is then replanted with seeds to grow even-aged or tree-farm varieties. More than two-thirds of the timber produced in the United States, and almost one-third of the timber in national forests, is harvested by clear-cutting. A clear-cut reduces biological diversity by destroying habitat, can make trees in bordering areas more vulnerable to winds, and creates an area that may take decades to regenerate.

FOREST FIRES

Forest fires can be divided into three types: surface, crown, and ground fires. Surface fires tend to burn only the undergrowth and leaf litter on the forest floor. Most mature trees easily survive these kinds of fires, as does wildlife. These fires occur every five years or so in forests with an abundance of ground litter and help prevent more destructive crown and ground fires. Such fires can even release and recycle valuable mineral nutrients, stimulate certain tree seeds, and help eliminate insects and pathogens.

Crown fires are very hot fires that burn both ground cover and tree tops. They normally occur in forests that have not experienced fires for several decades. Strong winds allow these fires to spread from deadwood and ground litter to treetops. They are capable of killing all vegetation and wildlife, leaving the land prone to erosion. Ground fires are most common in northern bogs. They can begin as surface fires but burn peat or partially decayed leaves below the ground surface. They can smolder for days or weeks before anyone notices them, and they are difficult to douse.

Natural forest fires can be beneficial to some species of trees, such as the giant sequoia and the jack pine, which release seeds for germination only after being exposed to intense heat. Grassland and pine forest ecosystems that depend on fires to regenerate are called fire climax ecosystems. They are managed for optimum productivity with prescribed fires.

The Society of American Foresters has begun advocating a concept called new forestry, in which ecological health and biodiversity, rather than timber production, are the main objectives of forestry. Advocates of new forestry propose that any given site should be logged only every 350 years, wide buffer zones should be left beside streams to reduce erosion and protect habitat, and logs and snags should be left in forests to help replenish soil fertility. Proponents of such forestry also endorse the involvement of private landowners in the cooperative management of lands.

Toby Stewart and Dion Stewart

FURTHER READING

Bettinger, Pete, et al. *Forest Management and Planning.* Burlington, Mass.: Academic Press, 2009.

Colfer, Carol J. Pierce. *The Equitable Forest: Diversity, Community, and Resource Management.* Washington, D.C.: Resources for the Future, 2005.

Crow, Thomas R. "Landscape Ecology and Forest Management." In *Issues and Perspectives in Landscape Ecology,* edited by John Wiens and Michael Moss. New York: Cambridge University Press, 2005.

Davis, Lawrence S., et al. *Forest Management: To Sustain Ecological, Economic, and Social Values.* 4th ed. Boston: McGraw-Hill, 2001.

McNeely, Jeffrey A., et al. *Conserving the World's Biological Diversity.* Washington, D.C.: Island Press, 1990.

Robbins, William G. *American Forestry.* Lincoln: University of Nebraska Press, 1985.

Fossil fuels

CATEGORIES: Energy and energy use; resources and resource management

DEFINITION: Fuels formed over long spans of time from buried dead organisms

SIGNIFICANCE: Fossil fuels are the most widely used sources of energy production throughout the world and are essential to human activity in modern society. The use of such fuels, however, is the cause of significant environmental degradation through air and water pollution and habitat destruction. The carbon dioxide emitted by the burning of fossil fuels has been linked to global warming.

Fossil fuels—coal, oil, and natural gas—are found in the earth's crust. They are the result of the decomposition of dead plants and animals under heat and pressure as they were covered with sediment, becoming part of the earth's crust, as either landmass or seabed. These fuels are nonrenewable resources; they have required millions of years to form.

Fossil fuels are composed of high percentages of carbon and hydrocarbons, and the ratio of carbon to hydrogen varies considerably from one type of fossil fuel to another. A gas such as methane has a low ratio and burns quickly, whereas a substance such as anthracite coal, composed almost entirely of carbon, has a lower ratio and burns more slowly. When burned, all fossil fuels produce large amounts of energy, and this characteristic led them to play a significant role in the industrialization and modernization of the world. According to the Energy Information Association, in 2007 fossil fuels accounted for the production of 86.4 percent of the energy consumed worldwide. Although fossil fuels are capable of meeting the energy production needs of the world, they are a resource that is diminishing, and their extraction and use both cause considerable environmental problems.

The major concern in regard to the use of fossil fuels is their emission of carbon dioxide (CO_2), one of the greenhouse gases that has been linked to global warming. According to the U.S. Department of Energy, the burning of fossil fuels produces almost twice as much CO_2 as natural processes can absorb each year.

COAL AND EFFECTS ON THE ENVIRONMENT

The three types of coal—anthracite, bituminous, and lignite—are retrieved either by deep-shaft underground mining or by opencast (surface) mining. Both types of mining cause considerable damage to the area mined, as they destroy land and pollute air and rivers. The pollution from lignite mining is particularly harmful to forests.

When coal is burned it emits a number of harmful substances, including sulfur dioxide, nitrogen oxide, mercury, particulates, and carbon dioxide. Sulfur dioxide, nitrogen oxide, and particulates contribute to the formation of acid rain, which can cause respiratory illness. Mercury that enters rivers, streams, or lakes combines into the chemical methylmercury. It is highly toxic to water plants, to fish, and to animals and people who consume the fish. It is, however, the CO_2 produced by the burning of coal that is of the greatest environmental concern. CO_2 is the major pollutant that causes global warming, and coal-fired power plants are responsible for the greatest amount of CO_2 released into the air. The transport of coal further contributes to the release of pollutants into the air. Although some coal is transported as slurry through pipelines, the majority of coal is transported by train using diesel-fueled locomotives, which in turn emit more CO_2 and other pollutants.

ENVIRONMENTAL IMPACTS OF OIL

Crude oil or petroleum is composed of hydrogen and carbon compounds. It is a liquid form of fossilized biomass derived from the decomposition of dead plants and animals found in underground reservoirs

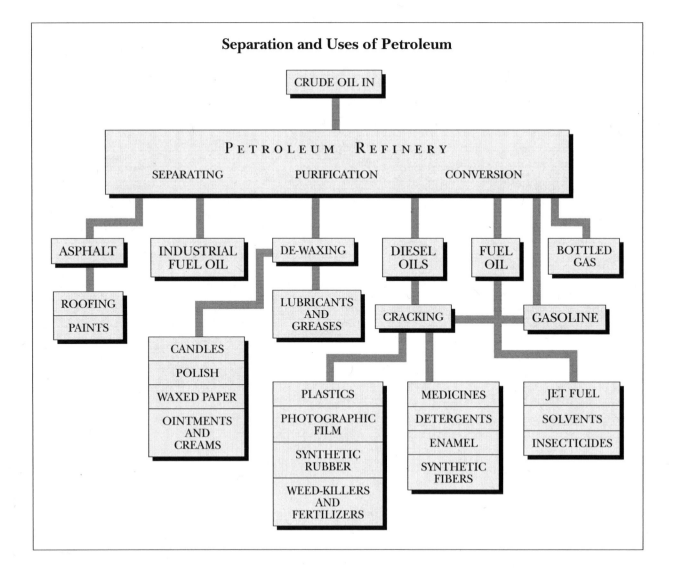

Separation and Uses of Petroleum

in sedimentary basins on land areas and in seabeds. Oil is extracted from the earth by pumping, using wells and oil rigs, and it is transported long distances through pipelines or in ships. The major danger to the environment from these activities is the occurrence of oil spills, which have serious impacts on wildlife, especially marine life, seabirds, and sea mammals.

Gasoline, diesel fuel, jet fuel, and liquid propane gas are all derived from oil. It is also the feedstock or raw material from which plastics, polyurethane, and many other products are made. Oil plays a vital role in

World Proved Fossil Fuel Reserves, 2003			
REGION	OIL	COAL	NATURAL GAS
Far East	8,041	140,362	16,317
Middle East and North Africa	105,662	1,322	71,385
Europe	11,845	135,783	48,433
Sub-Saharan Africa	6,500	33,348	4,497
North America	6,493	125,311	6,209
Central America and West Indies	2,550	690	1,037
South America	14,120	8,601	5,608
Oceania	611	41,748	2,679
Total	156,700	501,172	158,198

Source: International Energy Agency.
Note: In millions of metric tons of oil equivalent.

the everyday life of the modern world. Gasoline, diesel, and jet fuel are the most commonly used sources of energy in transportation. Gasoline is the primary fuel used in private cars; diesel fuel is used in freight trucks, in train engines, and in such heavy equipment as construction and farm vehicles. Diesel is also the fuel of choice for other kinds of machinery used in agriculture and construction. The generators used to provide electricity to such facilities as hospitals and nursing homes in times of emergency are usually powered by diesel fuel. Propane, which is a cleaner-burning fuel than either gasoline or diesel, is used in indoor equipment.

Oil's greatest impacts on the environment come from its use as fuel. In 2008, consumption of oil worldwide amounted to 85.4 million barrels per day. When oil is burned in any of its forms, it emits a number of harmful substances into the atmosphere. These include CO_2, carbon monoxide (CO), sulfur, and lead. Lead in particulate matter is classified as a carcinogen. Sulfur dioxide contributes to the formation of acid rain, which is harmful to animals, plants, and human beings. The nitrogen oxide and volatile organic compounds found in emissions from the burning of oil are among the causes of ground-level ozone. Many of these pollutants contribute to lung irritation, asthma, bronchitis, and lung disease.

ENVIRONMENTAL IMPACTS OF NATURAL GAS

Natural gas is composed of hydrogen and carbon; it is primarily methane. Like coal and oil, natural gas is formed over millions of years from the decomposing remains of plants and animals covered by sand and silt

and subjected to heat and pressure. Deposits of natural gas are found in both landmasses and seabeds. Extraction of the gas, achieved through drilling and the establishment of wells, has impacts on the wildlife in the area of the drilling through the disruption of habitat. Natural gas is transported by pipelines to refineries. At both drilling sites and along the pipelines, leaks can occur that can result in serious explosions.

Natural gas has many uses. It is used to generate electricity, as a fuel in industry, and for heating homes and powering home appliances. Natural gas also serves as a raw material for producing a wide variety of products ranging from fertilizers to medicines. When burned, natural gas emits fewer pollutants, especially sulfur and nitrogen, than either oil or coal. It does, however, produce CO_2.

EFFORTS TO REDUCE NEGATIVE IMPACTS

Fossil fuels continue to play an important role in all major areas of the world's economy. The generation of electricity, transportation, construction, and food production are all highly dependent on the use of fossil fuels. Governments around the world and the fossil-fuel industries are involved in ongoing efforts to combat the adverse effects of fossil fuels on the environment. Both by passing legislation within their own borders, such as the Clean Air Act in the United States, and by entering into international agreements such as the Kyoto Protocol, governments have set limits on the amounts of pollutants that may be emitted from fossil fuels and have set targets for reducing greenhouse gas emissions. Through research and new technology, as well as habitat reclamation programs, the fossil-fuel industries have worked to reduce the negative impacts of fossil fuels on the environment.

Because coal-fired power plants are the greatest emitters of CO_2, the primary greenhouse gas, citizens' groups in several countries, especially the United Kingdom, have argued for the elimination of coal mining and of the use of coal as a fuel. Methane has replaced coal as the fuel of choice in a number of power plants. The coal industry has responded with strong efforts to develop technologies aimed at reducing CO_2 emissions from the burning of coal and improving mining techniques to reduce adverse effects on land and communities in the areas where coal is mined. The reclamation of land at strip mines is one of these efforts.

In the United Kingdom, the technique of extracting coal through underground coal gasification has been investigated. The procedure involves injecting a mixture of steam and oxygen down a borehole through which gas is extracted from the coal and brought to the surface. This technique, however, may cause contamination of underground water supplies in onshore locations and the collapse of the burned-out coal seams both on- and offshore.

Coal-fired power plants using a technology known as integrated gasification combined cycle (IGCC) have also been introduced; IGCC plants convert coal into a synthetic gas before it is used to generate electricity. These plants have the capability of reducing pollutant emissions significantly, including the capture and separation of up to 95 percent of CO_2, which is then stored underground.

Other technologies and procedures implemented by the oil and gas industries to reduce the negative effects of their products on the environment include horizontal drilling techniques that can increase the area from which oil or gas can be extracted from one well. Reducing the number of wells drilled reduces the impacts on habitat and wildlife. In addition, the oil and gas industries use double-hulled tankers and double-lined pipelines to help reduce oil spills. In response to governmental mandates, oil companies have funded research that has resulted in the reformulation of gasoline and diesel fuels to reduce the emissions they produce.

Shawncey Webb

FURTHER READING

Archer, David. *Global Warming: Understanding the Forecast.* Malden, Mass.: Wiley-Blackwell, 2006.

Higman, Christopher, and Maarten van der Burgt. *Gasification.* 2d ed. Boston: Elsevier, 2008.

Kelley, Ingrid. *Energy in America: A Tour of Our Fossil Fuel Culture.* Lebanon, N.H.: University Press of New England, 2008.

Martin, Raymond S., and William L. Leffler. *Oil and Gas Production in Nontechnical Language.* Tulsa, Okla.: Pennwell, 2005.

Shogren, Jason F. *The Benefits and Costs of the Kyoto Protocol.* Washington, D.C.: AEI Press, 1999.

Williams, A., et al. *Combustion and Gasification of Coal.* New York: Taylor & Francis, 1998.

Gasoline and gasoline additives

CATEGORIES: Energy and energy use; pollutants and toxins

DEFINITION: Liquid fuel produced from petroleum, and chemicals that may be added to such fuel to change the way it performs, cleans, lubricates, or appears

SIGNIFICANCE: Gasoline plays a significant role in the transportation industry throughout the world, and gasoline additives play an important role in increasing both octane and performance of gasoline-fueled vehicles. The burning of gasoline, however, has many negative impacts on the environment and on human health.

Gasoline is a liquid fuel that contains a mixture of liquid hydrocarbons. Refined from crude oil, gasoline is shipped to storage terminals from refineries in pipelines that are also used to transport other liquid products. It is then trucked from the storage terminals to retail outlets.

Gasoline varies widely in its composition owing to refineries' mixing of crude oil from various locations, the mixing that may occur between gasoline and other products shipped in shared pipelines, and the various additives mixed in by individual companies. The invention of the automobile in the late nineteenth century transformed gasoline from a useless by-product of oil refining to a valuable transportation fuel. By the 1920's automobiles, gasoline, and gasoline stations were major elements of everyday life in the United States. Gasoline companies began putting additives in gasoline for marketing purposes, to distinguish their products from those of competitors.

Among the many different types of gasoline additives are hybrid compound blends, alcohols that act as oxygenators, ethers, antioxidants, and antiknock agents. Many gasoline additives produce emissions that are harmful to the environment and can cause health problems; others are beneficial to the environment in that they reduce air pollution. The first gasoline additive used was tetraethyl lead, which increased the octane of the gasoline and also acted as a lubricant. Benzene and toluene have been commonly used as additives. Methyl tertiary-butyl ether (MTBE) is an additive that increases octane and reduces the emission of pollutants by increasing the amount of oxygen in gasoline.

Gasoline and the Environment

When gasoline is burned it releases a number of harmful pollutants into the air, including carbon monoxide, nitrogen oxide, particulate matter, and carbon dioxide, a major greenhouse gas that has been linked to global warming. In addition, the leakage of gasoline from storage tanks and from pipelines has the potential to contaminate water supplies.

Both gasoline and the additives it contains can pose health hazards when the gasoline is burned or vaporized. Exposure to lead, which was until the 1970's the additive of choice, is known to cause cancer and other serious health problems. Benzene vapor from gasoline can cause headaches and dizziness, and high levels can cause rapid heart rate and tremors; benzene is also a carcinogen. Exposure to toluene can cause headaches, respiratory irritation, and nausea.

MTBE, which replaced lead as an octane enhancer in 1979, is an oxygenate that has had positive effects on the environment. It reduces the amount of toxic emissions as it causes more of the gasoline to burn. Inhalation of MTBE is not believed to pose a hazard to health; however, some concerns have been expressed regarding the additive's potential to contaminate drinking water, and it has been banned in many U.S. states.

Environmental Regulations

As early as 1924, exposure to lead was determined to be a serious health hazard. Nevertheless, the levels of lead in gasoline increased through the 1950's as motorists wanted larger, faster cars, and increasing the amount of lead in the gasoline increased both octane and engine performance. As a result of further research and greater awareness of the damage to both the environment and human health caused by the use of leaded gasoline, the 1970 amendments to the Clean Air Act set air-quality standards and included a plan for eliminating lead in gasoline. This legislation also set limits of acceptability for the amount of carbon monoxide, hydrocarbons, and nitrogen oxides in vehicle emissions. In 1976, all new vehicles were required to be equipped with catalytic converters to reduce pollutants in emissions. Only unleaded gas, which had been introduced in 1975, could be used in the vehicles with catalytic converters. The manufacture of these cars did much to phase out the use of lead in gasoline. On January 1, 1996, the use of leaded gasoline in on-road vehicles was banned in the United States.

Many other laws have been enacted that include provisions aimed at making gasoline less harmful to the environment and less of a health hazard. The 1990 amendments to the Clean Air Act set a target date of 1995 for all gasoline sold in certain metropolitan areas to be reformulated so that it would burn cleaner. This measure was taken to reduce ground-level ozone, a serious problem in many large cities, such as Dallas, Chicago, and New York. In 1990, the U.S. Environmental Protection Agency (EPA) also required the replacement of all buried single-lined gasoline storage tanks with double-lined tanks to decrease the possibility of leakage. In 2006, the reduction of sulfur levels in gasoline became a priority. Refineries were required to reduce sulfur levels in gasoline, and new vehicles were mandated to have pollution-control devices that need low sulfur content to operate properly.

The negative effects of gasoline and gasoline additives on the environment and on health are issues of major concern throughout the world. Although leaded gasoline is still used in Asia, Africa, and some Latin American countries, many countries, such as Brazil, have converted to the use of pure ethanol as a motor vehicle fuel and have reduced or eliminated lead usage. As of January 1, 2000, leaded gasoline was no longer available in Europe except in a few eastern and southeastern countries. In 2009, the European Union passed legislation requiring gasoline stations to install systems for capturing and recycling toxic emissions.

Shawncey Webb

Further Reading

Dinan, Terry, and David Austin. *Reducing Gasoline Consumption: Three Policy Options.* New York: Novinka Books, 2003.

Reynolds, John G., and M. Rashid Khan. *Designing Transportation Fuels for a Cleaner Environment.* Philadelphia: Taylor & Francis, 1999.

United Nations Environment Programme. *Phasing Lead Out of Gasoline: An Examination of Policy Approaches in Different Countries.* New York: United Nations Publications, 2000.

Geographic information systems

CATEGORY: Resources and resource management

DEFINITION: Software-based mapping systems capable of linking qualitative and quantitative geographic information from databases with interactive computerized maps

SIGNIFICANCE: Geographic information systems, which enable the computerized spatial analysis of various phenomena, have many environment-related applications. For example, they are useful for tracking nonpoint pollution, mapping out the positions of various biomes, monitoring the spread or dispersal of river sediments, and observing the migratory and nesting patterns of various animal species.

The use of geographic information system (GIS) technology in spatial analysis is a relatively new area of the field of applied geographic studies. Rudimentary GIS technology became available in the 1970's and was employed mostly for corporate and university use. It was not until the arrival of object-oriented operating systems and the spread of the personal computer, however, that GIS became a user-friendly software application. Today both online and hard-drive-resident GIS software programs are being used for a variety of applications.

If a question being investigated has a spatial dimension to it, a GIS can no doubt be used to express the data in a mapped format. The power of the GIS for environmental investigation comes from its ability to display data easily and quickly in a mapped form. In addition, the GIS can manipulate the data by applying various forms of statistical analysis and showing the changes and predictions of the phenomenon on the computerized map.

GIS software is often coupled with Global Positioning System (GPS) technology to identify absolute locations of points or areas of various phenomena or features in the field. The coordinates (latitude and longitude) of these observations are then brought into the GIS and automatically displayed in the form of a map.

GIS COMPONENTS

Like the application of a spreadsheet with a database, GIS uses data and then attaches the data to a form of geographic coordinate system to allow for expression of the data in a spatial or mapped form. The basic GIS is composed of a computer software program that can open existing digital map files and manipulate the active features within these files. The software also can build digital maps when it is supplied with spatial digital data. Although the utility of a digital map has many advantages over a hard copy, GIS software also makes possible the production of large- and small-scale hard-copy maps for display purposes.

The power of GIS software is derived from its unique handling of spatial information. GIS software takes data and expresses them in the form of mapping layers that can be laid over one another to compose a map showing various features in the contexts of time and space. Furthermore, these features can be linked as hot spots to provide users of the resulting map with additional information about the features. Conventional mapping protocols such as color, shading, and line also can be utilized interactively by the user of a GIS. Additionally, zooming in and out of features and layers is easily accomplished. By using advanced applications and algorithms, a GIS user can quickly and easily model spatial information to show impacts of the variables in mapped form.

One of the major challenges of early GIS use was that many maps existed only on paper, and they needed to be converted to digital format. Map digitizer hardware was used to scan paper maps into a digital format, in a tedious process that required the digitizer operator to trace over each detail on each map using a device similar to a conventional computer mouse, called a puck. Digitizers are still used in some cases, but large-area map scanners have taken over much of this work. Additionally, with the advancements in GPS technology that took place in the 1990's, the process of getting features from the real world into digital format was revolutionized. Modern GPS systems allow operators to collect points and polygons in the field in the form of geographic coordinates and bring these into GIS databases.

ENVIRONMENTAL APPLICATIONS

The processes of environmental research, environmental assessment, and the aggregation and collection of ecological assets have all been greatly enhanced by the use of GIS mapping software. Examples of applications of GIS software in environmental research are diverse. Energy managers have utilized GIS to locate optimal power-generating sites for wind turbines. Wildlife managers use the analysis capabilities of GIS technology to help them manage wildlife within conservation areas by mapping data on such things as nesting sites and game runs. Resource and ecological agencies have used GIS in the mapping of nonpoint pollution sources.

GIS technology also has a considerable presence within urban planning agencies. The software is used to manage transportation systems, to locate potential sites for urban parks, and to maintain database records for zoning map purposes. Fire districts use GIS applications in managing their dispatch and communications systems. GIS has been a crucial tool for on-site analysis in some emergency management applications, and it has been used to chart the flow of hazardous chemical spills as well as to alert community residents who might be in danger from these environmental hazards.

M. Marian Mustoe

FURTHER READING

Amdahl, Gary. *Disaster Response: GIS for Public Safety.* Redlands, Calif.: ESRI Press, 2001.

Clarke, Keith C., Bradley O. Parks, and Michael P. Crane, eds. *Geographic Information Systems and Environmental Modeling.* Upper Saddle River, N.J.: Prentice Hall, 2002.

Davis, David E. *GIS for Everyone: Exploring Your Neighborhood and Your World with a Geographic Information System.* 3d ed. Redlands, Calif.: ESRI Press, 2003.

Easa, Said, and Yupo Chan, eds. *Urban Planning and Development Applications of GIS.* Reston, Va.: American Society of Civil Engineers, 2000.

Greene, R. W. *Confronting Catastrophe: A GIS Handbook.* Redlands, Calif.: ESRI Press, 2002.

MacArthur, R. "Geographic Information Systems and Their Use for Environmental Monitoring." In *Environmental Monitoring and Characterization,* edited by Janick F. Artiola, Ian L. Pepper, and Mark Brusseau. Burlington, Mass.: Elsevier Academic, 2004.

Geothermal energy

CATEGORY: Energy and energy use

DEFINITION: Renewable source of heat and power that draws on the earth's internal heat

SIGNIFICANCE: Although the extraction of geothermal energy is not without some negative environmental impacts, geothermal resources represent a renewable, low-carbon energy source that can be used for a variety of energy services.

Geothermal energy is predominantly the product of three sources: decay of radioactive isotopes in the earth's crust, heat remaining from the time of the earth's formation, and incoming solar radiation. The creation of an extractable geothermal resource requires a heat source, a reservoir in which to collect heat, and an insulating barrier to preserve accumulated heat. Though the most highly valued reservoirs feature temperatures of several hundred degrees Celsius, lower-temperature resources, those under 150 degrees Celsius (302 degrees Fahrenheit), can still be economical to utilize. In addition to temperature, the depth and the presence or absence of water also help determine the use and usefulness of geothermal resources.

The presence of water in geothermal reservoirs creates hydrothermal, or hot water, resources. Human beings have used hot springs for therapeutic bathing throughout history, and for several millennia, communities located near warm water sources have used those resources directly for space heating. In the modern world, networks of piped hot groundwater are used for a variety of purposes, including space and district heating, greenhousing and aquaculture, and industrial drying and processing. The appropriateness of using a hydrothermal resource for a given direct-heating purpose is dependent on several factors, including water temperature and mineral content, and proximity to the site of use. If used efficiently, a single flow of hot water can provide multiple heating services. Worldwide, geothermal energy provides almost 30,000 megawatts of heating services.

Geothermal heating and cooling of buildings is feasible in the absence of hydrothermal resources. In many places in the world, the top 3 meters (10 feet) of the ground remain a near-constant 10 to 15 degrees Celsius (50 to 59 degrees Fahrenheit) throughout the year. In summer or winter, when the ambient air tem-

Geothermal Power Plants

Geothermal power plants use three different technologies to convert hydrothermal fluids to electricity: dry steam, flash steam, and binary cycle. The first geothermal power generation plants were of the dry steam type. As of the early twenty-first century, flash steam plants were the most common type in operation. Most geothermal plants in the future will be binary-cycle plants.

- **Dry steam power plants:** Steam goes directly to a turbine that drives a generator to produce electricity. Steam technology is used at the Geysers field in Northern California, the world's largest single source of geothermal power.

- **Flash steam power plants:** Hydrothermal fluids above 182 degrees Celsius are used to make electricity. Fluid is sprayed into a tank that is held at a pressure much lower than the fluid, so that the fluid vaporizes (or flashes) rapidly. The vapor drives a turbine that in turn drives a generator to produce electricity. Liquid that remains in the tank is flashed again in another tank to produce more energy.

- **Binary-cycle power plants:** Energy is extracted from the moderate-temperature water (204 degrees Celsius) that exists in most geothermal areas through a process in which hot geothermal fluid and a second fluid with a boiling point much lower than that of water are passed through a heat exchanger. The secondary fluid flashes to vapor from the heat of the geothermal fluid, and the vapor drives a turbine, which drives a generator.

Source: U.S. Department of Energy, Office of Energy Efficiency and Renewable Energy, Geothermal Technologies Program, "Geothermal Power Plants" (2004).

vaporizes), producing steam that drives a turbine. When hydrothermal resources are at relatively low temperatures (below 150 degrees Celsius), a binary-cycle power plant that employs a secondary working fluid, such as *n*-pentane or ammonia, can be employed. In such a plant, the heat from the hydrothermal resource is used to boil the secondary fluid, thereby providing the vapor required to operate the turbine.

Because most unexploited hydrothermal resources occur at lower temperatures, future geothermal power plants built around natural hydrothermal resources are likely to employ the binary-cycle design. Nearly all major geothermal power plants built before 2010 are located at tectonic plate junctions, sites that are prone to high terrestrial heat flow. Accessing this heat flow often requires drilling boreholes up to 3 kilometers (1.9 miles) deep. Next-generation enhanced geothermal systems (EGS) are being designed that can access hot, dry rock up to 10 kilometers (6 miles) below the surface and, through the injection of water, artificially create a hydrothermal resource. EGS technology could allow large geothermal power plants to be built in areas far from plate junctions.

perature is substantially higher or lower than that of the subsurface, a heat pump can be used to circulate air through a system of underground pipes to cool or warm that air before its reintroduction into the building.

POWER PLANT TYPES

The first power plant that used geothermal energy to create electricity was built in 1904, and by 2009 plants producing more than 10,000 megawatts of generation capacity had been installed around the world. Different power plant types have been designed to create electricity from different hydrothermal resource types. When hydrothermal resources exist as steam (that is, hot water vapor), they can be used directly in conventional turbine generators. When liquid water is present at high temperatures (above 150 degrees Celsius) and under high pressure, a flash steam power plant pumps the water into low-pressure tanks, where the water "flashes" (depressurizes and

ADDITIONAL CONSIDERATIONS

A feature of geothermal energy that distinguishes it from other renewable energy sources, such as sunshine or wind, is that it is almost continuously available. For this reason, geothermal power plants present a viable option for base-load electricity generation, a power plant class long dominated by coal and nuclear fuels.

Although geothermal energy is a highly available resource, care must be taken not to mine heat at a faster rate than it is replenished by natural processes, as this practice degrades the geothermal resource and diminishes the efficiency of electricity production. Similarly, many geothermal power plants must be designed to reinject any water extracted by pumping so as to maintain the stock of on-site hydrothermal resource.

Geothermal energy is often touted by environmentalists as offering a way to generate electricity without releasing large volumes of greenhouse gases, unlike fossil-fuel-powered plants. Geothermal energy extraction does, however, have other environmental consequences. Depending on the system, utilizing geothermal energy can require drilling holes ranging in depth from a couple of meters to several kilometers. This process can change surface morphology, disrupt plants and wildlife, and pose a threat to groundwater sources. The operation of geothermal power plants can promote the release of toxic gases (such as hydrogen sulfide and ammonia) and minerals (such as arsenic and mercury). The discharge of spent hydrothermal resources into waterways can lead to thermal pollution, and the drilling of deep wells, such as those required for enhanced geothermal systems, may lead to increases in seismic activity.

Although the total amount of thermal energy stored in the earth is immense, much of that energy is either too deep or too diffuse to be extracted readily. However, several estimates of the power available in economically accessible geothermal reservoirs support the claim that geothermal energy can contribute a substantial portion of the energy needed to meet worldwide demand, either through direct use for heating and cooling or through indirect use for electricity production. Using existing technologies with high-quality geothermal resources, geothermal plants can produce power and heat at prices competitive with such widely used energy sources as coal and natural gas.

Joseph Kantenbacher

FURTHER READING

Dickson, Mary H., and Mario Fanelli, eds. *Geothermal Energy: Utilization and Technology.* Bangalore, India: United Nations Educational, Scientific, and Cultural Organization, 2003.

DiPippo, Ronald. *Geothermal Power Plants: Principles, Applications, Case Studies, and Environmental Impact.* 2d ed. Burlington, Mass.: Butterworth-Heinemann, 2008.

Gupta, Harsh, and Sukanta Roy. *Geothermal Energy: An Alternative Resource for the Twenty-first Century.* Boston: Elsevier, 2007.

MacKay, David J. C. *Sustainable Energy—Without the Hot Air.* Cambridge, England: UIT Cambridge, 2009.

Grazing and grasslands

CATEGORIES: Resources and resource management; land and land use

DEFINITIONS: Grazing is the consumption of any plant species by any animal species; grasslands are ecosystems where grasses and other nonwoody vegetation predominate

SIGNIFICANCE: While grazing is of mutual benefit to plants and animals, overgrazing is ultimately detrimental to both the plant and animal populations, as well as to grassland ecosystems. Maintaining a balance between grazing animals and the plants on which they feed prevents deleterious consequences.

Grasslands are characterized by the presence of low plants, mostly grasses, and are distinguished from woodlands, tundra, and deserts. Grasslands experience sparse to moderate rainfall and are found in both temperate and tropical zones. Grassland plants coevolved over millions of years with the grazing animals that depended on them. Wild ancestors of cattle and horses, as well as antelope and deer, were found in Eurasian grasslands. On the North American prairie, bison and antelope prospered. Wildebeest, gazelle, zebra, and buffalo dominated African savannas, whereas the kangaroo was the preponderant grazer in Australia. Grasslands occupied vast areas of the world more than ten thousand years ago, before the development of agriculture and industrialization, and the subsequent explosive growth of the human population.

Grazing is a symbiotic relationship whereby animals gain their nourishment from plants, which in turn benefit from the activity. Grazing removes the vegetative matter required for grasses to grow, facilitates seed dispersal, and disrupts mature plants, permitting young plants to take hold. Urine and feces from grazing animals recycle nutrients to the plants. The grassland ecosystem also attracts other animals, including invertebrates, birds, rodents, and predators. The grasses, grazing animals, and grassland carnivores, such as wolves or cat species, constitute a food chain.

Grasses are generally well suited to periods of low rainfall because of their extensive root systems and can go dormant during periods of drought. Humans have been an increasing presence in grassland areas, where more than 90 percent of modern crop production occurs and much urbanization and industrialization have taken place. The remaining grasslands, unsuitable for crops because of inadequate rainfall or difficult terrain, are used for grazing by domesticated or wild herbivores. In addition, many woodland areas around the world have been cleared and converted to grasslands where animals can graze.

IMPACTS OF OVERGRAZING

Continued heavy grazing of a given area leads to deleterious environmental consequences. Even repeated removal of leaf tips will not adversely affect the regeneration of grasses, provided that the basal zone of the plant remains intact. Whereas animals can generally safely eat the upper half of the grass shoot, if they ingest the lower half, which sustains the roots and fuels regrowth, they will eventually kill the plants. Overgrazing leads to denuding of the land, invasion by less nutritious plant species, erosion caused by decreased absorption of rainwater by soil, and starvation of animal species. Because the loss of plant cover changes the reflectance of the land, climate changes can follow that make it virtually impossible for plants to return, with desertification an ultimate consequence.

The number of animals is not the only factor in overgrazing; the timing of the grazing can also be detrimental. Grasses require time to regenerate, and continuous grazing will inevitably kill them. Consumption too early in the spring can stunt their development. Semiarid regions are particularly prone to overgrazing because of low and often unpredictable rainfall; regrettably, these are the areas of the world to which much livestock grazing has been relegated, because the moister grassland areas have been converted to cropland.

Overgrazing has contributed to environmental devastation worldwide. Excessive grazing by cattle, sheep, goats, and camels is partly responsible for the deserts of the Middle East. Uncontrolled livestock grazing during the late nineteenth century and early twentieth century negatively affected many areas in the American West, where sagebrush and juniper trees invaded the grasslands. Livestock overgrazing has similarly devastated areas of Africa and Asia. Feral horses in the American West and the Australian outback continue to damage those environments.

Overgrazing by wildlife can also be deleterious. The Kaibab Plateau deer disaster in Arizona is one such example, where removal of natural predators and livestock that competed with the deer for food led first to a deer population explosion, then to overgrazing by the deer, followed by starvation and large die-offs within the deer population. Protection of elk and bison in Yellowstone National Park has similarly led to high populations, excessive grazing, and changes to the environment. Only the provision of winter feed has prevented the die-offs that would otherwise naturally ensue. Ironically, winter feeding has perpetuated the problem by maintaining these populations at levels higher than grazing can sustain. Feeding has also encouraged the animals to congregate in unusually large numbers, which has contributed to the spread of disease. In 2010 a coalition of conservation groups lost a lawsuit to stop the supplemental feeding of elk and bison on the National Elk Refuge in Wyoming.

GRASSLANDS MANAGEMENT

Grassland areas need not deteriorate if they are properly managed, whether for livestock, wild animals, or both. The land's carrying capacity, or the number of healthy animals that can be grazed indefinitely in a given area, must not be exceeded. Because of year-to-year changes in weather conditions and hence food availability, determining carrying capacity is not simple; worst-case estimates typically have been used as guidelines to minimize the risk of exceeding carrying capacity. The goal should be a grassland rendered and kept healthy by optimizing, not maximizing, the number of animals. For private land, optimizing livestock numbers is in the long-term self-interest of the landowner. For publicly held land, managed in common or with unclear or disputed ownership, restricting animals to the optimum level is particularly difficult to achieve. Personal short-term benefit often leads to long-term disaster, in a phenomenon known as the tragedy of the commons.

Managing grasslands involves controlling the numbers of animals and enhancing the habitat. Cattle and sheep can be physically restricted through the use of herding and fencing, although requiring such restrictions can be difficult to achieve through political means. Much more problematic is controlling wildlife when natural predators have been eliminated and hunting is severely restricted. As for habitat improvement, the prudent use of chemical, fire, mechanical, and biological approaches can increase carrying capacity for domesticated and wild herbivores. Removing woody vegetation by burning or mechanical means can increase grass cover, fertilizing can stimulate grass growth, and reseeding with desirable species (plants native to the particular region) can enhance the habitat. Effective grassland management also requires matching animals with the grasses on which they graze.

An approach to grazing known as holistic management may have the potential not only to stave off ecosystem damage of grasslands but also to reverse desertification. This approach operates on the essential principle that, because herbivores and perennial grasses evolved together, the grasses will thrive only in combination with herbivores grazing and roaming naturally. Contrary to common wisdom regarding best management practices for grazing, holistic management involves grazing livestock in ultradense, constantly moving herds that mimic big-game grazing patterns. The livestock till the soil with their hooves and fertilize it with their excrement. By grazing the grasses, they allow sunlight to reach the grasses' growth buds; by contrast, when grazing is so restricted that the vegetation is able to die upright, the growth buds are shielded from the sun and the entire plant dies the following year. The common management practice of allowing grazed land an extended period to rest and recover, then, may not promote a resurgence of vegetative cover; rather, this practice may cause the land to remain barren and dry.

In 1992 holistic management pioneer Allan Savory began a program in Zimbabwe, Africa, in which livestock herds were increased by 400 percent on 2,630 hectares (6,500 acres) of land that had been barren for hundreds of years. By 2010, after years of holistic planned grazing, this area had become healthy grassland with open water. Other holistic management practitioners around the globe have enjoyed similar successes.

GRAZING IN THE UNITED STATES

There are roughly 312 million hectares (770 million acres) of rangelands (grasslands, forests, wetlands,

A flock of sheep grazes in a grassland region. (©Serban Enache/Dreamstime.com)

and other ecosystems that are suitable for grazing) in the United States, more than half of which are privately owned. The federal government manages 43 percent, and the remainder is under state and local government control.

Laws pertaining directly to grazing in the United States include the Taylor Grazing Act of 1934, the Federal Land Policy and Management Act of 1976, and the Public Rangelands Improvement Act of 1978. The Taylor Grazing Act introduced measures to control the unregulated grazing practices of homesteaders that had led to overgrazing, enhanced erosion, damage to streams and springs, and the land's reduced productivity; however, rancher needs still tended to take precedence over range condition. Four decades later, heightened environmental awareness led to passage of the Federal Land Policy and Management Act, which established a multiple-use mandate for land management agencies to serve present and future generations in their practices. Not long after came passage of the Public Rangelands Improvement Act, which sought to improve the condition of public rangelands so that they might meet their potential for grazing and other uses. U.S. laws pertaining to environmental quality and endangered species also have impacts on rangeland management.

The Bureau of Land Management (BLM) manages livestock grazing on 64 million hectares (157 million acres) of the 99 million hectares (245 million acres) of public lands that it administers. The BLM administers roughly eighteen hundred permits and leases, which are held mostly by cattle and sheep ranchers. The U.S. Forest Service, which administers the 77 million hectares (191 million acres) of national forest system lands, manages some 39 million hectares (96 million acres) of rangelands. The Forest Service became the nation's first grazing control agency in the early 1900's. In 1934 the Department of the Interior's Division of Grazing Control (soon renamed the Division of Grazing) joined it; this division became the Grazing Service in 1939, which merged with the General Land Office in 1946 to form the BLM.

Both the Forest Service and the BLM implement a regulatory system of permits, rental fees, herd size limits, and grazing seasons. They must maintain a balance among several often-conflicting objectives: providing forage for grazing and browsing animals, ensuring the land's long-term health and productivity, protecting watersheds, managing wildlife habitat, administering permitted mineral and energy resource

exploration and extraction, offering recreational opportunities, and preserving the land's distinctive character and aesthetic appeal. In order to meet the array of resource needs, rangeland management agencies inventory, classify, and monitor rangeland conditions. Where rangeland health needs improvement, they implement measures to restore ecosystem functions. Public land decision makers must take into account a variety of factors that affect rangelands, including severe and extensive wildfires, invasive plant species, rural residential development driven by population increases, and global climate change.

James L. Robinson
Updated by Karen N. Kähler

FURTHER READING

Arnalds, Olafur, and Steve Archer, eds. *Rangeland Desertification*. Norwell, Mass.: Kluwer Academic, 2000.

Cheeke, Peter R. *Contemporary Issues in Animal Agriculture*. 3d ed. Upper Saddle River, N.J.: Prentice Hall, 2004.

Chiras, Daniel D., and John P. Reganold. "Rangeland Management." In *Natural Resource Conservation: Management for a Sustainable Future*. 10th ed. Upper Saddle River, N.J.: Prentice Hall, 2010.

Gibson, David J. *Grasses and Grassland Ecology*. New York: Oxford University Press, 2009.

Gordon, Iain J., and Herbert H. T. Prins, eds. *The Ecology of Browsing and Grazing*. Berlin: Springer, 2008.

Lemaire, G., et al., eds. *Grassland Ecophysiology and Grazing Ecology*. New York: CABI, 2000.

Manning, Richard. *Grassland: The History, Biology, Politics, and Promise of the American Prairie*. New York: Penguin Books, 1995.

Vallentine, John F. *Grazing Management*. 2d ed. San Diego, Calif.: Academic Press, 2001.

Woodward, Susan L. *Grassland Biomes*. Westport, Conn.: Greenwood Press, 2008.

Green Revolution

CATEGORY: Agriculture and food

DEFINITION: Implementation of advances in agricultural science to raise food production levels, particularly in developing countries

SIGNIFICANCE: The input-intensive agriculture associated with the Green Revolution has increased crop yields but has also created a number of environmental problems, such as rising nitrate levels in water supplies from the use of fertilizers, community health threats linked to pesticides, and damage to soil quality that includes compaction and salinization.

The Green Revolution can be traced back to a 1940 request from Mexico for the United States to provide technical assistance to increase Mexican wheat production. By 1944, with the financial support of the Rockefeller Foundation, a group of U.S. scientists began to research methods of adapting the new high-yield variety (HYV) wheat that had been successfully used on American farms in the 1930's to Mexico's varied environments. A major breakthrough in this effort is attributed to Norman Borlaug, who, by the late 1940's, was director of the research in Mexico. For his research and his work in the global dissemination of the Mexican HYV wheat, Borlaug won the 1970 Nobel Peace Prize.

From wheat, research efforts shifted to rice production. Through the work of the newly created International Rice Research Institute in the Philippines, researchers used advanced methods of plant breeding to develop an HYV rice. This so-called miracle rice was widely adopted in developing countries during the 1960's. Since that time, researchers have sought to spread the success of the Green Revolution to other crops and to more countries.

Approximately one-half of the yield increases in food crops worldwide since the 1960's are attributable to the Green Revolution. Had there not been a Green Revolution, the amount of land used for agriculture would undoubtedly be higher today, as would the prices of wheat, rice, and maize, three species of plants that account for more than 50 percent of total human energy requirements. There is a concern, however, that the output benefits of the Green Revolution have had some negative equity and environmental effects.

In theory, a small farmer will get the same advantages from planting HYV seeds as will a large farmer. In practice, however, small farmers have had more difficulty in gaining access to the Green Revolution. To use the new seeds, farmers need adequate irrigation and the timely application of chemical fertilizers and pesticides. In many developing countries, small farmers' limited access to credit makes it difficult for them to obtain the variety of complementary inputs they need for success with HYV seeds.

The Green Revolution has promoted input-intensive agriculture, which has, in turn, created several problems: Greater usage of fertilizers is associated with rising nitrate levels in water supplies, pesticides have been linked to community health problems, and long-term, intensive production has resulted in compaction, salinization, and other soil-quality problems. Because agriculture is increasingly dependent on fossil fuels, food prices will become more strongly linked to energy supplies of this type, a fact that has raised concerns about the sustainability of the new agriculture. Biotechnological approaches to generating higher yields, the expected future path of the Green Revolution, will raise an additional set of equity and environmental concerns.

Bruce G. Brunton

FURTHER READING

Conkin, Paul K. *A Revolution Down on the Farm: The Transformation of American Agriculture Since 1929.* Lexington: University Press of Kentucky, 2008.

Federico, Giovanni. *Feeding the World: An Economic History of Agriculture, 1800-2000.* Princeton, N.J.: Princeton University Press, 2005.

Hanford Nuclear Reservation

CATEGORIES: Nuclear power and radiation; waste and waste management

IDENTIFICATION: Site in Washington State that was formerly used in the production of plutonium for nuclear weapons

SIGNIFICANCE: Procedures used at the Hanford Nuclear Reservation when its reactors were operational allowed radioactive wastes to be discharged directly into the soil, slightly radioactive cooling water to be discharged into the Columbia River, and radioactive iodine to be released into the atmosphere. Environmental cleanup at the site continues into the twenty-first century.

The Hanford Nuclear Reservation is a roughly circular area 40 kilometers (25 miles) in diameter lying on the Columbia River in south-central Washington State. As a key part of the Manhattan Project to build the atomic bomb, several nuclear reactors were

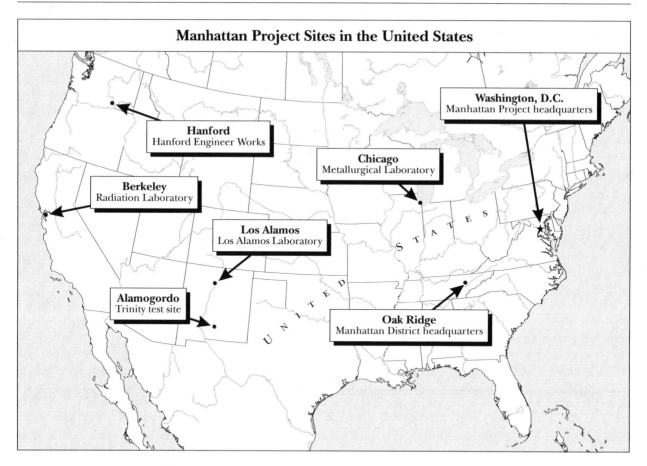

Manhattan Project Sites in the United States

constructed at Hanford beginning in 1943. Plutonium produced in these reactors was extracted from spent nuclear fuel and then shipped off-site for fabrication into nuclear weapons. Although the river water used for cooling spent only one or two seconds in the reactor core, the intense neutron bombardment made some trace elements in the water radioactive. Radioactivity was also picked up from uranium fuel elements on which the aluminum cladding had corroded. After leaving the reactor, the cooling water was held in basins to allow short-lived radioactive elements to decay, after which it was returned to the river.

Radioactive elements that were eventually detected downstream from Hanford include sodium 24, phosphorus 32, and zinc 65. The latter two were found to be concentrated in the flesh of fish and waterfowl. People who ate fish and drank water from the Columbia River were estimated to experience a maximum increased dose from this radioactivity of about 10 percent above natural background radiation, a value believed to be safe.

The chemical procedures used to extract pluto-

nium from spent fuel at Hanford released significant amounts of radioactive iodine 131 into the air, particularly in 1945. This was believed to be safe because iodine 131 has a short half-life (eight days), and its concentration is greatly diluted as it disperses across the countryside. It has since been learned that cows and goats concentrate iodine in their milk if they are fed grass contaminated with iodine and that the iodine is concentrated further in the thyroids of people who drink this milk. Infants and small children who drank a great deal of milk from grass-fed cows or goats near Hanford may have received harmful doses in 1945, but no such individuals have yet been identified.

The reactors at Hanford were shut down in the 1970's. During the years of reactor operation, Hanford stored some 256,000 cubic meters (9 million cubic feet) of highly radioactive liquid waste in 177 concrete-encased steel tanks. Some tanks contained chemical mixtures that could become explosive under certain conditions, so great vigilance was required. Approximately one-half of the waste was stored in tanks with only a single steel liner, and over the years some of these tanks leaked an estimated 4 million liters (1 million gallons) of highly radioactive waste into the soil. In addition, 800 billion liters (200 billion gallons) of low-level radioactive wastes were discharged directly into the soil, as it was believed that they would not migrate far. In fact, some elements migrated farther than anticipated, but only low levels of radioactivity have been found to have migrated off-site.

In 1989, the Washington Department of Ecology, the U.S. Environmental Protection Agency, and the U.S. Department of Energy initiated the legal steps needed to begin environmental cleanup at the Hanford Nuclear Reservation. The cleanup project, which has continued into the twenty-first century, is the largest such cleanup ever undertaken. It includes stabilization or removal of contaminated soil and the placement of restrictions on groundwater usage. The liquid waste stored at Hanford is to be vitrified (incorporated into glass) and taken to a permanent storage site; construction of the plant to be used in the vitrification process is expected to be completed in 2018.

Charles W. Rogers

Further Reading

Gephart, Roy E. *Hanford: A Conversation About Nuclear Waste and Cleanup.* Columbus, Ohio: Battelle Press, 2003.

Gerber, Michele Stenehjem. *On the Home Front: The Cold War Legacy of the Hanford Nuclear Site.* 2d ed. Lincoln: University of Nebraska Press, 2002.

McCutcheon, Chuck. *Nuclear Reactions: The Politics of Opening a Radioactive Waste Disposal Site.* Albuquerque: University of New Mexico Press, 2002.

Heat pumps

Category: Resources and resource management

Definition: Devices that transfer heat from air, earth, or water to heat or cool buildings

Significance: Heat pumps use heat sources that are naturally occurring, plentiful, and environmentally sustainable, and because they replace the use of fossil fuels for heating, they substantially reduce the production of greenhouse gases, which are linked to global warming. Heat pump systems are among the most reliable green heating technologies.

All types of heat pumps operate on the basic principle of heat transfer from an existing source rather than a source that requires the burning of fuel to create heat. A heat pump uses a small amount of energy to pull heat out of a relatively low-temperature area and then pumps it into a higher-temperature area. Heat is moved from a heat source (ground, air, or water) into a heat sink, a building. When switched to the reverse mode, a heat pump can cool a building. Heat pumps operate most efficiently in moderate climates.

The four major components of any heat pump system are a compressor, a condenser, an evaporator, and a metering device. Modern heat pumps use hydrofluorocarbons or other refrigerants that have little to no ozone-depleting effect. The main environmental impacts associated with using heat pumps are the pollution produced by the use of the electricity to power the pumps (most electricity is generated from the burning of fossil fuels, which contributes to pollution) and the possibility of toxic refrigerants leaking into the environment.

The efficiency rating of a heating system, known as the coefficient of performance (COP), is the ratio of the benefit obtained from the pump (heat moved) divided by the work that must be paid for to move heat from the source to the sink. For an electric furnace, the COP is 1; for a high-efficiency natural gas furnace, the COP can exceed 2. For heat pumps, the COP ranges from 1 to greater than 4. The COP of a heat pump used in the cooling mode is often referred to as the energy-efficiency ratio (EER) or seasonal energy-efficiency ratio (SEER).

Types of Heat Pumps

The most common type of heat pump is an air-source device that takes heat from the air outside a building and pumps it inside through refrigerant-filled coils. The basic constituents of this kind of heat pump are two fans, refrigerator coils, a reversing valve, and a compressor. The reversing valve reverses the flow of the refrigerant so that the pump can work in the opposite direction. In the reverse mode, the refrigerant absorbs heat from inside the building and releases it to the outside environment as an air conditioner would. The refrigerant cools and flows back inside to pick up more heat. Although air-source heat pumps work well, the operating costs are relatively high because of the electricity needed to run them. Typical COP ranges are between 1.0 and 2.9.

A water-source heat pump is an open-loop system that takes water drawn from a well directly to a heat exchanger, where heat is obtained. The water is then discharged back to an aboveground body of water or into a separate well. It uses water as its source of heat in the winter and water to move heat from a building in the summer. Typical open-loop systems move approximately 45 liters (12 gallons) of water per minute. Water-source heat pumps have the highest COP, but they require more maintenance than do other heat pump types. The COP typically ranges between 3.2 and 4.2. Potential environmental concerns with open-loop systems include possible contamination of surface water by accidental release of refrigerant and temperature changes in surface water that can affect aquatic habitats.

A ground-source heat pump is a closed-loop system. In the winter, it collects heat from a continuous loop of piping that is buried in the ground. During the summer, the pipes absorb heat to cool a building. Ground-source heat pumps are very dependable, but they are more costly to install than other types of heat pumps, and they also pose landscaping concerns. Typical COP ranges are between 2.6 and 3.4. The carbon dioxide output of both water-source and ground-source heat pumps is less than half of that produced by electric or gas furnaces or air conditioners.

ADVANCES IN TECHNOLOGY

Electric-powered heat pumps are the most common kinds in use, but a 5-horsepower, single-cylinder, glycol-cooled motor that runs on natural gas has been developed to power heat pumps. Pumps using the motor have been shown to have operating costs about 50 percent lower than electric heat pumps. With such advancements, applications of heat pumps have expanded to include heating swimming pools and heating water for household use.

For large-scale applications, absorption heat pumps have been developed. They differ from standard air-source heat pumps in that rather than compressing a refrigerant, an absorption pump absorbs ammonia into water, which is pressurized by a low-power pump. The heat source then boils the ammonia out of the water, and the process is repeated.

New types and blends of refrigerants are being developed for heat pumps that will produce minimal negative impacts on the environment. Environmentally friendly gases, such as hydrogen, helium, nitrogen, and plain air, are being used in Stirling-cycle heat pumps. Isobutane, which does not deplete ozone and is friendly to the environment, is also being used in heat pumps.

Alvin K. Benson

FURTHER READING

Banks, David. *An Introduction to Thermogeology: Ground Source Heating and Cooling.* Malden, Mass.: Blackwell, 2008.

Langley, Billy C. *Heat Pump Technology.* 3d ed. Upper Saddle River, N.J.: Prentice Hall, 2001.

Silberstein, Eugene. *Heat Pumps.* Clifton Park, N.Y.: Delmar Cengage Learning, 2002.

Hoover Dam

CATEGORY: Preservation and wilderness issues
IDENTIFICATION: Dam on the lower Colorado River, on the border between Arizona and Nevada
DATE: Completed in 1936
SIGNIFICANCE: Hoover Dam, which was built to regulate the flow of the lower Colorado River in order to prevent floods, provide consistent water levels necessary for irrigation, and produce hydroelectric power, also altered the environment of the southwestern United States, often in unanticipated ways.

At the time of its construction, Hoover Dam, then known as Boulder Dam (it was officially renamed in 1947), was rightfully hailed as an engineering marvel, with its concrete wall 221 meters (726 feet) high and 379 meters (1,244 feet) long at its crest. Spanish explorers named the Colorado River for its reddish-brown color, a result of the sediment that the river carries. The new dam captured the sand and silt, which settled to the bottom of the water collected behind the dam, in the reservoir named Lake Mead. Experts knew that the silt would eventually fill the reservoir, but they estimated that this process would take several hundred years. In the meantime, they sought ways to reduce the amount of silt deposited.

Arguing that overgrazing by Navajo sheep herds was causing soil erosion, which was the major source of silt in the Little Colorado and San Juan rivers (two tributaries of the Colorado), government officials successfully forced the Navajo to accept a stock reduction program. Nonetheless, silt continued to build up

Aerial view of Hoover Dam. (©Photoquest/Dreamstime.com)

duced, it could not carry the silt great distances, and sand quickly built up where the river widened near Needles. Plants soon filled the river bottom, providing yet another obstacle to water flow. The magnitude of the problem became apparent in 1941, when water releases from the dam increased in size and frequency. The sand, silt, and plant life diverted the rushing waters into the nearby town, forcing the evacuation of several families. During the 1940's the region became a veritable swamp. Flooded cesspools polluted the groundwater, creating a health hazard. In response, the federal government authorized levee construction and river dredging, expensive solutions to problems caused by a dam that was intended to prevent flooding.

One of the benefits to which the government pointed in publications praising the dam was the creation of new wildlife habitats along the shores of Lake Mead. A 1985 brochure noted that more than 250 species of birds had been identified in the region, including migratory species that use the lake as a stopover. It also claimed that the lake provides water for native animals, including desert bighorn sheep. In addition, several species of game fish live in the lake, a boon to the area's reputation as a recreational site and a plus for the region's economy.

The brochure neglected to mention the negative impacts of the dam on wildlife. For centuries the Colorado had deposited its sediment in a delta located at the river's mouth at the Gulf of California. This delta was a haven for wildlife, such as deer, birds, bobcats, and numerous other species. The reduced flow of the river and the reduction in sediment altered the delta, and wildlife began to disappear; some observers likened the changed area to a desert. Changes also occurred upriver from the dam. The game fish in Lake Mead competed with native fish upriver, possibly contributing to the extinction of some species in the lower reaches of the Grand Canyon.

behind the dam, and by 1949 the sediment was more than 82 meters (270 feet) deep in some areas. This changed the flow of the river upstream, slowing rapids in the Grand Canyon more than 160 kilometers (100 miles) north of the dam. Silt buildup in Lake Mead slowed after the completion of the Glen Canyon Dam north of the Grand Canyon in 1963.

Ironically, the reduction in the Colorado's flow downstream of the dam caused severe floods in Needles, California, during the 1940's. The water released from the newly finished dam picked up large deposits of sediment that stood at the base of the dam, carrying it downriver. Because the river's flow had been re-

The construction of the dam may have also increased the possibility of earth-quakes in the region. When Lake Mead began to fill during the late 1930's, scientists recorded several seismic shocks, a phenomenon that had not been noted in the area prior to the dam's construction. Arguing that several faults exist in the region, some scientists dismissed any notion of a general link between earthquakes and the weight of water in reservoirs. However, earthquakes in the regions of several major dams around the world during the 1960's led engineers to reconsider the connection between seismic activity and dams. Two major shocks in the Lake Mead area in 1972 confirmed suspicions that the reservoir contributes to earthquake activity.

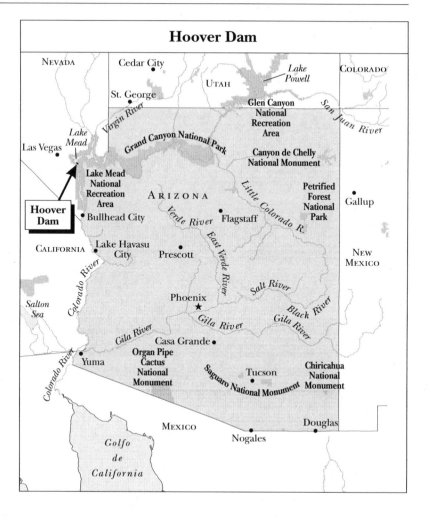

Perhaps the two most important environmental impacts of Hoover Dam are the precedent its construction created and the population growth that it fostered in the American Southwest. The success of the dam prompted the construction of several dams on the Colorado River, including the Glen Canyon Dam, which significantly altered the ecosystem within the Grand Canyon. In addition, the electricity generated at Hoover Dam and the lure of Lake Mead increased human migration to the area, which in turn led to increased pollution and greater demand for water from the already beleaguered Colorado River.

Thomas Clarkin

FURTHER READING

Berkman, Richard L., and W. Kip Viscusi. *Damming the West.* New York: Grossman, 1973.

Billington, David P., and Donald C. Jackson. *Big Dams of the New Deal Era: A Confluence of Engineering and Politics.* Norman: University of Oklahoma Press, 2006.

Goldsmith, Edward, and Nicholas Hildyard. *The Social and Environmental Effects of Large Dams.* New York: Random House, 1984.

Kleinsorge, Paul Lincoln. *The Boulder Canyon Project: Historical and Economic Aspects.* Palo Alto, Calif.: Stanford University Press, 1940.

McCully, Patrick. *Silenced Rivers: The Ecology and Politics of Large Dams.* Enlarged ed. London: Zed Books, 2001.

Mann, Elizabeth, and Alan Witschonke. *The Hoover Dam: The Story of Tough Times, Tough People, and the Taming of a Wild River.* New York: Mikaya Press, 2001.

Reisner, Marc. *Cadillac Desert: The American West and Its Disappearing Water.* Rev. ed. New York: Penguin Books, 1993.

Stevens, Joseph E. *Hoover Dam: An American Adventure.* Norman: University of Oklahoma Press, 1988.

Watkins, T. H., et al. *The Grand Colorado: The Story of a River and Its Canyons.* Palo Alto, Calif.: American West, 1969.

Hybrid vehicles

CATEGORY: Energy and energy use

DEFINITION: Motorized vehicles that combine electric motors and internal combustion engines so that they can be powered by gasoline, batteries, or a combination of the two

SIGNIFICANCE: Because hybrid vehicles use less gasoline than do vehicles powered by gasoline only, they produce substantially lower amounts of toxic carbon emissions than do conventional vehicles. Thus at the same time they help conserve fossil-fuel resources, they reduce air pollution.

The gasoline-powered automobiles of the twentieth century replaced the steam-powered automobiles of the late nineteenth and early twentieth centuries. As early as 1889, when Karl Benz and Gottlieb Daimler built the first automobiles, steam had already been used extensively to power locomotives. Among the earliest automobiles was the Stanley Steamer, which was fueled exclusively by steam. In 1900, car manufacturers in the United States sold 1,681 steam vehicles, 1,575 electric cars, and a mere 936 vehicles powered by gasoline. In 1906, twin brothers Francis E. Stanley and Freelan O. Stanley raced one of their steam-powered automobiles to a top speed of 127.7 miles per hour at Daytona Beach, Florida. Stanley Steamers were still being sold as late as 1920.

The development of gasoline-powered internal combustion engines greatly increased the range that automobiles could travel, and increasing numbers of such cars were manufactured as the twentieth century progressed. Gasoline was inexpensive and readily available, and the development of hybrid vehicles was seen as unnecessary and economically infeasible. The fuel shortages of the 1970's, however, awakened the public and automobile companies to the urgent need to produce automobiles that could offer drastically increased fuel economy in such places as the United States, much of Europe, and many Asian countries. Much of the world had become increasingly dependent on automobiles for transportation, especially in countries such as India and China, where rapidly emerging middle classes provided a market for automobiles.

Nevertheless, American automobile companies, especially Detroit's Big Three—Chrysler, Ford, and General Motors—were slow to move toward the production of compact cars and hybrids because the profit margin on small cars is considerably less than that on the full-size sedans and trucks that American companies had promoted strenuously. Eventually, however, public demand forced struggling American automobile companies to move quite vigorously into the development, manufacture, and sale of hybrids.

FUEL ECONOMY

The electrical power component of most hybrid vehicles is provided by lithium-ion batteries. In a typical hybrid car, every time the driver depresses the brake, the friction caused by braking automatically begins recharging the batteries the car carries. When the vehicle stops, such as for a traffic light, the gasoline-powered engine automatically shuts off to save fuel; it is then restarted immediately when the accelerator is pressed. The batteries in some hybrids are recharged through connection to the electrical grid (that is, by being plugged into electrical outlets); these plug-in hybrids are very expensive, owing to the cost of the batteries they use. Also, although plug-ins are fuel-efficient, they shift energy consumption to the electrical grid, which often uses electricity produced by the burning of fossil fuels.

Contrary to what many drivers expect, hybrid vehicles deliver better gas mileage in stop-and-start situations than they achieve on the open road at highway speeds. As is true of gasoline-powered vehicles, the mileage that hybrids deliver depends to some extent on the drivers' habits. Mileage is reduced by fast starts, for example. Even drivers who do not achieve optimal gas mileage in modern-day hybrid vehicles, however, can generally depend on getting more than 40 miles per gallon of gasoline on a regular basis.

Although experimental hybrid vehicles were produced throughout much of the twentieth century, the first commercially produced hybrid automobile, the Toyota Prius, was not available to the general public until October, 1997, when it was marketed in Japan. Honda marketed a hybrid, the Insight, in the United States in December, 1999, and seven months later, in July, 2000, Toyota's Prius, produced in limited quantities, was made available to American buyers. The Prius and the Insight have regularly accomplished fuel economies approaching 50 miles per gallon, and experimental versions of these hybrids have achieved double that fuel economy. Hybrid vehicles are generally more expensive than comparable conventional cars, but for consumers the higher prices are offset by the fuel savings that hybrids provide, along with incentives such as the tax credits the U.S. government allows hybrid buyers to claim under specified conditions.

Since the first hybrid vehicles were introduced, automakers have added many additional models to their hybrid lines, offering sport utility vehicles (SUVs), trucks, minivans, and mid- and full-size cars along with compacts. Some manufacturers that had not previously pursued the hybrid market, including the American companies Ford and General Motors, have developed or are planning to develop hybrid lines of their own. European automobile companies, notably Audi, BMW, Mercedes-Benz, Porsche, Volvo, and Volkswagen, have also shown concern for fuel economy and the use of alternative fuels, but rather than developing hybrids they have concentrated their efforts on developing efficient diesel-powered vehicles.

R. Baird Shuman

FURTHER READING

Chan, C. C., and K. T. Chau. *Modern Electric Vehicle Technology.* New York: Oxford University Press, 2001.

Ehsani, Mehrdad, et al. *Modern Electric, Hybrid Electric, and Fuel Cell Vehicles: Fundamentals, Theory, and Design.* Boca Raton, Fla.: CRC Press, 2005.

Erjavec, Jack, and Jeff Arias. *Hybrid, Electric, and Fuel-Cell Vehicles.* Clifton Park, N.J.: Thomson Delmar Learning, 2007.

Halderman, James D., and Tony Martin. *Hybrid and Alternative Fuel Vehicles.* Upper Saddle River, N.J.: Pearson/Prentice Hall, 2009.

Husain, Iqbal. *Electric and Hybrid Vehicles: Design Fundamentals.* Boca Raton, Fla.: CRC Press, 2003.

Nerad, Jack R. *Hybrid and Alternative Fuel Vehicles: Get the Lowdown on Today's Green Machines.* New York: Alpha Books, 2007.

Hydroelectricity

CATEGORY: Energy and energy use

DEFINITION: Electricity produced through hydropower, which is energy from water in motion, such as flowing or falling water

SIGNIFICANCE: Hydropower is the leading renewable energy source, producing 24 percent of the world's electricity for more than one billion people.

Hydropower is a natural, inexpensive, clean, and replenishable energy source, but the building and operation of hydroelectric plants often have adverse environmental impacts on local natural habitats.

As early as 4000 B.C.E., hydropower was used in the waterwheel, a device that used the power of running water striking wooden paddles mounted around a wheel to drive machinery to grind grain. Eventually, waterwheels were used to irrigate crops, drive pumps, provide drinking water, and power the machinery used in textile mills and sawmills. During the nineteenth century, the waterwheel gave way to the water turbine, which was then replaced by the steam engine in mills. The development of the electric generator and an improved hydraulic turbine, combined with a growing need for electricity, led to the first commercial hydroelectric power plant in 1882 in Appleton, Wisconsin. Typical large modern hydroelectric plants have dams with reservoirs for storing water, which flows through turbines that activate generators. Electrical substations or grids transmit the electricity to consumers.

ADVANTAGES AND DISADVANTAGES

Compared with other energy sources, hydropower has numerous advantages. Water is a naturally free, inexpensive, clean, and renewable power source. Because water can be stored in reservoirs and the amount of electricity generated through the turbines can be increased or decreased rapidly in response to fluctuations in demand, hydropower is economical and efficient. Hydroelectric plants have relatively low maintenance and operational costs, and hydropower is more flexible than limited resources such as coal and oil or intermittent renewable energy sources such as wind or solar energy.

Another advantage to the use of hydroelectricity is that it does not require the combustion of fuels that produce air pollution. Unlike oil, coal, and gas, water is a nonpolluting fuel source that does not create toxic by-products. Hydroelectric plants do not release carbon dioxide, a greenhouse gas emitted with the burning of fossil fuels, and they have no problems with waste disposal, in contrast to nuclear power plants.

As a domestic energy source, hydropower decreases American dependence on foreign oil and thus reduces the nation's vulnerability to fluctuating world economic and political conditions. Other significant benefits of hydropower include the contributions of dams and reservoirs to the management of water supplies (for both municipal needs and irrigation) and flood control. In addition, the reservoirs and lakes formed by dams are often used by the public for recreational activities. For example, the Grand Coulee Dam, completed in 1942, is the largest U.S. hydroelectric producer. Located in Washington State, the dam provides irrigation water for more than 243,000 hectares (600,000 acres) of land and controls floods on the Columbia River. The dam also forms Franklin D. Roosevelt Lake. The Lake Roosevelt National Recreation Area was established in 1946 for activities such as swimming, boating, hunting, camping, and fishing.

Hydroelectric power generation does raise some negative environmental concerns, however. Among these is that methane, a potent greenhouse gas, can form in reservoirs and be released into the air. In addition, the building of dams, along with the reservoirs that dams create, changes the environment in the areas in which the dams are located. Often the natural habitats of local fish, animal, and plant species are disturbed, either modified or destroyed, and local human populations may be displaced by the flooding of reservoirs. Further, hydroelectric plant structures can restrict fish migration upstream or downstream. The operation of hydropower plants can also change water quality and the flow rates of rivers and streams.

Worldwide Usage of Hydroelectricity

Hydropower accounts for some 70 percent of the renewable energy market and more electricity-generating capacity than any other renewable energy source. China is the leading producer of hydroelectricity, with more than half of the world's hydropower dams and plans to build more. Some nations have maximized the development of their available waterways for generating hydroelectricity; these include Canada, Norway, and Switzerland, which received 70 percent, 95 percent, and 74 percent, respectively, of their electricity from hydropower in 2010. Other major users of hydroelectricity include Brazil and Paraguay, which jointly built the Itaipu Dam on the Paraná River, which forms the border between the two countries. The Itaipu Dam is the world's largest hydroelectric plant in terms of generating capacity. In the United States, 10 percent of the electricity generated nationwide comes from hydropower plants at only three hundred dams (some eighty thousand dams

Leading World Producers of Hydroelectricity, 2006

Rank	Country	Kilowatt-Hours (billions)
1	China	431.43
2	Canada	351.85
3	Brazil	345.32
4	United States	289.25
5	Russia	173.65
6	Norway	118.21
7	India	112.46
8	Japan	84.90
9	Venezuela	81.29
10	Sweden	61.11

Source: Energy Information Administration, 2008.

exist in the United States, but most are used primarily for irrigation).

With increasing demand for clean, renewable energy to replace finite fossil fuels, interest has grown in using untapped water resources in Central Africa, China, India, and Latin America for the construction of more hydroelectric plants. Electrical power could improve the economies and the standards of living in many of the world's developing areas. Environmental issues must be addressed, however, such as how to develop hydroelectrical power while protecting the planet's remaining pristine rivers and forests and protecting needed agricultural lands. Emerging technologies may be able to mitigate some of the negative environmental impacts of hydroelectric power by eliminating the need to build more dams. Alternatives for generating hydropower without building dams include technologies that capture the power of waves or tides. Such hydrokinetic hydroelectricity would not require changes to the watercourse. Small systems, known as micro hydroelectric or micro hydel systems, producing 100 kilowatts or less can generate enough power for individual farms or homes. Small-scale hydro projects using small canals instead of dams to move water through turbines would also help preserve ecosystems.

Alice Myers

Further Reading

Craddock, David. *Renewable Energy Made Easy: Free Energy From Solar, Wind, Hydropower, and Other Alternative Energy Sources.* Ocala, Fla.: Atlantic, 2008.

Førsund, Finn R. *Hydropower Economics.* New York: Springer, 2007.

Miller, Frederic P., Agnes F. Vandome, and John McBrewster. *Hydroelectricity.* Beau Bassin, Mauritius: Alphascript, 2009.

Nersesian, Roy L. *Energy for the Twenty-first Century: A Comprehensive Guide to Conventional and Alternative Sources.* Armonk, N.Y.: M. E. Sharpe, 2010.

Surhone, Lambert M. et al., ed. *Wave Farm: Wave Power, Wave Hub, Electricity, Generation, Renewable Energy, Hydroelectricity, Ocean Thermal Energy Conversion.* Beau Bassin, Mauritius: Betascript, 2010.

Tiwar, Ramakant. *Hydroelectricity, Environment, and Quality of Life.* Scottsdale, Ariz.: Regal, 2010.

Hydrogen economy

CATEGORY: Energy and energy use

DEFINITION: An economy in which energy needs are met by molecular hydrogen produced predominantly from water

SIGNIFICANCE: Conversion to a hydrogen economy would drastically reduce pollution because using molecular hydrogen as an energy source generates only water, in contrast to the greenhouse gases produced by the burning of fossil fuels. In addition, the hydrogen gas used for fuel can be made from renewable resources.

The term "hydrogen economy" first appeared during the energy crisis of the 1970's. The use of hydrogen as a fuel source was proposed as a way to avoid energy crises resulting from the use of nonrenewable fuels. Interest in a hydrogen economy was resurrected in the 1990's when increasing numbers of people started to understand that the burning of fossil fuels generates carbon dioxide (CO_2), a greenhouse gas that has been linked to global warming; the use of molecular hydrogen (H_2), or hydrogen gas, as a fuel does not generate CO_2. It is interesting to note that nineteenth century science-fiction author Jules Verne imagined the use of hydrogen as a fuel in 1874, in his novel *Le Secret de l'île* (*The Mysterious Island*, 1875).

HYDROGEN AS A FUEL

H_2 is an ideal fuel for transportation, because the energy content of hydrogen is three times greater than that of gasoline and four times higher than that of ethanol. By the early years of the twenty-first century, growing numbers of automobile manufacturers around the world had begun making prototypes of hydrogen-powered vehicles.

H_2 can be used as a fuel in vehicles with internal combustion engines, but a more environmentally friendly way to use hydrogen power in motor vehicles is to replace their internal combustion engines with fuel cells that generate no greenhouse gases. Hydrogen is used in such fuel cells to produce electricity that powers the vehicle. Fuel cells are like batteries—that is, they generate electricity through a chemical reaction, in this case, between H_2 and oxygen (O_2). The resulting emissions consist of just water and heat with no CO_2 or other greenhouse gases. In addition, a fuel cell is two and one-half to three times more efficient than an internal combustion engine in the conversion of H_2 energy.

One problem with creating a hydrogen economy is that H_2 is not abundant on the earth. Although many microorganisms produce H_2 during fermentation, it is used almost immediately by other microbes because it is an excellent source of energy. If H_2 is to be used as a primary fuel source, it must be generated from other energy sources. Hydrogen as a chemical element (H) is the most plentiful element in the universe, and it is a part of the most abundant chemical compound on the earth—water. Therefore, to make H_2 widely available for fuel, cost-effective and environmentally friendly ways must be found to generate H_2 from water or other chemical compounds. H_2 has been obtained mainly from natural gas (methane and propane) through steam reforming. Although this approach is practically attractive, it is clearly not sustainable.

Molecular hydrogen can be also produced by electrolysis. In this case, electrical energy is used to split water into H_2 and O_2. However, the process is not efficient, and it requires significant expenditure of energy and purified water. One promising sustainable method of H_2 production is a biological approach. A great number of microorganisms produce H_2 from inorganic materials (for example, water) or from organic materials (for example, sugar) in reactions catalyzed by enzymes—hydrogenase, nitrogenase, or both. Hydrogen produced by microorganisms is called biohydrogen. For industrial applications, the most attractive method of H_2 production is one using photosynthetic microbes. These microorganisms, such as microscopic algae, cyanobacteria, and photosynthetic bacteria, use sunlight as an energy source and water to generate hydrogen. Hydrogen production based on photosynthetic microbes holds the promise of generating a renewable hydrogen fuel, as large amounts of solar light and water are available.

OBSTACLES

Several technological and economic problems have so far hindered progress toward a hydrogen economy. These problems include difficulties in storing and distributing H_2, as well as in convincing the general public of its safety. Hydrogen has gained an unwarranted reputation as a highly dangerous substance. Like other fuels, H_2 may produce explosions, but it has been used for years in industry and has earned an excellent safety record when handled properly.

Hydrogen has much lower energy density by volume than other fuels, and as a gas it requires three thousand times more space for storage than gasoline. Hydrogen storage, especially in motor vehicles, represents a challenge for scientists and engineers. For storage, H_2 is generally pressurized in cylinders or liquefied in cryostatic containers at −253 degrees Celsius (−423 degrees Fahrenheit). Both processes require a significant expenditure of energy and generate large quantities of waste CO_2. In most hydrogen-powered vehicles, H_2 is stored as compressed gas.

Another problem hindering the growth of a hydrogen economy has been the scarcity of refueling stations for hydrogen-powered cars. Gasoline stations cannot be converted into hydrogen stations, because H_2 stations require different pump technologies. Considerable monetary investment will be required to build and operate sufficient H_2 fueling stations to increase the attractiveness of owning hydrogen-powered vehicles.

Sergei A. Markov

FURTHER READING

Ball, Michael, ed. *The Hydrogen Economy. Opportunities and Challenges.* New York: Cambridge University Press, 2009.
Cammack, Richard, Michel Frey, and Robert L. Robson. *Hydrogen as Fuel: Learning from Nature.* London: Taylor & Francis, 2001.
Ogden, Joan. "High Hopes for Hydrogen." *Scientific American*, September, 2006, 94-99.
Rifkin, Jeremy. *The Hydrogen Economy: The Creation of the Worldwide Energy Web and the Redistribution of Power on Earth.* New York: J. P. Tarcher/Putnam, 2002.
Service, Robert F. "The Hydrogen Backlash." *Science* 305 (August 13, 2004): 958-961.

Internal combustion engines

CATEGORIES: Energy and energy use; atmosphere and air pollution
DEFINITION: Engines containing chambers in which the fuel that powers the engines is burned
SIGNIFICANCE: Internal combustion engines are the most commonly used engines in vehicles and in other applications where portability is important. Most internal combustion engines burn fossil fuels, so they are significant sources of greenhouse gases and other air pollutants.

Technically, any engine powered by combustion inside the engine is an internal combustion engine, including rockets and jet engines. Standard practice, however, is to limit the term to engines that convert the thermodynamic energy of the burned fuel directly into mechanical work inside the engine rather than relying on the expulsion of the combustion by-products to provide work, as in jet engines and rockets.

Most modern internal combustion engines are of a reciprocating piston design that relies on the four-stroke cycle described by German inventor Nikolaus August Otto in 1876. This four-stroke Otto cycle takes in the fuel and air mixture in the first step of the process. The mixture is then compressed and ignited. The release of energy in the combustion process pushes on the piston, providing the work of the engine. The piston then pushes the waste gas out of the engine. Valves are carefully timed to admit gas when the piston is moving down and to permit the exhaust of gas when the piston is moving up. A related cycle of steps is performed in the rotary engine devised by German inventor Felix Wankel in 1957.

The Otto cycle produces work only once for every two times that the pistons move up and down. A somewhat more complicated engine, called a two-stroke engine, combines some of the steps of the Otto cycle. Since they produce work with every cycle of the piston, two-stroke engines provide more power for their

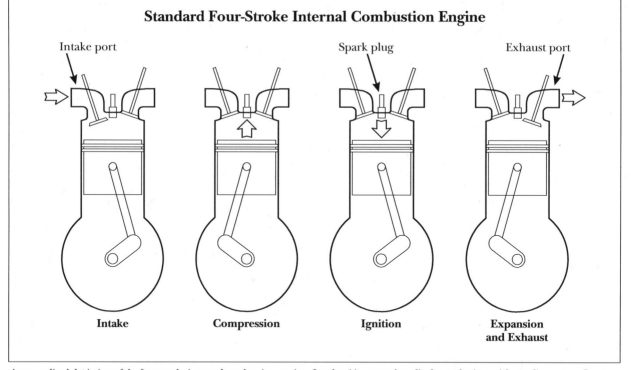

Standard Four-Stroke Internal Combustion Engine

Intake port   Spark plug   Exhaust port

Intake   **Compression**   **Ignition**   **Expansion and Exhaust**

A generalized depiction of the four-stroke internal combustion engine. Intake: Air enters the cylinder and mixes with gasoline vapor. Compression: The cylinder is sealed, and the piston moves upward to compress the air-fuel mixture. Ignition: The spark plug ignites the mixture, creating pressure that drives the piston downward. Expansion (exhaust): The burned gases exit the cylinder.

size than do four-stroke engines. In a two-stroke engine, fuel and air are admitted into the engine as the exhaust gas is being expelled. Since both the inlet and the outlet valves are open at the same time, some mixing is inevitable, so two-stroke engines almost always cause more pollution than four-stroke engines through unburned fuel being released in the exhaust. Two-stroke engines, however, produce more power for their size and are thus often used when high portability is desired, such as on lawn maintenance equipment.

Because fuel must be admitted into the engine, gas or liquid fuels are most suited for internal combustion engines. While almost any combustible fuel may be used, most modern internal combustion engines use either diesel oil or gasoline as fuel. These fuels often contain contaminants that are released into the atmosphere when they are burned. Early engines also relied on lead additives in gasoline to control ignition and to prevent damage to the engines; however, these additives can release toxins into the environment. Modern engines are designed to operate

with different additives performing the same function, thus reducing pollution from gasoline. Historically, engines have been designed to produce power with little concern over any air pollution they may create. Many engines thus do not completely burn their fuel, releasing the partially burned fuel as more pollution.

Because for many years gasoline and diesel fuel were comparatively inexpensive and plentiful, most engines were designed with little regard for fuel efficiency. The energy shortages of the 1970's, however, encouraged automobile manufacturers to build more efficient engines. Higher fuel efficiency also reduces tailpipe emissions of air pollutants, including greenhouse gases. The linking of these gases to global warming is another factor in the push for greater fuel efficiency of internal combustion engines.

Raymond D. Benge, Jr.

FURTHER READING
Hoag, Kevin L. *Vehicular Engine Design.* Warrendale, Pa.: SAE International, 2006.

Knight, Ben. "Better Mileage Now." *Scientific American*, February, 2010, 50-55.

Parker, Barry. *The Isaac Newton School of Driving: Physics and Your Car.* Baltimore: The Johns Hopkins University Press, 2003.

International Atomic Energy Agency

CATEGORIES: Organizations and agencies; nuclear power and radiation; energy and energy use

IDENTIFICATION: International body that promotes the peaceful use and deters the military use of nuclear energy

DATE: Established on July 29, 1957

SIGNIFICANCE: The International Atomic Energy Agency serves the important functions of providing nuclear safety and security information, monitoring possible sources of radioactive pollution, and conducting research aimed at developing radiation technology.

The International Atomic Energy Agency (IAEA) was established by the International Atomic Energy Agency Statute, an international treaty. Although it reports to the United Nations General Assembly and the United Nations Security Council, the IAEA operates independent of the United Nations. The purposes of the IAEA are to develop, expand, and promote the peaceful use of nuclear technology, to provide education regarding nuclear safety procedures, and to guard against the military use of nuclear energy. The IAEA has no power to force the cooperation of any of its member states, however; each state can choose to follow or ignore the guidelines set by the IAEA.

The IAEA is headquartered in Vienna, Austria, and has regional and liaison offices in Toronto, Tokyo, New York, and Geneva. The agency is staffed by approximately 2,200 professional and support personnel from more than ninety countries. The IAEA also operates scientific laboratories in Vienna and Seibersdorf, Austria; Monaco; and Trieste, Italy. These include the International Seismic Safety Centre, which examines seismic conditions related to nuclear facilities, and the Marine Environment Laboratory, which studies the amounts and the effects of radiation in the world's oceans. Radiation technology developed in IAEA laboratories has shown success in fighting the screwworm fly and some types of grain fungi. The laboratories have also engaged in research into nuclear techniques for eradicating the olive fruit fly and the tsetse fly.

Critics of the IAEA assert that the agency cannot simultaneously push for greater use of nuclear energy and protect against the proliferation of nuclear weapons, because more widespread use of nuclear techniques will necessarily lead to the production of radioactive materials suitable for weapons use. Even given the IAEA's limited power to force compliance, however, most nations have agreed to cooperate with the agency's guidelines. After the accidents that took place at the Three Mile Island nuclear power plant in Pennsylvania in 1979 and at the Chernobyl nuclear plant in the Soviet Union in 1986, the IAEA bolstered its efforts to promote nuclear safety.

When the Comprehensive Nuclear-Test-Ban Treaty was approved by the U.N. General Assembly in 1996, much of the monitoring of residual nuclear materials remaining from the production of weapons was delegated to the IAEA. The agency monitors the storage of radioactive materials from dismantled weapons, measures pollution from nuclear ships that have sunk in the Arctic, and monitors the pollution of nuclear test sites. Another responsibility of the IAEA is to develop protections against the procurement and use of nuclear materials by terrorists.

In 2005 the IAEA and its general director at the time, Mohamed ElBaradei, were awarded the Nobel Peace Prize "for their efforts to prevent nuclear energy from being used for military purposes and to ensure that nuclear energy for peaceful purposes is used in the safest possible way."

C. Alton Hassell

FURTHER READING

Fischer, David. *History of the International Atomic Energy Agency: The First Forty Years.* Vienna: IAEA, 1997.

Olwell, Russell B. *The International Atomic Energy Agency.* New York: Chelsea House, 2009.

Pilat, Joseph F, ed. *Atoms for Peace: A Future After Fifty Years?* Baltimore: The Johns Hopkins University Press, 2007.

International Institute for Sustainable Development

CATEGORIES: Organizations and agencies; resources and resource management

IDENTIFICATION: Nonprofit organization devoted to promoting human innovation to achieve sustainable development

DATE: Founded in March, 1990

SIGNIFICANCE: The International Institute for Sustainable Development plays an important role in environmental protection by working with other nongovernmental organizations and with government agencies to conduct research and disseminate information about the benefits of sustainable development.

In 1983, the United Nations convened the World Commission on Environment and Development to address rising international concerns about a degraded global environment and endangered natural resources. The findings of this commission (commonly known as the Brundtland Commission, for its chair, Gro Harlem Brundtland) were compiled and published in 1987 under the title *Our Common Future*. This report introduced the rubric "sustainable development," a long-term view of development that incorporates concerns for the needs of future generations in efforts to meet present-time goals. Sustainable development emphasizes direct assistance in meeting the needs of the world's impoverished communities and clear-eyed assessment of the influences of technology and social organization on efforts to meet the present and future needs of the global community. *Our Common Future*, also known as the Brundtland Report, was the first document of its kind to connect economic activity to the state of the global environment.

In 1988, Canadian prime minister Brian Mulroney announced to the United Nations General Assembly that Canada was planning to build a center for sustainable development in Winnipeg, Manitoba. Its mission would be to work on issues related to sustainable development with the United Nations Environment Programme and other international institutions dedicated to environmental affairs. The funding agreement to create the International Institute for Sustainable Development (IISD) was signed in March, 1990.

IISD was conceived as an institution independent of government and business entities. This independent stature enabled its founders to attract highly skilled directors and to create funding structures that would not create conflicts of interest within the intergovernmental network. The stated mission of IISD is to promote human innovation to achieve sustainable development as defined and measured by environmental health, economic prosperity, and better living standards for all peoples. The institute focuses on six key programs: trade and investment, sustainable natural resources management, measurement and assessment, climate change and energy, global connectivity, and reporting services. IISD is headquartered in Winnipeg and has branch offices in Ottawa, Ontario, New York City, and Geneva, Switzerland. More than two hundred organizations around the world have worked with IISD on its various projects and programs.

IISD was one of the first institutions to recognize the potential of the Internet to disseminate timely information about sustainable development. It created the online *Earth Summit Bulletin* in 1992 to report on the proceedings of the United Nations Conference on Environment and Development (also known as the Earth Summit) held in Rio de Janeiro, Brazil, in June of that year. IISD continues to publish the bulletin online under the title *Earth Negotiations Bulletin*; it covers all U.N. conferences and summits related to the environment. Representatives of IISD attended the 2009 United Nations Climate Change Conference, held in Copenhagen, Denmark, to promote the mitigation of and adaptation to climate change.

Victoria M. Breting-García

FURTHER READING

Hayward, Lillian. "A Successful Institution in a Struggling System: The Story of the International Institute for Sustainable Development and Sustainable Development in Canada." In *The New Humanitarians: Inspiration, Innovations, and Blueprints for Visionaries*, edited by Chris E. Stout. Westport, Conn.: Praeger, 2009.

International Institute for Sustainable Development. *Sustaining Excellence: The 2008-2009 Annual Report of the International Institute for Sustainable Development.* Winnipeg: Author, 2009.

World Commission on Environment and Development. *Our Common Future.* Washington, D.C.: Author, 1987.

Light pollution

CATEGORIES: Energy and energy use; urban
environments
DEFINITION: Human-caused illumination of areas beyond where light is intended and wanted
SIGNIFICANCE: In addition to its adverse effects on the
work of astronomers and the wasted energy it represents, light pollution can have deleterious impacts on animals, including humans.

The most obvious effect of light pollution is aesthetic. Stray light from human-made lighting
sources makes the sky bright at night, which makes
stars and constellations less easily visible. The field of
astronomy is adversely affected by light pollution for
this reason; in fact, in many highly populated areas,
astronomers are unable to see most galaxies and neb-
ulae, even with the use of telescopes. Because of the
impact of this situation on their field of study, astronomers have been among the most vocal critics of light
pollution, but environmentalists have increasingly
joined in efforts to address the problem.

Light pollution is often an unintended consequence of intentional lighting. The light from human-
made sources, if not properly directed, often goes beyond the areas that are meant to be illuminated. Many
people who install outdoor lighting fixtures do not
even think about how the light they generate affects
others. In this way, light pollution is much like noise
pollution. Light pollution is also like noise pollution in
that for many years it was thought of solely as a nuisance
issue, a problem without any real consequences for the
environment.

ENVIRONMENTAL EFFECTS

One of the biggest environmental impacts associated with light pollution is the waste of energy represented by light that goes beyond where it is intended
to go. When light shines beyond the area that needs to
be illuminated, the light source is using more energy
than is really necessary to do the intended job. It has
been estimated that the energy used for outdoor
lighting could be cut in half if all lighting fixtures were
appropriately shielded to direct their light more precisely. Aside from the economic benefits, such a reduction in energy consumption would have a significant impact on the need for electricity generation,
which often has negative environmental effects.

Light pollution has also been found to be detrimental to wildlife. Nocturnal animals are adapted to
life in the dark, and the lack of full darkness in areas
with high levels of light pollution can influence the activities of such animals; for example, it can affect the
relationship between predator and prey, as the prey
cannot hide in darkness as they normally would.
Some studies have shown that migratory animals, particularly birds, are also affected by light pollution, and
other research has found that increased light affects
the breeding practices of many animals. Excess
nighttime lighting can affect plant growth as well.

Humans also appear to be physically affected by
light pollution. An increasing body of evidence indicates that the human circadian rhythm developed to
include a certain number of hours of darkness per
day. Disruptions of a person's circadian rhythm can
result in serious health problems, ranging from sleep-
lessness to irritability and depression.

MITIGATION

Outdoor lighting is essential for safety and security,
but not all outdoor lighting generates the same level of
light pollution. Reducing light pollution can be as easy
as replacing conventional outdoor lighting fixtures
with fixtures that are shielded so that they direct light
where it is wanted and limit the amount of light that
goes in other directions. Such fixtures can achieve the
same level of illumination in intended areas with lower-
wattage bulbs than are needed in conventional fixtures, resulting in energy savings in addition to reductions in stray light. Shielded light fixtures tend to cost
more than unshielded fixtures, but the savings in electricity costs may offset the greater initial expense over
time. Retrofitting existing lights with shielding on a
large scale, however, can be prohibitively expensive.

The biggest impediment to the reduction of light
pollution is a general lack of awareness and understanding of the effects of light pollution among the
public. The deleterious effects of air and water pollution are generally well understood, but the effects of
light pollution—other than on astronomy—are often
not immediately recognized. Because of this lack of
awareness, outdoor lighting is often installed by
nonexperts. Municipalities, businesses, and home
owners could reduce light pollution by consulting
with lighting engineers who can design lighting plans
to ensure sufficient illumination of desired areas with
minimal waste of light and energy.

Raymond D. Benge, Jr.

FURTHER READING

Bakich, Michael E. "Can We Win the War Against Light Pollution?" *Astronomy*, February, 2009, 56-59.

Gallaway, Terrel, Reed N. Olsen, and David M. Mitchell. "The Economics of Global Light Pollution." *Ecological Economics* 69, no. 3 (2010): 658-665.

Klinkenborg, Verlyn. "Our Vanishing Night." *National Geographic*, November, 2008, 102-123.

Luginbuhl, Christian B., Constance E. Walker, and Richard J. Wainscoat. "Lighting and Astronomy." *Physics Today*, December, 2009, 32-37.

Mizon, Bob. *Light Pollution: Responses and Remedies.* New York: Springer, 2002.

Rich, Catherine, and Travis Longcore, eds. *Ecological Consequences of Artificial Night Lighting.* Washington, D.C.: Island Press, 2006.

Love Canal disaster

CATEGORIES: Disasters; human health and the environment; waste and waste management

THE EVENT: Devastation of a community in Niagara Falls, New York, as the result of the burial of toxic chemical wastes in the area some years before

DATES: 1976-1980

SIGNIFICANCE: The events that took place at Love Canal demonstrate the environmental damage and dangers to human health posed by the improper disposal of toxic wastes. The Love Canal case also shows how informed and active citizens can influence legislators and policy makers to address environmental problems.

The discovery and identification of dangerous chemical wastes in the Love Canal neighborhood of Niagara Falls, New York, in 1976 transformed a community where the residents' livelihoods depended on the chemical companies long established in the area. Houses were boarded up and abandoned, a school was left empty and falling down, warning signs were posted, and the entire area was fenced off. The completeness of the human and ecological devastation at Love Canal made it the standard against which all subsequent chemical waste disasters have been compared. The toxic terror generated by Love Canal was caused by chemical waste buried at a time when the term "pollution" was not yet part of the American vocabulary.

In 1892 entrepreneur William Love arrived in Niagara Falls with plans to construct a navigable power canal between the upper and lower portions of the Niagara River and use the 90-meter (300-foot) drop in water level to generate electric energy. Digging began in May, 1894, but the depressed state of the economy at the time resulted in a withdrawal of investment capital, which ended the project with the canal less than one-half finished. Love Canal became the property of the Niagara Power and Development Company, which gave the Hooker Electrochemical Corporation permission in 1942 to dump wastes in the canal. The site was considered to be ideal for disposal of chemical wastes as the walls were lined with clay, which has a low level of permeability. Hooker purchased the property in 1947.

Between 1942 and 1952, Hooker disposed of 21,800 tons of chemicals at the site, burying them at depths of 6 to 8 meters (20 to 25 feet). The majority of the chemicals were contained in metal and fiber barrels, although some waste was reputedly dumped directly into the canal. The customary method for disposal of chemical wastes throughout the United States in the 1950's was to dump them directly into unlined pits, lagoons, rivers, lakes, or surface impoundments; wastes were also sometimes burned. Apart from disposal into bodies of water, these methods were legal up until 1980.

In 1953 Hooker filled the canal and topped it with a 0.5-meter (2-foot) clay cap. Beneath lay 43.6 million pounds of eighty-two different chemical residues. Included were benzene, a chemical known to cause anemia and leukemia; lindane, exposure to which results in convulsions and excess production of white blood cells; chloroform, a carcinogen that attacks respiratory, nervous, and gastrointestinal systems; trichloroethylene, a carcinogen that attacks genes, livers, and nervous systems; and methylene chloride, which can cause recurring respiratory distress and death. The most dangerous chemical in the waste, however, was dioxin, a component of the 200 tons of trichlorophenol dumped in the canal. Dioxin has been described as one of the most powerful known carcinogens.

Shortly after the canal was filled, the Niagara Falls Board of Education purchased the canal property for the token sum of one dollar on the condition that the board warn future owners of the buried chemicals, use the land only as a park with the school in close proximity, and build no houses on the property.

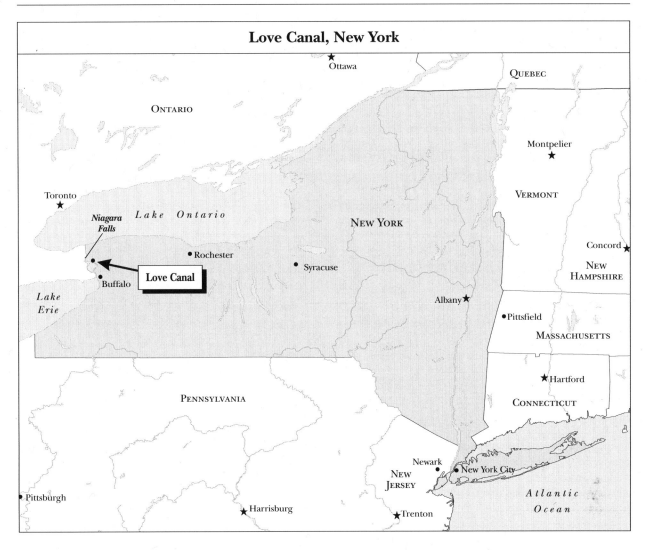

Love Canal, New York

Shortly after taking possession, however, the school board removed 13,000 cubic meters (17,000 cubic yards) of topsoil from the canal for grading at the site of the 99th Street School and the surrounding area. City workers then installed a sewer that punctured both the canal walls and the clay covering to facilitate adjacent housing tracts. Breaks in the clay cap and walls of the canal created openings through which the toxic chemicals eventually flowed.

During the winter of 1975-1976, heavy snowfall caused the groundwater level to rise in the Love Canal area, filling the uncovered canal. Portions of the landfill subsided, and waste storage drums surfaced in a number of locations. Surface water, heavily contaminated with chemicals, was found in the backyards of houses bordering the canal. Residents complained of discomfort and illness caused by unpleasant chemical odors coming from the canal.

Lois Gibbs, president of the Love Canal Homeowners Association, united the community and became an effective and persuasive advocate for families seeking government aid. Gibbs involved herself in December, 1977, when her son, Michael, began to experience asthma and seizures just four months after he entered kindergarten at the 99th Street School. She went door-to-door and questioned other residents about their health in an attempt to discover the full extent of contamination. In 1979 Gibbs traveled to Washington, D.C., where she testified before Congress on behalf of the Love Canal home owners.

In 1977 studies conducted by Niagara Falls city and New York state health officials showed extensive pollution affecting 57 percent of the homes at the southern end of the canal and a "moderate excess of spontaneous abortions and low birth weight infants occurring in households on 99th Street bordering the landfill." In August, 1978, the New York state health commissioner closed the 99th Street School and evacuated 240 families living within two blocks of the canal. In October, 1980, after the release of the alarming results of a health study conducted by the U.S. Environmental Protection Agency (EPA), President Jimmy Carter ordered a total evacuation of the community.

The chemical disaster at Love Canal left behind a legacy of lawsuits and bitterness. In October, 1983, a tentative settlement of the billions of dollars in lawsuits was reached by lawyers of the Hooker Electrochemical Corporation, the city of Niagara Falls, the Niagara Falls Board of Education, Niagara County, and former residents of the Love Canal area. Claims against Hooker and the public agencies totaled $16 billion. On February 19, 1984, former residents of Love Canal received payments ranging from $2,000 to $400,000.

In November, 1980, Congress passed legislation to deal with the cleanup of toxic wastes. The Comprehensive Environmental Response, Compensation, and Liability Act (CERCLA), commonly referred to as Superfund, established a $1.6 billion fund for the cleanup of hazardous substances to be administered by the EPA. The money was to be used when "no responsible party could be identified or when the responsible party refuses to or is unable to pay for such a cleanup."

Peter Neushul

FURTHER READING

Blum, Elizabeth D. *Love Canal Revisited: Race, Class, and Gender in Environmental Activism.* Lawrence: University Press of Kansas, 2008.

Gibbs, Lois. *Love Canal: My Story.* Albany: State University of New York Press, 1982.

_____. *Love Canal: The Story Continues . . . .* Stony Creek, Conn.: New Society, 1998.

_____. "What Happened at Love Canal." 1982. In *So Glorious a Landscape: Nature and the Environment in American History and Culture,* edited by Chris J. Magoc. Wilmington, Del.: Scholarly Resources, 2002.

Layzer, Judith A. "Love Canal: Hazardous Waste and the Politics of Fear." In *The Environmental Case: Translating Values into Policy.* Washington, D.C.: CQ Press, 2002.

Levine, Adelaine Gordon. *Love Canal: Science, Politics, and People.* Lexington, Mass.: Lexington Books, 1982.

Nanotechnology

CATEGORY: Human health and the environment

DEFINITION: Diverse field of science and technology that seeks to understand and control matter at dimensions of 1 to 100 nanometers

SIGNIFICANCE: Nanotechnology receives large-scale public and private investment around the world. The field holds the promise of revolutionizing much of science and technology, but the potential impacts of the products of nanotechnology on the environment, health, and safety are poorly understood. Preliminary research findings suggest that much further study is needed.

Nanotechnology is a relatively new field concerned with a wide range of materials and processes. The increasing speeds and decreasing sizes of personal electronic devices owe much to nanotechnology, which enables the production of lighter and stronger materials that reduce energy usage and prolong the life spans of the devices made with them. Battery and lighting systems have been developed that use nanotechnology to be more fuel-efficient. Nanotechnology has also contributed to the development of improved medical diagnostic devices and drug-delivery systems. Research into the use of nanotechnology to detect pollutants and build more effective water-purification systems is ongoing. The promise of nanotechnology is immense, but the field is new, and much remains uncertain about its overall impacts on the environment and human health.

DEFINITION

The term "nano" is a prefix for one-billionth, or 1×10^{-9}, of a unit. Nanotechnology is concerned with the study, development, and control of materials at nanoscale—that is, in the range of 1 to 100 nanometers (or 1 to 100 billionths of 1 meter). Nanotechnology includes processes and instruments that engineer materials at nanoscale, and nanoparticles have at least one dimension in the nanoscale range.

Many naturally occurring materials have nanoscale dimensions, including proteins, the genetic molecule deoxyribonucleic acid (DNA), and viruses. Volcanoes and forest fires produce nanoparticles, and many soils contain organic and inorganic nanoparticles. Nanoparticles are also produced by human activities, such as cigarette smoking and the burning of fuels in combustion engines. The polymer and plastics industry makes chemical molecules with nanoscale dimensions. Environmental issues associated with nanotechnology thus overlap other areas.

A significant segment of nanotechnology is concerned with newly discovered nanoparticles. These can have completely different electrical, magnetic, or biological properties compared to larger particles of the same substance. For example, gold nanoparticles can be red, blue, or gold, depending on their precise size. Titanium dioxide and zinc oxide are used in sunscreens to block the sun's ultraviolet (UV) rays, but large particles of these substances leave a white coating on the skin; as nanoparticles, the same substances are transparent and more appealing to sunbathers. Questions have arisen, however, about what else might be different about these nanoparticles and what effects they might have when they get into the body or are washed into the environment.

Richard E. Smalley has been called the grandfather of nanotechnology. In 1986 he and others discovered a completely new form of carbon. They named it buckminsterfullerene, but as the molecules look like soccer balls, they are more commonly called buckyballs. Several sizes and shapes have been identified and collectively are called fullerenes. They are being investigated as possible devices to transport drug molecules to specific tissues and cells.

Many different kinds of nanoparticles have been developed and given names such as dendrimers, nanowires, and quantum dots. Carbon nanotubes are particularly interesting. Identified in 1991, they are highly organized carbon atoms that form sheets that roll into long tubes. Having different forms, they usually are a few nanometers wide and can be millimeters long. They are extremely strong for their weight, can transport other materials, and have unique electrical properties. They may have uses in reinforcing car and airplane bodies and in making comfortable bulletproof clothing; they may also have applications in medicine and in new battery technology. Carbon nanotubes have been at the center of early debate over the potential environmental impacts of nanotechnology.

Preliminary Nanotoxicology

Nanoparticles can enter living cells, making them useful as drugs but also raising concerns. Some nanoparticles enter the nuclei of cells, where genetic material is stored. This may have beneficial uses, but it could also lead to genetic damage. Nanoparticles smaller than 35 nanometers can penetrate the blood-brain barrier, which prevents most chemicals from reaching the brain. This property could help deliver drugs for brain disorders, but it might also cause harmful side effects.

The field of science that investigates such concerns is known as nanotoxicology. Some early nanotoxicological studies have provided worrisome results. Nanosilver has antibacterial properties and has been used in special clothing and on surfaces where bacteria might grow. Bulk silver is normally safe, but laboratory experiments have shown that nanosilver might interfere with the human immune system.

Carbon nanotubes account for much of nanoparticle manufacturing, and their production is predicted to increase dramatically. However, a 2009 review of research into the toxicity of carbon nanotubes found that only twenty-one studies had yet been conducted, and all had shown some damage to tissues and animals. None of the research studies had examined the effects of carbon nanotubes on humans.

Hardly any research has examined nanoparticles after they enter the environment from normal wear and tear or when products are discarded. One of the first studies exposed largemouth bass to buckyballs for forty-eight hours. Most of the organs of the fish were unharmed, but their brains showed evidence of oxidative damage. Because buckyballs are highly fat-soluble and thus prone to cause environmental damage, the researchers urged the widespread application of the precautionary principle to avoid the sort of environmental damage seen from earlier chemicals with similar solubility profiles.

Nanobots and Gray Goo

The vision for nanotechnology originated in a 1959 talk by American physicist Richard Feynman. He predicted the development of very fast and small computers, as well as tiny machines that could circulate through the body. Such hypothetical devices have come to be called nanobots or nanites and are commonly included in science-fiction scenarios. They also come up in discussions about the potential environmental impacts of nanotechnology.

Another early proponent of nanotechnology, K. Eric Drexler, published *Engines of Creation: The Coming Era of Nanotechnology* in 1986. This book had a significant impact on the development and popular understanding of nanotechnology. Drexler's proposal, called molecular manufacturing, involved building nanomachines (or assemblers) that would make things with atomic precision. Drexler's proposal remains scientifically controversial, with critics such as Richard Smalley asserting that the approach is physically impossible.

Others have used the idea of such assemblers to portray nanotechnology as extremely dangerous. Drexler suggested that nanomachines could be programmed to assemble copies of themselves. This would increase production but raises concerns about how to control them. Nanotechnology molecular assemblers have become associated with self-replication, although the ideas are not necessarily linked. Science-fiction authors have invented scenarios in which marauding nanobots wreak environmental havoc.

Drexler eventually distanced himself from the idea of assembler self-replication, but he coined the term "gray goo" to describe a situation in which self-replicating nanomachines get out of control and consume everything around them. In a later edition of his book, Drexler lamented how nanotechnology had become associated with so-called gray goo scenarios. He used the term in only one passage of the book, while repeatedly stressing nanotechnology's potential either to destroy the world or to remake it, curing illness and restoring the environment.

Such grand claims make it more difficult to evaluate the real potential and actual threat of nanotechnology. A distinction must be made between "normal" nanotechnology and "futuristic" nanotechnology. Molecular assemblers and gray goo scenarios belong well into the future, although the steps that current scientists take may determine whether or when these might develop. Normal nanotechnology in the early twenty-first century focuses on recent discoveries about nanoparticles and their properties. Because of the newness of the field, much remains unknown and uncertain, either positive or negative, and practical environmental concerns are being raised.

EXAMINING ENVIRONMENTAL CONCERNS

Given the scientific uncertainty about the impacts of nanoparticles, many scientists and policy makers have called for caution in the study and use of such particles. The European Union has adopted a precautionary approach in its chemical regulatory agency and in its voluntary code of conduct for nanotechnologists. Worldwide, concerted efforts have been undertaken to understand and regulate nanoparticles. The U.S. Environmental Protection Agency launched a major research initiative in 2009 into the health and environmental concerns raised by nanotechnology.

While nanotoxicology is starting to be addressed, many remain concerned about the funding of research into environmental concerns. In the United States, the National Nanotechnology Initiative (NNI) coordinates federal investment in nanotechnology. Between 2005 and 2010, less than 4 percent of the $9 billion invested went directly to the examination of environmental, health, and safety issues. In 2008 the NNI published its strategy for such research, but the National Research Council was critical of the approach, concluding that it overestimated how much research had already been conducted and thereby underestimated the funding necessary to address environmental issues adequately.

The potential benefits of nanotechnology are enormous, but they will be realized only if concerns about possible negative health and environmental impacts are addressed. A gray goo scenario is not necessary for nanoparticles to damage the environment, and much research has yet to be done in this young field before the risks of nanotechnology are fully understood and steps can be taken to ensure that any potential harms are minimized.

Dónal P. O'Mathúna

FURTHER READING

Allhoff, Fritz, et al., eds. *Nanoethics: The Ethical and Social Implications of Nanotechnology.* Hoboken, N.J.: Wiley-Interscience, 2007.

Drexler, K. Eric. *Engines of Creation: The Coming Era of Nanotechnology.* New York: Anchor Books, 1986.

Edwards, Steven A. *The Nanotech Pioneers: Where Are They Taking Us?* Weinheim, Germany: Wiley-VCH, 2006.

O'Mathúna, Dónal P. *Nanoethics: Big Ethical Issues with Small Technology.* London: Continuum, 2009.

Ray, Paresh Chandra, Hongtao Yu, and Peter P. Fu. "Toxicity and Environmental Risks of Nanomaterials: Challenges and Future Needs." *Journal of Environmental Science and Health*, Part C, Environmental Carcinogenesis and Ecotoxicology Reviews 27, no. 1 (2009): 1-35.

Natural Resources Conservation Service

CATEGORIES: Organizations and agencies; agriculture and food; resources and resource management

IDENTIFICATION: Federal agency under the U.S. Department of Agriculture that is responsible for coordinating the conservation of soil and water

DATE: Established on April 27, 1935

SIGNIFICANCE: By partnering with nearly three thousand local conservation districts, as well as with conservation organizations and state governments, the Natural Resources Conservation Service helps to protect soil, water, and wetlands from erosion, contamination, and overuse. The agency's scientists and engineers have done much of the research underlying modern understanding of watersheds and soil.

The Natural Resources Conservation Service (NRCS) began during the 1920's with soil scientist Hugh Hammond Bennett, sometimes called the father of soil conservation. Bennett, who worked for the U.S. Department of Agriculture, recognized the threat posed by soil erosion and coauthored a 1928 government report on the problem titled *Soil Erosion: A National Menace*. He also published articles in popular magazines in which he proposed conservation measures to preserve topsoil. In 1933, Bennett became the first director of a new agency under the Department of the Interior, the Soil Erosion Service, and began an experimental project with farmers in the Coon Creek watershed in Wisconsin to put into practice particular farming methods that best suited the land and watershed in each area. The project demonstrated that intelligent land use could prevent erosion and support clean air and water, as well as safeguard plants and animals.

The Dust Bowl of the 1930's helped Bennett convince the U.S. Congress to take further action, and in 1935 the Soil Conservation Act was passed; this legislation created the Soil Conservation Service (SCS) as a part of the Department of Agriculture, with Bennett at its head. The SCS expanded quickly under President Franklin D. Roosevelt's New Deal and soon was conducting more than one hundred demonstration projects with local farmers, as well as running more than 450 Civilian Conservation Corps (CCC) work

camps and employing thousands of Works Progress Administration (WPA) workers. Conservation districts were established, and farmers and local government officials worked with the SCS to tailor plans for each district.

The work of the SCS continued to expand under new laws, including the Flood Control Act of 1944, the Watershed Protection and Flood Prevention Act of 1954, the Clean Water Act of 1972, the Rural Development Act of 1972, and the Food Security Act of 1985. During the 1980's, the SCS collaborated with the U.S. Army Corps of Engineers and the U.S. Fish and Wildlife Service to develop mapping techniques and conventions to identify wetlands on private land. The agency also conducts periodic inventories of soil erosion, cropland, water conservation needs, and natural resources. In 1994, the SCS was reorganized and its name was changed to the Natural Resources Conser-

A member of the Natural Resources Conservation Service discusses a laser leveling project in Yuma, Arizona, with local officials. (USDA/NRCS)

vation Service, to better reflect the scope of the agency's responsibilities. The NRCS continued to work with watersheds and soil, with new emphasis on the damage caused to water resources by chemical runoff from large farms and on the impacts on water quality of the large meat and dairy operations known as concentrated animal feeding operations, or CAFOs. In the twenty-first century, the NRCS began working with organic farmers to develop targeted conservation practices for organic agricultural operations.

Cynthia A. Bily

FURTHER READING

Blanco, Humberto, and Rattan Lal. *Principles of Soil Conservation and Management.* New York: Springer, 2008.

Conrad, Daniel. "Implementation of Conservation Title Provisions at the State Level." In *Soil and Water Conservation Policies and Programs: Successes and Failures,* edited by Ted L. Napier, Silvana M. Napier, and Jiri Tvrdon. Boca Raton, Fla.: CRC Press, 2000.

National Science Teachers Association. *Dig In! Hands-On Soil Investigations.* Arlington, Va.: NSTA Press, 2001.

Sampson, R. Neil. *For Love of the Land: A History of the National Association of Conservation Districts.* Tucson, Ariz.: Wheatmark, 2009.

Nuclear fusion

CATEGORIES: Nuclear power and radiation; energy and energy use

DEFINITION: Reaction between light atomic nuclei that produces a heavier nucleus and releases energy

SIGNIFICANCE: Nuclear fusion can produce much more energy for a given weight of fuel than any other available energy technology. Controlled fusion reactors could generate high levels of power with uninterrupted delivery and no greenhouse gas emissions. The fusion process produces far less radioactive material than fission reactors, and the by-products generated are less damaging biologically. The radioactive wastes produced by fusion reactors would cease to be dangerous after reasonably short periods of time.

Deuterium, the primary fuel used for nuclear fusion, is abundant in seawater. When a deuterium atom and a tritium atom, both isotopes of hydrogen, are fused together, helium is formed, with the release of a neutron and 17.6 million electronvolts (MEV) of energy. To undergo fusion, the interacting nuclei need kinetic energies on the order of 0.7 MEV to overcome the electrical repulsion between their positive charges. These energies are available at temperatures around 10 million kelvins (18 million degrees Fahrenheit), which poses a major problem for containment of the fusion fuel. In some experiments, the resulting plasma generated by heat from an electrical discharge is contained in the reactor core with appropriately shaped magnetic fields (magnetic confinement). In other experiments, fusion is initiated through the heating and compressing of pellets of the light nuclei with a high-intensity laser beam (inertial confinement). Methods of achieving fusion at lower temperatures, known as cold fusion, continue to be studied, but none has been found that produces more energy than is consumed in the fusion process.

ENVIRONMENTAL ADVANTAGES AND CONCERNS

The natural product resulting from the fusion of deuterium with tritium is helium, which poses no threat to life and does not contribute to global warming. Although tritium is radioactive, it has a short half-life of twelve years, has a very low amount of decay energy, and does not accumulate in the body. It is cycled out of the human body as water, with a biological half-life of seven to fourteen days. Since fusion requires precisely controlled conditions of temperature, pressure, and magnetic field parameters in order to generate net energy, there is no danger of any catastrophic radioactive accident, as heat generation in a fusion reactor would quickly stop if any of these parameters were disrupted by a reactor malfunction. In addition, since the total amount of fusion fuel in the reactor vessel is very small (a few grams) and the density of the plasma is low, there is no risk of a runaway reaction, because fusion would cease in a few seconds if fuel delivery were stopped.

Because of the generation of high-energy neutrons in the deuterium-tritium reaction, the typical structural materials of fusion reactors, such as stainless steel or titanium, tantalum, and niobium alloys, will become radioactive when bombarded by the neutrons. The half-lives of the resulting radioisotopes are typically less than those generated by nuclear fission.

Most of this radioactive material would reside in the fusion reactor core and would be dangerous for about fifty years. Low-level wastes would be dangerous for about one hundred years. Since the choice of materials used in a fusion reactor is quite flexible, low-activation materials, such as vanadium alloys and carbon fiber materials, that do not easily become radioactive can be used.

Most fusion reactor designs use liquid lithium as a coolant and for generating tritium when it is bombarded by neutrons coming from the fusion reaction. Because lithium is highly flammable, a fire could release its tritium contents into the atmosphere, posing a radiation risk. Estimates of the amount of tritium and other radioactive gases that might escape from a typical fusion power plant indicate that they would be diluted to safe levels by the time they reached the perimeter fence of the plant.

Another safety and environmental concern associated with fusion reactors is the potential that the neutrons generated in a fusion reactor could be used to breed plutonium for an atomic bomb. In order for a reactor to be used in this way, however, it would have to be extensively redesigned; thus the plutonium production would be very difficult to conceal. The tritium produced in fusion reactors could be used as a component of hydrogen bombs, but the likelihood is minimal.

Development of Commercial Fusion Reactors

Despite fusion research that started during the 1950's, a commercial fusion reactor will most likely not be available until at least 2050. Several deuterium-tritium fusion reactors using the tokamak design have been built as test devices, but none of them produce more thermal energy than the electrical energy consumed.

The United States, Japan, Russia, China, South Korea, and the European Union are joint funders of the International Thermonuclear Experimental Reactor (ITER), which is being constructed at Cadarache in southern France. ITER is planned to fuse atomic nuclei at very high temperatures inside of a giant electromagnetic ring. In May, 2009, Lawrence Livermore National Laboratory announced the development of a high-energy laser system that can heat hydrogen atoms to temperatures that exist in the cores of stars. Such a system would provide the ability to produce more energy from controlled, inertially confined nuclear fusion than is necessary to produce the reaction.

Alvin K. Benson

Further Reading

Braams, C. M., and P. E. Stott. *Nuclear Fusion: Half a Century of Magnetic Confinement Fusion Research.* Philadelphia: Institute of Physics Publishing, 2002.

Bryan, Jeff C. *Introduction to Nuclear Science.* Boca Raton, Fla.: CRC Press, 2009.

McCracken, Garry, and Peter Stott. *Fusion: The Energy of the Universe.* Burlington, Mass.: Elsevier Academic, 2005.

Seife, Charles. *Sun in a Bottle: The Strange History of Fusion and the Science of Wishful Thinking.* New York: Viking Press, 2008.

Nuclear power

Categories: Nuclear power and radiation; energy and energy use

Definition: Electricity generated through the harnessing of the heat energy produced by controlled nuclear fission

Significance: Nuclear power has long been the most controversial source of electricity. High plant construction costs, safety concerns, waste disposal problems, and public mistrust all served to slow the growth of the nuclear power industry during the late twentieth century. In the early twenty-first century, factors such as nuclear power's potential to meet electricity demand while reducing greenhouse gas emissions have increased its appeal.

Many of the environmental impacts of nuclear power plants are common to all large-scale electricity-generating facilities, regardless of their fuel. The most important are land use and related impacts on plants, animals, and ecosystems; nonradioactive water effluent and water quality; thermal pollution of adjacent waters; and social impacts on nearby communities. Unique to nuclear power plants is the hazardous radiation emitted by radioactive materials present in all stages of the nuclear fuel cycle. Such radiation is contained in uranium ore when it is mined and processed, in fabricated uranium reactor fuel, in spent fuel that has been fissioned, in contaminated reactor components, and in low-level radioactive waste—such as contaminated tools, protective clothing, and replaced reactor parts—generated by routine plant operation and maintenance.

Spent reactor fuel is highly radioactive and must be

isolated from the environment for tens of thousands of years or more. Spent fuel can be reprocessed to separate out usable uranium and plutonium, but doing so generates large volumes of low-level waste that present disposal challenges of their own. Other challenges in waste handling and disposal arise at the end of a plant's useful life, when the contaminated reactor must be dismantled and the radioactive and non-radioactive components disposed of in a process known as decommissioning.

Under normal operating circumstances, commercial nuclear power plants release negligible radioactive emissions. The principal safety concern is that a severe accident could release large quantities of dangerous radioactive materials into the environment, as happened in 1986 at the Chernobyl nuclear plant in Ukraine. Roughly a quarter century after one of Chernobyl's reactors exploded, radiation levels remain dangerously high within the deteriorating concrete containment structure surrounding the reactor, and levels within the exclusion zone that extends in a 30-kilometer (18.6-mile) radius around the plant site continue to be higher than normal background levels.

EARLY HISTORY

The nuclear power industry arose out of the technology developed during World War II to produce the atomic bomb. Postwar enthusiasm for new technology in general, combined with pressure to demonstrate peaceful uses for expensive and fearsome wartime nuclear technology, led to a strong U.S. government effort beginning during the early 1950's to induce industry to develop nuclear energy. Large government subsidies and preferential treatment assisted the industry from its early days. Between fiscal year (FY) 1948 and FY2007, nuclear power received 53.5 percent of all federal energy research and development funds, totaling $85.01 billion in constant FY2008 dollars. One of the industry's unique subsidies was the passage of the 1957 Price-Anderson Act, which limits the liability of nuclear power plant owners and equipment vendors in the event of a reactor accident.

The basic design of the first U.S. nuclear power plants was adapted from early pressurized water reactor technology developed for submarines and other naval propulsion applications. Roughly two-thirds of the 104 commercial reactors in use in the United States are pressurized water reactors. In this reactor

design, light (ordinary) water surrounds the nuclear fuel, which is made up of enriched uranium. The system is pressurized so that the fuel heats the water without boiling it. The resulting heat is used to boil a separate water supply, creating steam. The steam spins a turbine to generate electricity. The choice of this reactor design was largely driven by expediency and political considerations rather than an explicit effort to seek safe or reliable design features. The first large-scale commercial nuclear plant in the United States, which began operating at Shippingport, Pennsylvania, on a demonstration basis in 1957 and continued until 1982, was a conversion of a naval reactor project for which funding had been canceled. Some observers believe this early technology decision was largely responsible for the industry's problems in later years.

Another U.S. nuclear power plant that began operations in 1957, the Vallecitos plant near Pleasanton, California, was a research and development facility that became the first privately owned and operated nuclear power plant to provide significant quantities of electricity to a public utility grid. The Vallecitos facility employed a boiling-water reactor, a type of reactor in which the light water surrounding the enriched uranium fuel is converted directly into steam. The steam is piped to a turbine, which rotates to power an electric generator that produces electricity. The Vallecitos reactor was shut down in 1963. Approximately one-third of the commercial nuclear reactors operating in the United States are boiling-water reactors.

Yet another nuclear reactor technology emerged in the postwar years. Beginning in 1946, the United States developed a series of experimental prototype breeder reactors, a type of nuclear reactor in which the reaction is controlled in such a way that more fuel is produced than consumed. In 1963, the first commercial breeder reactor began low-power test operations at the Enrico Fermi Atomic Power Plant in Michigan. An accident in 1966 resulted in a partial core meltdown and caused reactor and fuel assembly damage that took almost four years to repair. Operations resumed in 1970 and continued until the decision was made in 1972 to decommission the reactor.

LATE TWENTIETH CENTURY DEVELOPMENTS

Government, industry, and public opinion were all largely positive about nuclear energy up through the late 1960's. Two-thirds of the U.S. commercial reactors operating in 2010 were issued construction per-

Leading World Producers of Nuclear Power, 2010

RANK	COUNTRY	KILOWATT-HOURS (BILLIONS)	PERCENTAGE OF ELECTRICITY	REACTORS
1	United States	798.7	20.2	104
2	France	391.7	75.2	58
3	Japan	263.1	28.9	55
4	Russia	152.8	17.8	32
5	South Korea	141.1	34.8	20
6	Germany	127.7	26.1	17
7	Canada	85.3	14.8	18
8	Ukraine	77.9	48.6	15
9	China	65.7	1.9	13
10	United Kingdom	62.9	17.9	19
11	Spain	50.6	17.5	8
12	Sweden	50.0	34.7	10
	Totals	2267.5	28.1	369
	World as a whole	2560.0	14.0	441

Source: World Nuclear Organization, November, 2010. Nations are listed in descending order of the amount of electricity they generate with nuclear reactors. The percentage column indicates what part of each nation's electricity consumption is supplied by nuclear power. "Reactors" indicates the number of nuclear reactors operating in November, 2010.

mits between 1966 and 1973, a time of great optimism about the technology. During this period, the National Environmental Policy Act of 1969 was enacted, which forced prospective reactor owners to address environmental impacts in plant proposals; the environmental movement arose, beginning with the first Earth Day in 1970; and there was a widespread increase in environmental activism on the part of the public. By the mid-1970's, several widely publicized safety hearings, plant incidents, and government studies had begun to focus public and media attention on nuclear plant regulatory and safety lapses, accident risks, and the problem of nuclear waste disposal. These forces combined to create a sizable antinuclear movement in the United States, which was bolstered by the 1979 accident at the Three Mile Island plant in Pennsylvania.

Although proponents of nuclear power frequently blamed licensing interventions by antinuclear activists for numerous plant cost overruns and delays, most analyses concluded that in the majority of cases other factors, such as capital availability and shifting regulatory requirements, were primarily responsible for a slowdown in the development of nuclear power. By the late 1980's a decline in the number of plants under construction and a shift of public concern to the threat of the nuclear arms race had begun to reduce the ranks of the antinuclear power movement.

Development of breeder reactor technology in particular slowed significantly in the United States during the late twentieth century. One reason for the decline was the unique safety challenges presented by breeder reactors. Unlike light-water reactor systems, fast-neutron breeder reactors employ molten sodium as a coolant. Sodium burns when exposed to air and reacts explosively with water. Economic considerations also put breeder reactors at a disadvantage. As long as uranium supplies remained abundant, light-water reactor facilities were the more competitive option. Finally, the quantities of plutonium that could be created in breeder reactors raised concerns that the material could be used for nuclear weapons applications. The threat of nuclear proliferation led to a directive from President Jimmy Carter in 1977 that indefinitely deferred commercial reprocessing of spent nuclear fuel and plutonium recycling. This effective ban severely curbed breeder reactor progress in the United States. Congressional funding continued for a demonstration breeder plant in Oak Ridge, Tennessee, despite Carter's opposition, but in 1983 Congress cut funding for the project, which effectively ended the country's breeder reactor development for the rest of the century.

Between 1987 and 1994 nuclear power proponents won long-sought changes in regulations governing emergency planning requirements, the licensing of new reactors, siting, and reactor design certification. The essence of these changes was to facilitate the process for approving new reactors while sharply reducing opportunities for public participation in the regulatory process. Nuclear opponents adamantly opposed many of these changes, especially a 1992 congressional decision authorizing the U.S. Nuclear Regulatory Commission (NRC)—the federal agency responsible for nuclear power licensing and safety regulation—to forgo a long history of issuing separate licenses for construction and operation, each of which allowed for hearings. Instead, Congress mandated the issuance of a single combined license for both activities that permits few opportunities for safety challenges after construction has been completed.

STATUS AND PROJECTIONS: UNITED STATES

The early twenty-first century has seen increasing receptivity to nuclear power in the United States. Among the factors contributing to this renewed interest are the need to meet the nation's continued growth in demand for electricity, the rising prices of fossil fuels, worries over possible interruptions in oil and gas availability, particularly from Middle Eastern sources, and concerns regarding the impact of the burning of fossil fuels on air quality and global climate. Some environmentalists tout nuclear power as a clean-air, carbon-free technology.

In the United States, nuclear power plants contributed approximately 20 percent of the electricity generated in 2009. In mid-2010 there were 104 licensed, operable reactors at sixty-five sites in thirty-one states. The newest of these received its construction license in 1973 and began its operational life in 1996. As of July, 2010, thirteen license applications were under active NRC review for up to twenty-two new reactors.

The nation's FY2011 budget authorized a total of $54.5 billion for nuclear power facilities, $36 billion of it in new loan authority established by the 2005 Energy Policy Act for DOE projects that cut greenhouse gas emissions. In February, 2010, President Barack Obama announced $8 billion in loan guarantees to go toward the construction of two new reactors at the existing Plant Vogtle nuclear power facility near Augusta, Georgia. These reactors are scheduled to come online in 2016 and 2017. If the NRC grants final approval for construction, these will be the first new nuclear reactors built in the United States in the twenty-first century.

All U.S. reactors were originally granted forty-year operating licenses. Under NRC regulations adopted in 1992, plant owners may seek twenty-year license extensions. In the case of some reactors, competitive economic pressures or the costs of expensive equipment upgrades make retirement preferable to an extended operating life; reactors may even be permanently shut down before their scheduled license expiration dates because competing power sources or needs for expensive repairs make continued operation economically undesirable. In other cases, equipment upgrades and license renewal prove more cost-effective than construction of a new power facility. (The license renewal process alone, not including equipment upgrades, costs $10 million to $15 million.) As of July, 2010, the NRC had granted license renewals to fifty-nine reactors, and more renewal applications were expected.

In 2006 President George W. Bush proposed the Global Nuclear Energy Partnership (GNEP), a program for reducing the risk of nuclear weapons proliferation while minimizing reactor wastes. Spent fuel reprocessing and advanced breeder technologies were components of GNEP. In 2009, under the Obama administration, the DOE announced that it would not be pursuing domestic commercial reprocessing; however, research and development on proliferation-resistant fuel cycles and waste management would continue.

STATUS AND PROJECTIONS: WORLD

As of November, 2010, 441 nuclear reactors were in operation in twenty-nine countries. The number of reactors in the United States (104), France (58), Japan (55), and the Russian Federation (32) accounted for more than half of the world's total operating reactors. The majority of these reactors were between twenty and thirty-nine years old. In eighteen countries, nuclear power supplied at least 20 percent of total electricity for 2009.

While most of the world's nuclear reactors are U.S.-designed pressurized water reactors and boiling-water reactors, other types are also in operation. Many of these employ graphite or heavy water (water enriched in deuterium) to moderate the nuclear reaction, which allows them to use less expensive natural (nonenriched) uranium as a fuel. The advanced gas-cooled reactors that predominate in the United Kingdom, for example, use graphite as a moderator and carbon dioxide instead of water as a coolant. In the pressurized heavy-water reactors common in Canada, heavy water serves as both coolant and moderator. The light-water graphite reactors of the Russian Federation are similar to boiling-water reactors but employ graphite moderators.

Although several countries established breeder reactor programs in the previous century, few of these programs were thriving as of 2010. The United Kingdom had not constructed a new breeder facility since it shut down its last breeder reactor in 1994. Germany's one fast-breeder reactor permanently ended operations in 1991. France shut down Superphénix, the world's only commercial-sized breeder reactor, in 1998, after a spotty history of malfunction and repairs that kept the plant offline for more than half of its operational life. France's Phénix reactor enjoyed a more successful run, but it came to a close in 2010 with no immediate plans for another breeder reactor. In Japan, after a 1995 sodium coolant leak and fire at the Monju reactor, repairs and public controversy suspended the facility's operations until 2010. The only countries constructing new fast-breeder reactors as of August, 2010, were the Russian Federation and India, both of which were motivated to pursue the technology at least in part by concerns regarding uranium supplies.

In 2010 sixty new reactors were under construction in fifteen nations, although some of them may ultimately not be brought online. Fifty-one of them were pressurized water reactors, four were boiling-water reactors, two were pressurized heavy-water reactors, two were fast-breeder reactors, and one was a light-water graphite reactor. China, the Russian Federation, the Republic of Korea (South Korea), and India accounted for roughly 70 percent of the reactors under construction.

Waste- and Contamination-Related Issues

Spent fuel and high-level radioactive waste can pose threats to human health and the environment for many thousands of years, so they must be properly isolated and secured. Deep subterranean storage appears to be the best solution, but finding a repository site with the right geological characteristics is a technical challenge that is invariably complicated by political controversy. In the United States, Congress designated Yucca Mountain, Nevada, as the nation's sole repository in 1987, and site suitability studies were conducted at Yucca Mountain for nearly two decades. Opponents, including the state of Nevada, charged that the DOE's studies were geared more toward preparing the site for operation than for objectively assessing its suitability. The DOE submitted its license application for the repository in 2008, ten years after the original target date for opening. In early 2010, under the Obama administration, funding for the site was cut, and the DOE withdrew its license application. Lawsuits have been filed to challenge Yucca Mountain's closure, which leaves high-level waste in temporary storage at nuclear facilities around the country.

Some countries—notably France, England, Russia, Japan, and India—reprocess spent fuel from nuclear reactors. Reprocessing strips the waste of uranium and plutonium, which can be used to fuel reactors. While reprocessing results in a small reduction of high-level nuclear wastes, it generates large volumes of low-level nuclear wastes, which also require environmentally responsible disposal. Reprocessing is more costly than the single use and disposal of spent fuel. Also, because it creates stockpiles of plutonium, reprocessing has the potential to contribute to nuclear weapons proliferation and terrorism. Separating plutonium from more highly radioactive spent fuel assemblies makes it easier for it to be stolen. With this danger in mind, President Jimmy Carter issued an executive order in 1977 that indefinitely deferred U.S. reprocessing of spent nuclear reactor fuel.

Concern about nuclear power plant accidents continues to trouble the public. Precise accident probability estimates are impossible to derive, given the complexity of nuclear reactor systems. Industry proponents point to several government-sponsored studies that have concluded that the probability of a plant accident with off-site consequences is extremely low. Critics have countered that these studies were methodologically flawed, omitted important factors, and underestimated the true risks. They also emphasize the catastrophic consequences that could result if a low-probability accident should nonetheless occur.

Arguments Pro and Con

Nuclear proponents cite several points in the technology's favor: a good safety record, improved operating performance since the Three Mile Island accident, studies concluding that the risk of a severe accident is low, and the fact that nuclear power plants emit no significant amounts of common air pollutants or gases that contribute to global warming. Critics of nuclear power point to the long-standing failure of any country to establish a site for the permanent disposal of spent fuel and high-level wastes; flaws, uncertainties, and omissions in accident probability studies; the catastrophic consequences that could result from a severe reactor accident; a large number of safety-related incidents and near accidents; and the high cost of nuclear plants compared to competing electicity-generating technologies and energy-efficiency improvements. In addition, for those countries that do not already have nuclear weapons arsenals, inherent proliferation risks are associated with nuclear power technology and fuels, which, if misused, could provide the expertise, infrastructure, and basic materials for a program to develop nuclear weapons.

High costs remain another obstacle to new plant orders. U.S. reactors completed during the 1990's cost $2 billion to $6 billion each, averaging more than $3 billion. Although proponents argue that new plant designs could be built more cheaply, the industry's history of large cost overruns discomforts prospective plant owners, capital markets, and state regulators. Many analysts believe that unpredictably high capital costs have been among the most important reason for the industry's decline. The picture has been complicated further by the deregulation of the electric utility industry that followed passage of the Public Utility Regulatory Policies Act in 1978 and the Energy Policy Act in 1992. Uncertainty surrounding the future economic and regulatory climate raises questions about the competitiveness of both new and many existing nuclear reactors.

Public opinion surveys in the United States after the events at Three Mile Island showed a growing majority opposing the construction of new nuclear power plants. Numerous influential policy assessments from the late twentieth century concluded that it was unlikely that new nuclear power plants would be built in the United States unless the key issues of waste disposal, costs, safety, and public acceptance were satisfactorily resolved. Although the situation differs from country to country, some combination of these factors served to hamper the growth of nuclear power in most countries during the late twentieth century. In the United States, additional factors that contributed to nuclear power's decline during the 1980's and 1990's included unexpectedly plentiful supplies of natural gas and slower-than-anticipated growth in electricity demand.

The public's mistrust of nuclear power is generally acknowledged as a roadblock to new plant orders. Risk perception studies have shown that the public's lack of trust is deeply rooted, widely felt, and resistant to change. Surveys assessing public support in the United States for the use of nuclear power reflected a decline between 1994, when 57 percent of those polled were in favor, and 2001, when 46 percent were in favor. Since 2001, however, support has increased, reaching 62 percent in 2010. Concerns about such environmental problems as greenhouse gas emissions and the cost and availability of fossil fuels played a role in this upswing in nuclear power's popularity. NRC officials and others have noted that, regardless of one's

explanation of the public's views, public acceptance plays an important role in determining whether new plants will be built in the United States.

Phillip A. Greenberg
Updated by Karen N. Kähler

FURTHER READING

Bodansky, David. *Nuclear Energy: Principles, Practices, and Prospects.* 2d ed. New York: Springer, 2004.

Garwin, Richard L., and Georges Charpak. *Megawatts and Megatons: The Future of Nuclear Power and Nuclear Weapons.* Chicago: University of Chicago Press, 2001.

Hagen, Ronald E., John R. Moens, and Zdenek D. Nikodem. *Impact of U.S. Nuclear Generation on Greenhouse Gas Emissions.* Washington, D.C.: Energy Information Administration, U.S. Department of Energy, 2001.

Hore-Lacy, Ian. *Nuclear Energy in the Twenty-first Century: The World Nuclear University Primer.* London: World Nuclear University Press, 2006.

Mahaffey, James. *Atomic Awakening: A New Look at the History and Future of Nuclear Power.* New York: Pegasus Books, 2009.

Murray, Raymond LeRoy. *Nuclear Energy: An Introduction to the Concepts, Systems, and Applications of Nuclear Processes.* Burlington, Vt.: Butterworth-Heinemann/Elsevier, 2009.

Wolfson, Richard. *Nuclear Choices: A Citizen's Guide to Nuclear Technology.* Rev. ed. Cambridge, Mass.: MIT Press, 1993.

Oil crises and oil embargoes

CATEGORY: Energy and energy use

DEFINITION: Disruptions of oil supply patterns between the Middle East and the industrialized West

SIGNIFICANCE: Oil crises and oil embargoes have typically occurred during times of political tension in the Persian Gulf region. Such episodes have strengthened support in Western nations for greater domestic energy production and for military policies enhancing oil security in the Persian Gulf.

The industrialized West depends on oil as a fuel and chemical feedstock. Given that the majority of the world's long-term oil reserves are located in the

Middle East, the West depends on a smooth flow of oil through world markets. On at least three occasions during the last few decades of the twentieth century, political events in the Middle East led to crises in the world oil markets. These crises illustrated the West's vulnerability to oil supply interruptions and price increases.

World Oil Market Interruptions

In the early years of international oil markets, the United States was the leading producer, accounting for more than one-half of the world's oil production until the 1950's. U.S. oil production, however, peaked at 11.3 million barrels per day in 1970 and began to decline as lower-cost reserves in the Middle East were tapped. Leading oil-producing nations in the Middle East had met in 1960 to form the Organization of Petroleum Exporting Countries (OPEC), but the new organization was largely ignored by the world community. Because oil flowed without significant interruption, there was also little notice of the increasing

dependence of the West on Middle Eastern oil into the early 1970's.

The security of oil supply became an immediate world issue on October 6, 1973, with an attack by Egyptian forces against Israeli positions along the Suez Canal. The United States supported Israel in the brief war that followed. In retaliation, King Faisal of Saudi Arabia ordered a 25 percent cut in Saudi oil output and a cutoff of shipments to the United States. The other Arab members of OPEC joined in the embargo and production cutbacks. World oil prices roughly quadrupled, from around three dollars per barrel to twelve dollars. In the United States, emergency conservation measures were implemented, and consumers waited in long lines for limited supplies of motor fuels. The embargo ended about six months later, on March 18, 1974.

The Western economies recovered, and oil prices were relatively stable from 1974 to 1978. Oil demand resumed its growth, and oil again flowed to the West. In 1979, however, the Iranian revolution removed much of Iran's production from world markets at a time when there was little excess capacity. World oil prices again rose sharply, reaching a peak of nearly thirty-five dollars per barrel by 1981. During this incident, unlike 1973-1974, there was no attempt to declare an embargo. OPEC members merely raised prices and continued to ship oil.

The high prices in the aftermath of the Iranian revolution did not persist, as a worldwide surplus of oil drove prices lower during the 1980's. A third crisis, the Persian Gulf War of 1990-1991, elevated prices so temporarily that some analysts referred to the period as "an oil spike," referring to the sharp upward, then downward, movement in oil prices. The upward movement was precipitated by Iraq's invasion of Kuwait in August, 1990. World oil prices reached their highest level in more than eight years, briefly peaking near the forty-dollar-per-barrel mark. Saudi Arabia and other producers began to replace Kuwait's lost output, and prices fell, with a dramatic drop after

Major Oil Crises and Oil Embargoes

Year	Event
1960	Oil-producing nations holding more than 90 percent of known oil reserves form the Organization of Petroleum Exporting Countries (OPEC) to seek higher and more stable crude oil prices.
1970	U.S. oil production peaks. After being the dominant oil producer in the first half of the twentieth century, the United States finds its production declining and begins to import an increasing fraction of its oil.
1970	Libya receives higher prices for its crude oil from Occidental Petroleum.
1973	World oil prices soar after Arab members of OPEC declare a cutback in production and an embargo on shipments bound for the United States and other allies of Israel.
1979	Oil prices double after the fall of the shah of Iran's government removes Iranian capacity from production.
1990	Oil prices briefly reach previous record highs after Iraqi forces invade Kuwait and take over Kuwaiti oil fields.
1991	Operation Desert Storm forces—led by the United States— defeat Iraqi forces, which set numerous oil well fires before retreating.
2003	U.S. occupation of Iraq disrupts Middle East oil markets and raises new concerns about the stability of world oil supplies.

Operation Desert Storm defeated Iraqi forces in Kuwait in January, 1991. Even the burning of Kuwaiti oil wells by Iraqi forces was unable to keep world prices at their previous high levels.

OIL CRISIS EFFECTS

The early stages of all three crises were characterized by panic buying, with producers and consumers scrambling to assure supplies. Later research showed that the crises affected price more than physical availability. Even during the most severe of the three episodes (1973-1974), the ordered cutbacks amounted to less than 10 percent of world oil supply. Further, after the embargo ended there was evidence that important quantities of supposedly embargoed oil had reached the United States and other Western nations.

During each of the three crises, Western economies entered recessions. Higher oil prices acted as a tax that transferred massive amounts of wealth from consuming nations to producing nations. Later declines in world oil prices had the opposite effect, stimulating the economies of the consuming nations.

The 1973-1974 embargo led to marked changes in energy policy in the United States. During the embargo, President Richard Nixon announced Project Independence, a program designed to enable the United States to achieve self-sufficiency in energy through crash programs along the lines of the Apollo moon missions and the Manhattan Project to develop the first nuclear weapons. Project Independence called for major development of nuclear and coal energy resources, placing a low priority on conservation and environmental concerns. Similar policies continued during the administration of President Gerald R. Ford but lost urgency as the embargo's effects were overcome. The Iranian disruption of 1979-1980 occurred during the term of President Jimmy Carter, adding force to Carter's characterization of energy problems as "the moral equivalent of war." Carter called for conservation and new technology to engineer a transition that he characterized as having the same importance as the transition from wood to coal during the Industrial Revolution. By the time of Operation Desert Storm in 1991, policy concern had shifted to the ability of Western nations to use military force to keep oil flowing. Iraq's initially successful invasion of Kuwait and the implied threat to Saudi Arabia quickly generated support for a military solution by a coalition of nations led by the United States.

The 1973 oil embargo imposed by the Organization of Petroleum Exporting Countries (OPEC) led to fuel shortages in the United States. (Library of Congress)

KNOWLEDGE GAINED FROM OIL CRISES

Although the oil crises have been extensively studied, their message for the future and the policy lessons to be learned from them are uncertain. One viewpoint holds that oil crises constitute an early warning of resource depletion. The 1973-1974 price increases were initially seen as a signal confirming predictions that the prices of nonrenewable resources would increase as depletion approached. This "depletionist" viewpoint calls for government-enforced conservation of existing resources and development of new technologies to postpone or avoid the consequences of oil depletion.

A second interpretation of the oil crises is that instead of reflecting a fundamental problem of depletion, they reflect a problem with distribution; that is, oil resources occur in patterns that are different from their patterns of use. Since large amounts of oil resources are held in the politically unstable Middle East but used in the West, cutoffs and price increases are always possible. The policy problem is viewed as a politically inspired cutoff of oil shipments. There is no threat, in this view, of a calculated economic cutoff of oil because producers would find it more profitable to sell oil at a high price than to cut it off altogether. An embargo would make sense only to demonstrate control of a resource and the will to sustain price increases.

A third interpretation characterizes the oil crises as simple products of monopoly power or conspiracy. During the 1970's oil crises—with their long lines for gasoline—and the rapid 1990 price increases that followed Iraq's invasion of Kuwait, such explanations were common. Early versions of this viewpoint denied resource scarcity as a problem and called for the breakup of oil companies to end the conspiracy. Later, as Middle Eastern oil-producing countries assumed control over operations from Western oil companies, the focus shifted to policy actions to combat the OPEC monopoly.

OPEC POWER

The degree of perceived power held by the OPEC oil cartel has fluctuated considerably since its formation in 1960. OPEC nations held 90 percent of the world's then-known oil reserves. Although this guaranteed the OPEC nations a key role in the future as reserves outside OPEC were depleted, the organization was weak during its first ten years. A hint of OPEC's possible power came in 1970 when a bulldozer accident broke a pipeline carrying oil from the Persian Gulf to the Mediterranean Sea. In the aftermath of the accident, which caused tight oil supplies, Libya insisted on and received higher prices for its crude oil.

During the 1973-1974 embargo OPEC's power was little questioned. The sharp upward movement of oil prices seemed to prove that OPEC had the ability to withhold enough oil to keep prices permanently higher. Further confirmation came with the 1979-1980 incident, when oil prices again doubled. Recessions following the oil crises made the West appear dependent on OPEC's indulgence for its future prosperity.

The collapse of oil prices after the three crises led to a different interpretation. In this view, oil prices were kept artificially low before 1970 by the rapid pumping of oil from Middle Eastern reserves by Western-based companies. The companies were seeking profit with little regard for the long-term future of the resource, since they realized that power would soon shift away from them. After 1970, as the host nations began to realize their power, oil prices recovered from their artificially low levels. The extraordinary oil price increases of 1973-1974, in this view, were from artificially low levels to normal levels. At the time they occurred, they had been seen as increases from normal levels to artificially high levels. Some analysts came to believe that OPEC was simply announcing, rather than causing, higher oil prices.

Energy analysts have observed that oil crises and embargoes have had a common pattern. First, demand growth catches up with world capacity, leading to generally tight market conditions. Next, a precipitating event occurs in the Middle East, leading to quick price increases and disruptions of ordinary supply channels. If there is no permanent loss of supply, however, the disruption soon ends. At the time of the crisis, policy priority goes to energy security over environmental concerns. With the passage of time, however, energy security loses some of its prominence as a policy goal.

William C. Wood

FURTHER READING

Danielsen, Albert L. *The Evolution of OPEC*. New York: Harcourt Brace Jovanovich, 1982.

Griffin, James M., and Henry B. Steele. *Energy Economics and Policy*. 2d ed. New York: Academic Press, 1986.

Hinrichs, Roger A., and Merlin Kleinbach. *Energy: Its Use and the Environment*. 4th ed. Belmont, Calif.: Thomson Brooks/Cole, 2006.

Parra, Francisco. *Oil Politics: A Modern History of Petroleum*. New York: I. B. Tauris, 2004.

Stobaugh, Robert, and Daniel Yergin, eds. *Energy Future: Report of the Energy Project at the Harvard Business School*. 3d ed. New York: Vintage Books, 1983.

Venn, Fiona. *The Oil Crisis*. New York: Longman, 2002.

Oil drilling

CATEGORIES: Energy and energy use; resources and resource management

DEFINITION: Activities involved in boring through earth and rock to tap petroleum reservoirs

SIGNIFICANCE: Careful management of oil drilling projects is crucial because the processes involved in such projects—including site preparation, equipment setup, drilling, fluid circulation, and waste disposal—all have the potential to degrade the environment.

The process of drilling a hole through the rock layers that overlie a petroleum reservoir is fairly simple, at least in principle. A diamond-tipped drill bit is attached at the base of a length of vertical pipe, and the pipe is rotated. The bit grinds away the rock, producing a hole the width of the drill bit and the length of the attached pipe, or drill string. As the top of the rotating drill string approaches ground level, a new piece of pipe is added, lengthening the drill string and allowing the depth of the hole to increase. The weight of the drill string is supported by a drilling rig, which helps keep the hole straight.

Meanwhile, a fluid known as drilling mud is pumped down the hole to keep the bit cool, help keep the hole from collapsing, carry rock chips (cuttings) up the hole, and prevent overpressurized, subsurface liquid or gas from causing a blowout. Blowouts occur when subsurface zones of high pressure force the fluid in the well to flow out of the hole at a high rate of speed, in some cases blowing the drill string completely out of the hole and destroying the drill rig. Drilling mud is pumped downhole through the interior of the drill string, out through holes in the bit at the bottom of the drill string, then back to the surface between the drill string exterior and the drill hole, a space known as the well annulus. At the surface, the cuttings are collected, and the mud is recirculated downhole. Drilling mud is carefully monitored for the correct viscosity and weight. Chemicals are added, as needed, to modify these characteristics.

At intervals during drilling, the drill string is removed, and a steel liner, or casing, is cemented into place downhole. This supports the sides of the hole and isolates the annulus from the surrounding downhole environment.

If insufficient amounts of oil are found to make the well economically viable, the well is termed a "dry hole." It must be carefully cased from top to bottom and filled with cement so that the hole is sealed permanently, a procedure known as plugging and abandoning the well. If oil is found in sufficient amounts, it is pumped from the well, a process known as primary production. After an oil well's output begins to decline significantly, alternative methods of production may be applied. The term "enhanced oil recovery" refers to these more complicated—and expensive—methods for increasing an oil well's production. The most common method, saltwater injection, involves pumping saltwater brine, produced from the subsurface with the oil, back into adjacent wells, forcing more oil to the surface. Chemicals such as surfactants may also be employed to help mobilize the oil.

ENVIRONMENTAL CONCERNS

The environmental concerns related to oil drilling on land are somewhat different from those related to drilling at sea. In either case, however, the effects of poor operations management can be devastating to the environment, particularly in ecologically sensitive areas. Methods of site access and preparation can have significant impacts on the ecology of land sites, especially in forest preserves, wetlands, and tundra. Soils, as well as surface-water and groundwater supplies, are at risk from oil spills and improper disposal of saltwater, drill cuttings, and drilling mud. Groundwater is also at risk from improper casing, saltwater injection, and well plugging and abandonment. Groundwater pollution may go undetected for years and can affect relatively large areas of the subsurface.

At sea, much larger areas may be at risk because of down-current transport of pollutants. Environments particularly threatened by marine drilling platforms include coral reefs, oyster banks, mangrove swamps, and tidal estuaries. Disposal of drilling mud and drill cuttings threatens the benthic (seafloor) environment surrounding the platform and the pelagic (open sea) environment down current. Improper operations can release oil and brine into the water column, and faulty casing can create oil and brine seeps on the seafloor.

In the United States, numerous federal laws regulate oil drilling, production, and transport on land and at sea. These include the Federal Water Pollution Control Act of 1972; the Outer Continental Shelf Lands Act of 1953; the Comprehensive Environmental Response, Compensation, and Liability Act (CERCLA) of 1980 (also known as Superfund); the Marine Protection, Research, and Sanctuaries Act of 1972; and the Safe Drinking Water Act of 1974. Most U.S. states have stringent permit requirements, site inspection programs, and accidental spill reporting and response programs for drilling operations. Industry compliance with these programs is generally excellent.

Oil spills from offshore platforms represent only

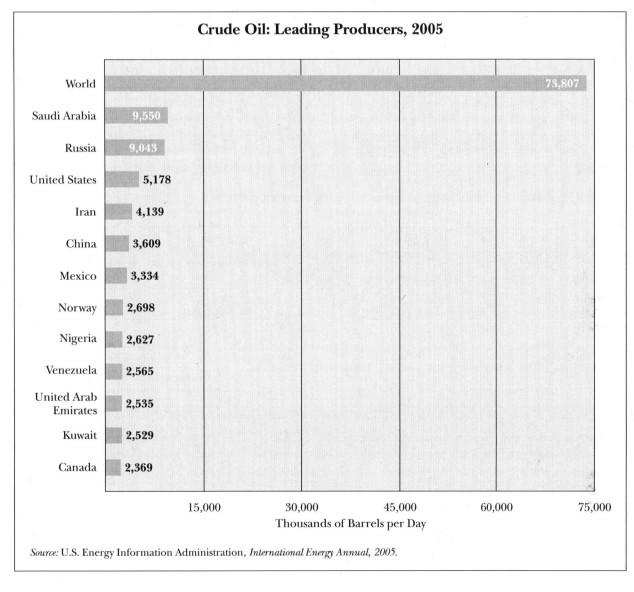

Crude Oil: Leading Producers, 2005

	Thousands of Barrels per Day
World	73,807
Saudi Arabia	9,550
Russia	9,043
United States	5,178
Iran	4,139
China	3,609
Mexico	3,334
Norway	2,698
Nigeria	2,627
Venezuela	2,565
United Arab Emirates	2,535
Kuwait	2,529
Canada	2,369

Source: U.S. Energy Information Administration, *International Energy Annual, 2005.*

about 1 percent of the petroleum released into the oceans each year. Natural oil seeps contribute about eight times this amount, and their contribution has increased steadily as onshore and offshore oil production has reduced the pressure in hydrocarbon reservoirs. Marine drilling platforms, while perhaps eyesores above water, provide habitats for marine species that otherwise would not be present—these structures might be likened to artificial reefs. Scuba divers and fishing boat captains alike seek out platform substructures for the lush growth of invertebrates encrusting them and the many fish that this growth attracts. When offshore drilling platforms are decommissioned, debates often ensue among environmen-

talists as to whether the structures should be completely dismantled or allowed to remain intact so that the marine community may benefit.

Clayton D. Harris

FURTHER READING

Boomer, Paul M. *A Primer of Oilwell Drilling.* 7th ed. Austin: Petroleum Extension Service, University of Texas, 2008.
Camp, William G., and Thomas B. Daugherty. "Fossil Fuel Management." In *Managing Our Natural Resources.* 4th ed. Albany, N.Y.: Delmar, 2004.
Mtsiva, V. C., ed. *Oil and Natural Gas: Issues and Policies.* Hauppauge, N.Y.: Nova Science, 2003.

Oil shale and tar sands

CATEGORIES: Energy and energy use; resources and resource management

DEFINITIONS: Oil shale is finely grained sedimentary rock that incorporates a solid hydrocarbon substance in its structure; tar sands are sands that are permeated with a tarlike petroleum that is too thick to flow

SIGNIFICANCE: The conversion of the hydrocarbons in oil shale and tar sands into oil could provide an energy source several times the amount of the earth's current known oil reserves, but the conversion process has a number of environmental costs.

Oil is not found in vast oil-filled underground caverns; rather, it is found in the spaces between mineral grains that make up rock. Permeable rock has more space between grains than does impermeable rock. If the oil is thin enough, it will slowly flow through permeable rock and into the borehole of a well, from which it can be brought to the surface.

The hydrocarbons in oil shale cannot flow because they are in a solid form called kerogen. When some types of kerogen are heated by natural processes (60 to 150 degrees Celsius, or 140 to 300 degrees Fahrenheit) they slowly release crude oil and natural gas. In place of nature's slow process, oil shale may be mined and then burned as a low-grade fuel, or it can be crushed and then heated in a retort to produce crude oil and natural gas. Aboveground retorting is usually done between 300 and 520 degrees Celsius (570 and 970 degrees Fahrenheit). It is also possible to process shale underground (in situ, or in place) by fracturing the rock underground and then using the heat of an underground fire to produce crude oil, which can be pumped to the surface. In place of the fire, steam or other hot fluid can be circulated underground. After retorting, the oil is usually upgraded through a process in which it is passed over a catalyst and treated with hydrogen gas to increase the hydrogen content and remove impurities such as sulfur, nitrogen, iron, and arsenic.

Shale oil is very expensive to produce, although expected increases in production and improvements in the process are projected to bring its cost down significantly over time. The process also has environmental costs. Processing oil shale releases the greenhouse gas carbon dioxide, which has been linked to global warming. Near-surface deposits of oil shale are open-pit mined or strip-mined, both processes that damage surrounding ecosystems; underground mining uses the less efficient room-and-pillar method. In any kind of mining of oil shale, one to five barrels of water are used for each barrel of shale oil produced; in addition, the process produces mountains of crushed rocks that must be disposed of.

The world's use of shale oil peaked in 1980, several years after the 1973 oil crisis. In 2008 Estonia was the top producer at 5,500 barrels per day, followed by Brazil at 3,100 barrels per day. It has been estimated that worldwide deposits of oil shale could produce 2.8 to 3.3 trillion barrels of shale oil. The United States has the largest share, with enough oil shale to produce 1.5 to 2.6 trillion barrels in the Green River Formation (a geologic formation located in parts of Utah, Wyoming, and Colorado). In comparison, the world's conventional oil reserves are estimated at 1.317 trillion barrels.

Different grades of oil shale yield different amounts of oil. About 16 percent of the Green River Formation yields 95 to 380 liters (25 to 100 gallons) of oil per ton of shale, about 33 percent yields 38 to 95 liters (10 to 25 U.S. gallons), and the final 51 percent yields 19 to 38 liters (5 to 10 U.S. gallons) per ton of shale. Unable to compete with cheap conventional oil, oil shale mining ceased in the United States in 1982, but in 2003 an oil shale development program was restarted.

TAR SANDS

Tar sands (also called oil sands) are mixtures of sand, clay, and bitumen, a tarlike form of petroleum. The largest deposits of tar sands are in Canada and Venezuela, each country having the equivalent of the world's reserves of crude oil. Canada's production of oil from tar sands reached 1.25 million barrels per day in 2009 (at a cost of about $27 per barrel) and provided 47 percent of the nation's oil production. This allowed Canada to become the biggest supplier of petroleum products to the United States. In Canada about two tons of tar sand are processed to produce one barrel of oil. Producing oil in this way has the same environmental problems as producing oil from oil shale: Strip mining degrades ecosystems, and the process releases more carbon dioxide into the atmosphere than does the production of conventional oil, uses large amounts of water, and leaves tons of spent sand that must be disposed of.

Bitumen may be extracted in situ through the injection of steam, hot air, or solvents to allow the bitumen to flow. Alternatively, a deposit may be strip-mined and the materials then hauled to a processing facility, where the bitumen is separated from water, sand, and other waste. Like shale oil, the heavy crude extracted from bitumen must be upgraded through a process in which it is passed over a catalyst and treated with hydrogen gas to increase the hydrogen content and remove impurities such as sulfur, nitrogen, and arsenic. It can then be used as feedstock for conventional refining.

The only significant tar sands in the United States are in eastern Utah. The Utah tar sand deposit is far smaller than Canada's, and the Utah sands are hydrocarbon-wetted rather than water-wetted as the Canadian sands are, so their use would require different processing techniques.

Charles W. Rogers

FURTHER READING

Bartis, James T., et al. *Oil Shale Development in the United States: Prospects and Policy Issues.* Santa Monica, Calif.: RAND Corporation, 2005.

Marsden, William. *Stupid to the Last Drop: How Alberta Is Bringing Environmental Armageddon to Canada (and Doesn't Seem to Care).* Toronto: Vintage Canada, 2008.

Speight, James G. *Enhanced Recovery Methods for Heavy Oil and Tar Sands.* Houston: Gulf, 2009.

Old-growth forests

CATEGORIES: Forests and plants; resources and resource management

DEFINITION: Forests containing many trees that have never been harvested by loggers

SIGNIFICANCE: Persons involved in the timber industry generally view the large trees found in old-growth forests as a renewable source of fine lumber, but environmentalists argue for protection of these trees, asserting that they are part of ancient and unique ecosystems that can never be replaced.

In the 1970's scientists began studying the uncut forests of the Pacific Northwest and the plants and animals that inhabit them. One of the first results of this research was the U.S. Forest Service publication *Ecological Characteristics of Old-Growth Douglas-Fir Forests*

(1981). In this report, biologist Jerry Franklin and his colleagues revealed that these forests are not just tangles of dead and dying trees; rather, they constitute unique, thriving ecosystems made up of living and dead trees, mammals, insects, and even fungi.

The lands usually referred to as old-growth forests are located primarily on the western slope of the Cascade Mountains in southeast Alaska, southern British Columbia in Canada, Washington, Oregon, and Northern California. The weather in these regions is wet and mild, ideal for the growth of trees such as Douglas fir, cedar, spruce, and hemlock. Some studies have shown that there is more biomass, including living matter and dead trees, per hectare in these forests than anywhere else on earth. The trees in old-growth forests may be as tall as 90 meters (300 feet) with diameters of 3 meters (10 feet) or more and can live as long as one thousand years. The forest community grows and changes over time in such a forest, not reaching biological climax until the forest consists primarily of hemlock trees, which are able to sprout in the shade of the sun-loving Douglas fir.

One of the most important components of the old-growth forest is the large number of standing dead trees, or snags, and fallen trees, or logs, on the forest floor and in the streams. The fallen trees rot very slowly, often taking more than two hundred years to disappear completely. During this time they are important for water storage, as wildlife habitat, and as "nurse logs" where new growth can begin. In fact, seedlings of some trees, such as western hemlock and Sitka spruce, have difficulty competing with the mosses on the forest floor and need to sprout on fallen logs.

Another strand in the complex web of the forest consists of micorrhizal fungi, which attach themselves to the roots of the trees and enhance the roots' uptake of water and nutrients. The fruiting bodies of these fungi are eaten by small mammals such as voles, mice, and chipmunks, which then spread the spores of the fungi in their droppings. Numerous species of plants and wildlife appear to be dependent on this ecosystem to survive. The most famous example is the northern spotted owl, whose endangered species status and dependence on the old-growth ecosystem has caused great political and economic turmoil in the Pacific Northwest.

By the 1970's most of the trees on the timber industry's private lands had been cut. Their replanted forests, known as second growth, would not be ready for harvest for several decades, so the industry became increasingly dependent on public lands for raw materials. Logging of old-growth trees in the national forests of western Oregon and Washington increased from 900 million board feet in 1946 to more than 5 billion board feet in 1986.

Environmentalists claimed that only 10 percent of the region's original forest remained, and they were determined to save what was left. The first step in their campaign was to encourage the use of the evocative term "ancient forest" to counteract the somewhat negative connotations of "old-growth." They then found an effective tool in the northern spotted owl. This small bird was determined to be dependent on the old-growth ecosystem, and its listing under the federal Endangered Species Act in 1990 was a bombshell that caused a decade of scientific, political, and legal conflict.

Under the law, the Forest Service was required to protect enough of the owl's habitat to ensure its survival. An early government report identified 3.1 million hectares (7.7 million acres) of forest to be protected for the bird. Later, the U.S. Fish and Wildlife Service recommended 4.5 million hectares (11 million acres). In 1991 U.S. District Court judge William Dwyer placed an injunction on all logging in spotted owl habitat until a comprehensive plan could be put in place. The timber industry responded with a prediction of tens of thousands of lost jobs and regional economic disaster. In 1993 President Bill Clinton convened the Forest Summit conference in Portland, Oregon, to work out a solution. The Clinton administration's plan, though approved by Judge Dwyer, satisfied neither the industry nor the environmentalists, and protests, lawsuits, and legislative battles continued.

As the twentieth century came to an end, timber harvest levels had been significantly reduced, the Northwest's economy had survived, and environmentalists were promoting additional reasons to value old-

A Roosevelt elk grazes in the old-growth forest of Olympic National Park in the state of Washington. (©Natalia Bratslavsky/Dreamstime.com)

growth forests: as habitat for endangered salmon and other fish, as sources for medicinal plants, and simply as repositories of benefits yet to be discovered. The decades-long controversy over the forests of the Northwest had a deep impact on environmental science as well as on U.S. government policy regarding the preservation of natural resources; it also encouraged new interest in other native forests around the world, from Brazil to Malaysia to Russia.

Joseph W. Hinton

FURTHER READING

Dietrich, William. *The Final Forest: The Battle for the Last Great Trees of the Pacific Northwest.* New York: Simon & Schuster, 1992.

Durbin, Kathie. *Tree Huggers: Victory, Defeat, and Renewal in the Northwest Ancient Forest Campaign.* Seattle: Mountaineers Books, 1996.

Keiter, Robert B. "Ecology Triumphant? Spotted Owls and Ecosystem Management." In *Keeping Faith with Nature: Ecosystems, Democracy, and America's Public Lands.* New Haven, Conn.: Yale University Press, 2003.

Kelly, David, and Gary Braasch. *Secrets of the Old Growth Forest.* Salt Lake City: Gibbs-Smith, 1988.

Maser, Chris. *Forest Primeval: The Natural History of an Ancient Forest.* 1989. Reprint. Corvallis: Oregon State University Press, 2001.

Wirth, Christian, Gerd Gleixner, and Martin Heimann, eds. *Old-Growth Forests: Function, Fate, and Value.* New York: Springer, 2009.

Overconsumption

CATEGORY: Resources and resource management

DEFINITION: Excessive and unsustainable utilization of resources, goods, and services

SIGNIFICANCE: Human life is impossible to sustain without consumption, but overconsumption often causes multiple external effects (such as air, water, and soil pollution) that have negative impacts on the health of ecosystems and organisms, including those of humans. Depending on the circumstances (culture, geography, social milieu, income, education, and so on), individuals and groups overconsume different kinds of things.

It is useful to distinguish among the reasons for and the agents, objects, and effects of overconsumption. Among the things that are overconsumed in certain parts of the world are natural resources (such as water and timber), energy (such as electricity), and commodities (such as electronic devices and automobiles); services and information may also be overconsumed. Overconsumption of different types can have various environmental effects. The overfishing and overhunting of animals can lead to the extinction of species and thus to the reduction of biodiversity; an example is the extinction of the Caribbean monk seal in the twentieth century as a result of overhunting. The intensive and extensive global usage of gasoline as fuel for combustion engines results in high levels of carbon dioxide emissions, which have been shown to contribute to global warming. Another example of the unsustainable—and intergenerationally unjust—utilization of nonrenewable resources is the consumption of scarce chemical elements such as lithium, tantalum, indium, and hafnium, which are used for semiconductors and liquid crystal displays (LCDs) in televisions, computers, and mobile phones.

REASONS FOR OVERCONSUMPTION

Whereas in the developed world overconsumption often takes the form of the excessive purchasing of consumer goods in affluent social milieus (for example, multiple televisions or vehicles per household), in developing nations overconsumption is more often related to excessive or unsustainable exploitation of raw materials coupled with overpopulation and poverty (such as unsustainable clear-cutting of trees for charcoal or timber export). Such problems raise questions concerning justice or equity within one generation (intragenerational justice) and between generations (intergenerational justice).

Overconsumption is not a modern phenomenon—since Paleolithic times humans have existed who destroyed their environment through excessive utilization of resources and then moved to unspoiled areas. The rate of consumption was intensified and accelerated to a globally unsustainable level by a combination of factors, including the dawn of modern science and technology, the growth of industrialization, the advancement of worldviews and ethics that endorse despiritualization, and the advent of a paradigm of productivity, economic growth, and capitalism. Since the early twentieth century the fields of marketing and advertising have not only intensified but also accelerated the rate of consumption even further by utilizing psychoanalytical, sociological, and cultural strategies. Such strategies play on people's unfulfilled personal desires and attach symbolic values (meta-goods) to commodities to lure potential customers to consume beyond their actual needs.

ATTEMPTS TO REDUCE OVERCONSUMPTION

In addition to causing environmental problems, overconsumption can have significant psychological effects, such as oniomania (compulsive buying disorder), and social effects, such as social isolation related to excessive use of electronic media. Environmentalists, educators, and psychotherapists have expressed concerns about marketing strategists' ulterior motives and the agendas of advertisement campaigns. Advertisements can trigger and foster overconsumption by intensifying—or even creating—desires.

Approaches to reducing overconsumption include education about the environmental impacts of consumption habits (for example, through the calculation of ecological footprints, or how much demand exceeds the regenerative capacity of a resource or the biosphere's supply). Other educational strategies focus on analyzing the psychology at work in advertising campaigns and on making consumers aware of social factors that stimulate overconsumption, such as peer pressure, symbolic consumption, and conspicuous consumption. Ecological economists—who locate the economic sector within the world and its ecology—design and suggest political strategies and legal mechanisms that attempt to form development in the sectors of economy, society, and ecology in a sustainable fashion. Campaigns against overconsumption can also take more radical forms that include acts of ecotage (or monkeywrenching) or ecoterrorism.

Roman Meinhold

FURTHER READING

Baudrillard, Jean. *The Consumer Society. Myths and Structures*. 1998. Reprint. Thousand Oaks, Calif.: Sage, 2004.

Meinhold, Roman. "Meta-Goods in Fashion-Myths: Philosophic-Anthropological Implications of Fashion." *Prajna Vihara. Journal of Philosophy and Religion* 8, no. 2 (2007): 1-15.

Penn, Dustin J. "The Evolutionary Roots of Our Environmental Problems: Toward a Darwinian Ecology." *Quarterly Review of Biology* 78, no. 3 (2003): 275-301.

Princen, Thomas. "Consumption and Its Externalities: Where Economy Meets Ecology." *Global Environmental Politics* 1, no. 3 (2001): 11-30.

Schmidtz, David, and Elizabeth Willcott. "Varieties of Overconsumption." *Ethics, Place, and Environment: A Journal of Philosophy and Geography* 9, no. 3 (2006): 351-365.

White, Lynn Townsend, Jr. "The Historical Roots of Our Ecologic Crisis." *Science* 155, no. 3767 (1967): 1203-1207.

Photovoltaic cells

CATEGORY: Energy and energy use

DEFINITION: Devices made of materials that create electrical energy directly from absorbed light

SIGNIFICANCE: Multiple photovoltaic cells can be grouped together in an array to form a panel capable of making electricity from sunlight. Most other forms of solar power generation require solar heating of materials, which are then used to do work. Because photovoltaics do not have moving parts, they require very little maintenance, have long service lives, and do not cost anything to operate once installed.

Light can be described as particles of energy called photons. Different wavelengths of light have different amounts of energy. When light of sufficient energy is absorbed by an object, it can excite an electron to sufficient energy to be lost by the atom. This effect, called the photoelectric effect, was described by Albert Einstein. Photovoltaic cells are generally fabricated from semiconductors. Silicon-based photovoltaic cells are most common, but other materials are also used. Electrons at sufficiently high energies in semiconductors can move within the material, creating electricity. The energy of light needed to accomplish this is called the band gap energy. Different materials have different band gaps, and the most efficient photovoltaic cells are constructed of different materials to take best advantage of the various wavelengths of light shining on them.

Not all of the light striking a photovoltaic cell is converted into electrical energy. To compute the overall power efficiency of a photovoltaic cell, one divides the power output by the power of the incoming light. The first photovoltaic cells used commercially

A bank of solar panels made up of photovoltaic cells, which collect solar energy and convert it to electricity. (©Milacroft/Dreamstime.com)

in solar panels had efficiencies of about 6 percent, meaning that only 6 percent of the energy of the sunlight striking the cells was converted into electric energy. Some high-efficiency commercially produced solar panels have efficiencies in excess of 20 percent. Research efforts focusing on the creation of very high-efficiency photovoltaics have yielded photovoltaic cell efficiencies in excess of 40 percent under laboratory conditions. Efficiencies are typically lower, however, in less-than-ideal field applications.

Photovoltaic cells can be fairly efficient at converting solar energy into electricity, compared with other methods, and they cost little to operate. The fabrication costs of photovoltaic systems are quite high, however, which reduces their cost-effectiveness. Most large photovoltaic systems cost so much that many years of use are required to recover the cost of installation. Some of the most recently developed photovoltaic cells use thin films, which use fewer raw materials, are more flexible, and are less expensive to build and install than earlier kinds of photovoltaics. Reduction

in the amount of materials needed for photovoltaic systems is also beneficial to the environment, because many of the chemicals used in manufacturing photovoltaics are extremely toxic.

The larger a solar panel is, the more sunlight shines on it, increasing the electrical power produced; large solar panels are more expensive than smaller ones, however. One method used to make photovoltaic systems more cost-effective involves lenses or mirrors that focus light onto the photovoltaic cells. These concentrator photovoltaic (CPV) systems increase the intensity of light falling on the solar panels, allowing smaller solar panels to produce as much electrical power as larger panels, thus cutting the cost of photovoltaic solar power generation. Plans for many modern large photovoltaic solar systems include the use of CPV systems. It has been hypothesized that modern CPV systems may be able to produce electricity at prices competitive with other forms of electric generation.

Raymond D. Benge, Jr.

FURTHER READING

Muñoz, E., et al. "CPV Standardization: An Overview." *Renewable and Sustainable Energy Reviews* 14, no. 1 (2010): 518-523.

Patel, Mukund R. *Wind and Solar Power Systems: Design, Analysis, and Operation.* Boca Raton, Fla.: Taylor & Francis, 2006.

Perlin, John. *From Space to Earth: The Story of Solar Electricity.* Ann Arbor, Mich.: Aatec, 1999.

Wenham, Stuart R. *Applied Photovoltaics.* Sterling, Va.: Earthscan, 2007.

Zweibel, Ken, James Mason, and Vasilis Fthenakis. "Solar Grand Plan." *Scientific American,* January, 2008, 64-73.

Planned obsolescence

CATEGORIES: Philosophy and ethics; resources and resource management

DEFINITION: Engineering of a product such that its style or function guarantees the product's replacement after a given period of time

SIGNIFICANCE: Manufacturers' policies of planned obsolescence promote the sales of new products by ensuring that consumers will be prompted to replace the products they own at an optimal rate of consumption. Environmentalists have noted that planned obsolescence harms the environment in several ways, including by increasing waste and contributing to the consumption of resources.

Planned obsolescence was identified as a promising approach for the makers of consumer products as early as the 1920's, when mass production, well under way in the developed world, attracted exacting empirical research that exposed to analysis not only every minute aspect of production processes but also consumer spending practices. In 1932 Bernard London's famed pamphlet *Ending the Depression Through Planned Obsolescence* made a virtue of planned obsolescence by blaming the Great Depression on consumers who used their old cars, radios, and clothing much longer than statisticians had expected they would.

The term "planned obsolescence" entered the popular vocabulary in 1954, when Brooks Stevens, an American industrial designer, used it in the title of an address he gave at an advertising conference in Minneapolis. Stevens defined planned obsolescence as in-

stilling in the buyer the desire to own something a little newer, a little better, a little sooner than is necessary. By 1959, the phrase was in such broad everyday usage that Volkswagen was able to capitalize on it by turning the virtue into a vice, launching what would become a legendary advertising campaign that distinguished Volkswagen as the automobile manufacturer that did not believe in planned obsolescence.

FORMS OF PLANNED OBSOLESCENCE

Planned obsolescence was further sealed in the public consciousness as a vice rather than a virtue in 1960, when the cultural critic Vance Packard published his book *The Waste Makers.* This study of modern society exposed planned obsolescence as the systematic strategy of unscrupulous business leaders who were taking advantage of a mindless public of greedy and wasteful consumers, who in turn were fast becoming debt-ridden in a frantic race to feed their advertising-inflamed desires with products they did not need. Packard distinguished between two forms of planned obsolescence: obsolescence of desirability, or psychological obsolescence, which involves the continual evolution of the aesthetic design of products to manipulate consumers into believing the products are out-of-date, even when they remain functional; and obsolescence of function, which involves the purposeful engineering of products with technical or functional limitations that limit the products' life spans so that customers will need to buy replacements.

A further form of planned obsolescence is systemic obsolescence, which is the practice of altering the systems in which certain products are used so that the products' continued use becomes difficult or impossible within those system settings. Software companies often employ this practice in their design strategies, introducing new software that is incompatible with the previous generation of software and thereby rendering the older software effectively obsolete. The lack of compatibility between generations of software products forces consumers to purchase new software prematurely. Developers of computer hardware products sometimes employ similar strategies, designing new products that are incompatible with older parts and connector plugs. Another way in which manufacturers effect systemic obsolescence is to cease production of replacement parts for older products and to stop offering maintenance services for those products.

INFLUENCE ON CONSUMERS

Planned obsolescence is a tempting policy for manufacturers because it trains the public in consuming practices that have high potential to increase sales of consumer products. Under the influence of planned obsolescence policy, consumers move beyond the limited realm of necessity purchasing and into the infinite realm of desire. From vehicles to deodorants, from real estate to technological products, people are conditioned to replace their belongings, not because their possessions no longer serve them well but simply because those belongings have been around for a while.

As fierce competition in globalizing trade markets puts growing pressure on producers to increase profits, planned obsolescence becomes an increasingly powerful temptation in corporate decision making about product engineering. Manufacturing companies constantly seek to minimize production costs, often using the least expensive components they can find, many of which are produced in countries where regulations on manufacturing processes are weak or nonexistent. Such practices further ensure that products will enjoy life spans that barely exceed their warranty periods.

Planned obsolescence has been a powerful force in shaping consumer practices across the globe. Arguments for and against planned obsolescence remain appealing to both producers and consumers. Producers defend planned obsolescence as an essential driving force behind manufacturing innovation and economic growth. They highlight its tendency to promote research and product development, pointing to the many products that have become less expensive, more useful, and better designed as a result of planned obsolescence policies. Although consumers resent the idea that functional everyday products are designed to break easily, they rarely complain about the policy of planned obsolescence as it pertains to the latest fashions and exciting new gadgets.

Although public outcry is muted, there is little doubt that planned obsolescence policies cause significant harms to society and to the environment. In encouraging consumption at the highest levels, planned obsolescence is hardly good for consumers, many of whom go into debt for the sake of owning products they really do not need. Continual replacement of products also results in the depletion of natural resources and increasing rates of environmental pollution, as new products are manufactured to keep up with consumer demand. What to do with old products that are replaced poses a growing challenge as well, as the management of trash has become an immense problem, especially in the cities of industrialized nations. Landfill space has become increasingly hard to find, and some consumer wastes, such as cast-off electronic devices, pose special pollution problems because they contain toxic components.

Environmentalists argue that consumers should seek to reduce their consumption of new products, reuse those already existing products they can, and recycle whatever materials they can from products that are no longer useful in their original forms. In these ways, people can counter the results of manufacturer policies of planned obsolescence.

Wendy C. Hamblet

FURTHER READING

Dobrow, Larry. *When Advertising Tried Harder: The Sixties—The Golden Age of American Advertising.* New York: Friendly Press, 1984.

Frank, Thomas. *The Conquest of Cool: Business Culture, Counterculture, and the Rise of Hip Consumerism.* Chicago: University of Chicago Press, 1997.

Orbach, Barak Y. "The Durapolist Puzzle: Monopoly Power in Durable-Goods Markets." *Yale Journal on Regulation* 21 (2004): 67-118.

Packard, Vance. *The Waste Makers.* 1960. Reprint. New York: Simon & Schuster, 1978.

Power plants

CATEGORY: Energy and energy use

DEFINITION: Facilities that generate electrical power through any of a variety of methods

SIGNIFICANCE: Many of the practices used in the generation of electrical power are environmentally destructive. In particular, power plants that rely on fossil fuels contribute to greenhouse gas emissions, acid precipitation, urban smog, and toxic mercury emissions. Power plants in general often also affect water quality, disrupt land use, and generate a variety of hazardous and toxic wastes.

Electric power is produced from a number of sources. Of the 4,119 million megawatt-hours of electricity generated in the United States in 2008, coal contributed 48.2 percent; natural gas, 21.4 percent;

nuclear, 19.6 percent; hydroelectric, 6.0 percent; other renewable resources such as solar, geothermal, wind, and biomass, 3.1 percent; petroleum, 1.1 percent; and other sources, 0.6 percent. In other countries, the relative utilization of fuels varies depending on what local resources are available. France has little coal and oil, so for most of its electricity (more than 75 percent) it depends on nuclear power. China's increasing industrialization is largely fueled by its vast coal resources, from which it generates roughly 80 percent of its electricity.

Large-scale electric power facilities and related infrastructure tend to present certain environmental challenges regardless of the fuels they consume. Massive centralized power generation facilities require substantial amounts of land, and environmentally irresponsible operations can leave the sites badly polluted and the neighboring land significantly devalued. Power transmission lines have a negative aesthetic impact, particularly in natural areas. These large structures can also disrupt wildlife habitats, and where they cross agricultural land they have the potential to impede farming operations. If a power plant diverts water from a river to serve as a coolant and then returns the heated water to the river, the resulting thermal pollution can cause a localized reduction in the river's dissolved oxygen levels and otherwise negatively affect aquatic organisms and ecosystems.

POWER GENERATION USING FOSSIL FUELS

Coal is the most abundant of the world's fossil fuels. Mining, transportation, and combustion of coal

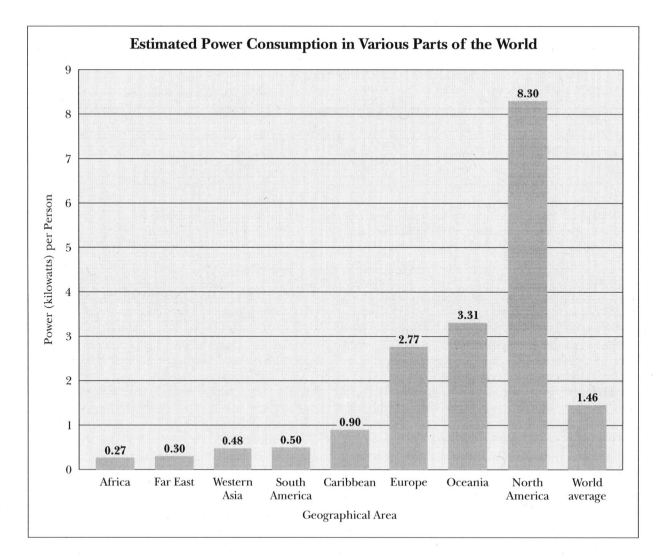

Estimated Power Consumption in Various Parts of the World

create a host of environmental problems. Surface mining of coal defaces the landscape and causes erosion. Deep mining is a hazardous occupation for miners because of long-term lung effects; the coal-mining industry also has a history of deadly underground explosions. Whenever coal is transported or stored, care must be taken to minimize the risk of spontaneous combustion.

Oil drilling, be it on land or offshore, can result in massive accidental releases to the environment, a well-known example being the BP *Deepwater Horizon* oil spill in the Gulf of Mexico that continued for months during the spring and summer of 2010. Oil is commonly transported by pipelines and ocean tankers, both of which have a history of ruptures and spills. Environmental releases of oil can harm aquatic organisms, waterfowl and seabirds, other wildlife, and their ecosystems. Natural gas pipelines are also problematic, as leaks can lead to damaging and deadly explosions such as the one that occurred in San Bruno, California, in 2010.

When coal, oil, or natural gas is burned at an electric power plant, high-pressure steam is produced to turn a turbine that is connected to a generator. Some coal contains as much as a 10 percent sulfur impurity, which is converted to gaseous sulfur dioxide during burning. Oxygen and nitrogen from the air also combine during combustion to form gaseous oxides. When these gases are released into the atmosphere, they combine with water to form sulfuric acid and nitric acid, which eventually return to earth as acid rain. The harmful effects of acid rain include loss of fish in acidified lakes, deterioration of forests, and surface erosion of marble buildings and monuments. Acid rain can be reduced through the use of cleaner fuel, such as natural gas or low-sulfur coal. Also, sulfur dioxide can be removed before it leaves the smokestack by means of chemical "scrubbers," but such technology adds expense. For some older coal plants, it makes more sense from an economic standpoint to phase out the plant than to retrofit it with scrubber technology.

Pollution-control measures can also minimize other harmful air pollutants generated during combustion, including ozone, mercury, and particulate matter. Ozone (the main component of smog) and particulates can have detrimental impacts on the lungs of humans and animals, in addition to reducing visibility. Trace amounts of mercury released from fossil fuels during burning can bioaccumulate in the environment to harm humans and ecosystems.

When fossil fuels are burned, carbon combines with oxygen from the air to form gaseous carbon dioxide. In the last decades of the twentieth century, concerns arose that increased carbon dioxide levels would cause the earth's atmosphere to act like the glass panels of a greenhouse, allowing solar radiation to enter the atmosphere but preventing infrared heat from escaping. Global warming from this greenhouse effect could melt polar ice caps and snow cover, which in turn could raise the levels of the oceans and cause disastrous flooding of coastal communities. Also, a hotter and drier climate could create worldwide problems for agriculture. The only way to reduce the production of carbon dioxide is to burn less coal, oil, and natural gas.

POWER GENERATION USING OTHER SOURCES

Nuclear power plants offer one alternative to fossil-fuel-burning plants. The major benefit of nuclear power is that no chemical burning takes place, so no fly ash, acid rain, or greenhouse gases are produced. A common objection to this power generation technology stems from the possibility that an accident could release radioactivity into the environment. Such a release occurred during the 1986 Chernobyl disaster in Ukraine, which remains the worst nuclear reactor accident in the history of the industry. Opponents of nuclear power also point to the problem of long-term nuclear waste storage, which presents both technical and sociopolitical challenges.

Hydroelectric power plants use water, a renewable, nonpolluting resource, to generate electricity, but they also have environmental disadvantages. When a new hydroelectric dam is built, the stored water often fills a scenic canyon or floods farmland near the river. During extended droughts, as happened in the Pacific Northwest during the 1980's, consumers of hydroelectric power are faced with electric power shortages. The impact of dam construction on downstream water supplies can cause friction among communities, states, or nations. The greatest hazard of a dam is the large quantity of water stored behind it. If a dam experiences catastrophic failure, as China's Banqiao Reservoir did in 1975, the resulting loss of life and property downstream can be staggering.

Geothermal energy from underground can be harnessed anywhere, but major electric power generation projects have generally focused on locations coinciding with geothermal hot spots near the earth's surface.

Tidal power technologies have been limited geographically to places on coastlines where large differences exist between high and low tides; new developments may make power production at other locations possible. Wind power, generated by the motion of wind turbines, requires an average wind speed of at least 16 kilometers (10 miles) per hour to be practical. Problems inherent to wind power include the difficulty of maintaining a constant turbine rotation speed regardless of wind speed variation in order to produce electricity at a constant frequency, the difficulty of preventing damage to turbine blades from high-velocity wind gusts and ice in winter, and the unavoidable noise pollution created by the rotating blades. Biomass power plants, which use materials such as wood, agricultural wastes, and gaseous fuels derived from them, generate greenhouse gases, nitrogen oxides, and particulates as part of the combustion process.

Solar energy generation, which uses sunlight, produces no air pollution or waste products and so seems to be an ideal method. However, since solar radiation is not available at night, an energy storage system is needed. One solar technology employs reflectors that concentrate sunlight to heat a liquid or gaseous medium, which in turn creates steam or pressurized gas that drives a turbine to generate electricity. Another solar technology uses photovoltaic cells that convert sunlight directly into electricity. Some environmentalists have proposed that the future of solar energy may lie not in the building of traditional centralized power plants but rather in the development of small collector systems for individual communities.

Hans G. Graetzer
Updated by Karen N. Kähler

FURTHER READING

Ayres, Robert U., and Ed Ayres. *Crossing the Energy Divide: Moving from Fossil Fuel Dependence to a Clean-Energy Future.* Upper Saddle River, N.J.: Wharton School Publishing, 2010.

McCully, Patrick. *Silenced Rivers: The Ecology and Politics of Large Dams.* Enlarged ed. London: Zed Books, 2001.

Murray, Raymond L. *Nuclear Energy: An Introduction to the Concepts, Systems, and Applications of Nuclear Processes.* 6th ed. Burlington, Vt.: Butterworth-Heinemann/Elsevier, 2009.

National Research Council. *Electricity from Renewable Resources: Status, Prospects, and Impediments.* Washington, D.C.: National Academies Press, 2010.

Visgilio, Gerald Robert, and Diana M. Whitelaw, eds. *Acid in the Environment: Lessons Learned and Future Prospects.* New York: Springer, 2007.

Race-to-the-bottom hypothesis

CATEGORY: Resources and resource management

DEFINITION: Theory that the mobility of international capital pits workers and governments against one another in a competition to underbid and under-regulate that results in increasingly primitive working conditions and increasingly lax environmental laws

SIGNIFICANCE: If the race-to-the-bottom hypothesis is correct, the expected outcomes include widespread environmental deregulation and consequent degradation, especially in the developing world.

According to the race-to-the-bottom hypothesis, globalization dilutes not only the bargaining power of laborers but also the ability of governments to regulate industrial pollution. Desperate to build and maintain their tax bases, states in the developing world compete to appease capital sources with increasingly business-friendly and environment-hostile standards.

Critics of the hypothesis argue that while it may be the case that environmental regulations, working conditions, and pay may have weakened in some regions in the short run, some investment is almost always better than no investment, and the trend will inevitably reverse when market equilibrium has been neared, unemployment has sufficiently diminished, and a requisite degree of regulations have been enacted in an adequate number of states. Some also assert that the process is a necessary growing pain of industrialization, and the developing world's quality of life and environmental integrity will continue to improve and eventually match that of the global North.

The empirical evidence is unclear. Anecdotal cases of capital flight can be cited, as well as Ireland's notable attempt to attract capital by lowering environmental standards, and some studies have shown a negative correlation between regulation and investment. Other studies, however, have found environmental regulatory improvement in so-called export processing zones, where one might expect any actual race to the bottom to be most evident. Proponents of the theory, however, maintain that given the profit motive of investors and unquestionably looser restrictions in poorer regions, it is at least reasonable to expect market forces to encourage a suboptimal hovering near the middle, if not an all-out race to the bottom.

Matt Deaton

Refuse-derived fuel

CATEGORIES: Energy and energy use; waste and waste management

DEFINITION: Solid fuel material created from the processing of municipal solid waste

SIGNIFICANCE: The burning of refuse-derived fuel has some advantages over the burning of coal in terms of reducing damage to the environment, but this alternative energy source is not completely clean.

Raw municipal solid waste (MSW) is a notoriously poor fuel because of its high moisture and low heat content. In addition, mass-burn incineration of MSW produces a broad range of atmospheric pollutants, and the ash produced may become concentrated in potentially toxic elements, such as cadmium or arsenic. One goal of the production of refuse-derived fuel (RDF) is to improve the combustion of MSW by producing a fuel of lower moisture content, more uniform size, greater density, and lower ash content than raw MSW. Another goal is to reduce the amount of material in landfills.

A typical process for the production of RDF involves passage of raw wastes through a screen to remove small, inert materials (such as stones, soil, and glass), pulverization of larger particles in a shredding device, separation of ferrous metals by magnetic extraction, and segregation of the lightweight, mostly organic fraction in an upward airstream (this step is known as air classification). The shredded organic waste fraction can be used directly as a fuel (fluff RDF), or it can be compressed into high-density pellets or cubettes (densified RDF). The latter material is popular because it is easy to transport and store and because of its adaptability in handling and combustion.

RDF can be utilized as a cofuel with coal or fired separately. A major advantage of RDF over coal is that its sulfur content is markedly lower (0.1 to 0.2 percent

compared with 5 percent or more for some coal samples), as is its nitrogen content. Both sulfur and nitrogen are among the more notorious atmospheric precursors to acid rain. Also, as a result of processing, RDF contains smaller amounts of potentially toxic metals than does MSW.

RDF possesses only 50-60 percent of the calorific value and 65-75 percent of the density of typical bituminous coals. As a consequence, considerably larger weights of RDF must be burned to obtain performance similar to that of coal. The use of RDF in a boiler may therefore have an adverse impact on the performance of the boiler's systems for air-pollution control and ash removal. In addition, the chlorine content of RDF is higher than typical coal. Other problems sometimes associated with the use of RDF concern odors and dust production in storage and particulate, carbon monoxide, and hydrogen chloride discharges during combustion.

John Pichtel

FURTHER READING

Hickman, H. Lanier, Jr. "Refuse-Derived Fuel and Energy Recovery: Fulfilling the Resource Recovery Promise." In *American Alchemy: The History of Solid Waste Management in the United States.* Santa Barbara, Calif.: Forester Communications, 2003.

Niessen, Walter R. "Refuse-Derived Fuel Systems." In *Combustion and Incineration Processes.* 3d ed. New York: Marcel Dekker, 2002.

Renewable energy

CATEGORY: Energy and energy use

DEFINITION: Energy derived from natural, unlimited, and replenishable sources

SIGNIFICANCE: The burning of fossil fuels such as coal, natural gas, and petroleum releases emissions that contain greenhouse gases and cause air pollution and acid rain, whereas most forms of renewable energy are nonpolluting. In addition, because the earth has a finite supply of fossil fuels, the development of renewable energy sources is important to the long-term future of humankind.

The environmental movement and the oil crises of the 1970's led to interest in the development of energy sources that would offer alternatives to the use of fossil fuels. Fossil fuels are limited resources, and the burning of fossil fuels to generate energy creates emissions of carbon dioxide, toxic chemicals, and air pollutants that harm the environment and human health. Because renewable, or clean, energy systems use natural, local sources that are inexhaustible and such systems have fewer negative impacts on human life and the environment, governments have provided increasing support for the development of renewable energy technologies.

BIOMASS

The oldest renewable energy source is biomass, which is organic animal and plant material and waste. Biomass resources include grass crops, trees, and agricultural, municipal, and forestry wastes. Since the discovery of fire, humans have burned biomass to release its chemical energy as heat. For example, wood has been burned to cook food and to provide heat. Biomass energy has also been used to make steam and electricity. Biomass oils can be chemically converted into liquid fuels or biodiesel, a transportation fuel. Ethanol, another transportation fuel, comes from fermented corn or sugarcane. Crops such as willow trees and switchgrass are also cultivated for biomass energy generation.

Biomass energy has many environmental benefits when compared with fossil-fuel energy. It contributes little to air pollution, as it releases 90 percent less carbon dioxide than do fossil fuels. Energy crops, such as prairie grasses, require fewer pesticides and fertilizers than do high-yield food crops such as wheat, soy beans, and corn, so they cause less water pollution. Energy crops also add nutrients to the soil. About 4 percent of the energy used in the United States is biomass energy.

SOLAR ENERGY

One of the most promising and popular kinds of renewable energy is solar energy, which uses radiant energy produced by the sun. Solar energy was used as early as the seventh century B.C.E., when a magnifying glass was used to concentrate sunlight to light fires. In 1767, Swiss scientist Horace-Bénédict de Saussure invented the first solar collector, a device for storing the sun's radiation and converting it into a usable form, such as by heating water to create steam. In 1891, American inventor Clarence Kemp patented the first commercial solar water heater.

Sunlight can be converted directly into electricity

at the atomic level by photovoltaic (PV) cells, also called solar cells. The photovoltaic phenomenon was first noted in the eighteenth century and became more practical with the use of silicon for the cells in the twentieth century. The cells are joined together in panels, often connected together in an array. They can be placed on rooftops and connected to a grid. In the twenty-first century, solar cells are used worldwide in home and commercial electrical systems, satellites, and various consumer products.

Solar energy has numerous environmental benefits. Photovoltaics produce electricity without gaseous or liquid fuel combustion or hazardous waste by-products. Decentralized PV systems can be used to provide electricity for rural populations, saving more expensive conventional energy for industrial, commercial, and urban needs. By providing electricity for remote and rural areas, solar energy also reduces the use of disposable lead-acid cell batteries, which can contaminate water and soil if they are not disposed of properly. The use of solar energy in rural areas also reduces air pollution by decreasing the use of diesel generators and kerosene lamps.

Since solar energy depends on sunlight, the efficiency and performance of solar energy systems are affected by weather conditions and location. Nevertheless, the amount of inexhaustible solar energy that could be generated around the globe exceeds the amount needed to meet the world's energy requirements. It has been estimated that if PV systems were installed in only 4 percent of the world's deserts, they could supply enough electricity for the entire world. As solar technologies improve and costs decrease, solar energy has the potential to be the leading alternative energy source of the future.

WIND ENERGY

One of the fastest-growing types of renewable energy during the 1990's, wind energy has been used by humans for centuries. Windmills appear in Persian drawings from 500 C.E., and they are known to have been used throughout the Middle East and China. The English and the French built windmills during the twelfth century, and windmills were indispensable for pumping underground water in the western and Great Plains regions of the United States during the nineteenth and early twentieth centuries. These windmills converted wind into mechanical power.

The modern windmills used to convert wind energy into electricity are called wind turbines or wind gener-

Top Consumers of Geothermal Energy, 2005

	MEGAWATT CAPACITY	GIGAWATT-HOURS PER YEAR
United States	7,817	8,678
Sweden	4,200	12,000
China	3,687	12,605
Iceland	1,844	6,806
Turkey	1,495	6,900
Japan	822	2,862
Hungary	694	2,206
Italy	607	2,098
New Zealand	308	1,969

Note: Worldwide installed capacity for direct use increased from 8,604 megawatts in 1995 to 28,268 megawatts in 2005. Yearly direct use increased from 31,236 gigawatt-hours per year in 1995 to 75,943 gigawatt-hours per year in 2005.

ators. In 1890 Poul la Cour, a Danish inventor, built the first wind turbine to generate electricity. Another Dane, Johannes Juul, built the world's first alternating current (AC) wind turbine in 1957. In the twenty-first century, large wind plants are connected to local electric utility transmission networks to relieve congestion in existing systems and to increase reliability for consumers. Wind energy is also used on a smaller scale by home owners in what is known as distributed energy; home-based wind turbines, with batteries as backup, can lower electricity bills by up to 90 percent.

The use of wind energy has long-term environmental benefits. Unlike nuclear and fossil-fuel electricity generation plants, wind generation of electricity does not consume fuel, cause acid rain and greenhouses gases, or require waste cleanups. For example, it has been estimated that when Cape Wind, America's first offshore wind farm under development in Nantucket Sound, becomes fully operational, its 130 wind turbines will reduce greenhouse gas emissions by 734,000 tons annually.

In 2010 the annual wind energy generating capacity of the United States was more than 35,000 megawatts, enough electricity to power 9.7 million homes. This amount of electricity generated by fossil-fuel-burning plants would have released some 62 million tons of carbon dioxide; avoiding the release of so much carbon dioxide is the equivalent of keeping 10.5 million cars off the roads.

Wind energy technology has advanced to the point that wind power is affordable and can compete successfully with fossil fuels and other conventional energy generation. According to a report by the U.S. Department of Energy, wind energy could provide 20 percent of the U.S. electricity supply by 2030. Wind power as a commercial enterprise has been established in more than eighty countries, and in 2009 wind energy capacity increased by 31 percent, with the main markets in Asia, North America, and Europe.

The main disadvantage of wind energy is that it is intermittent, because wind velocities are inconsistent even in areas of strong winds. In addition, some environmentalists have objected to the establishment of wind farms because of their potential to harm wildlife and the aesthetic damage they do to natural landscapes.

HYDROPOWER

Long before electricity was harnessed, in about 4000 B.C.E., ancient civilizations used hydropower, or energy from moving or flowing water, in the waterwheel, the first device employed by humans to produce mechanical energy as a substitute for animal and human labor. Running water in a stream or river moves the wooden paddles mounted around a waterwheel, and the resulting rotation in the shaft drives machinery. The earliest waterwheels were used to grind grain, and the technology went on to be used worldwide for that purpose, as well as to supply drinking water, irrigate crops, drive pumps, and power sawmills and textile mills.

In the nineteenth century, the water turbine replaced the waterwheel in mills, but then the steam engine replaced the turbine in mills. The hydraulic turbine reemerged, however, to power electric generators in the world's first hydroelectric power stations during the 1880's. By the early twentieth century, 40 percent of the U.S. electricity supply was hydroelectric power. Modern large hydropower plants are attached to dams or reservoirs that store the water for turning the turbines and are connected to electrical grids or substations that transmit the electricity to consumers.

Hydropower is the leading renewable energy source for generating electricity. It has both negative and beneficial effects on the environment. Building dams and reservoirs changes the environment and can harm native habitats and their fish, animal, and plant life. In addition, reservoirs sometimes emit methane, a greenhouse gas. Water is a natural and inexpensive energy source, however. No fuel combustion takes place in the generation of hydropower, so the process does not pollute the air, and energy storage is clean. Hydroelectric power accounts for 24 percent of electricity used worldwide, the electricity consumption of more than 1 billion people. It provides electricity for more than 35 million American households, equivalent to about 500 million barrels of oil a year.

Geothermal Energy

Geothermal energy comes from heat produced deep inside the earth. Deep wells and pumps bring underground hot water and steam to the earth's surface to heat buildings and generate electricity. Some geothermal energy sources come to the surface naturally, including hot springs, geysers, and volcanoes. The ancient Chinese, Native Americans, and Romans used hot mineral-rich springs for bathing, heating, and cooking. Food dehydration became the major industrial use of this form of energy. In 1904, the first electricity from geothermal energy was generated in Larderello, Italy.

Although not as popular a renewable energy source as wind or solar energy, geothermal energy has significant advantages and benefits for the environment. Because the earth's heat and temperatures are basically constant, geothermal energy is reliable and inexhaustible; it is also not affected by changes in climate or weather. It is very cost-efficient as well; heat pumps can be operated at relatively low cost. The steam and water used in geothermal systems are recycled back into the earth.

Geothermal plants are environmentally friendly. Because they do not burn fuel to generate electricity, they release little or no carbon dioxide and other harmful compounds. Geothermal plants produce no noise pollution and have minimal visual impacts on the surrounding environment, because they do not occupy large surface areas.

The U.S. Environmental Protection Agency and the Department of Energy support the use of geothermal heat pumps. The American Recovery and Reinvestment Act of 2009 (ARRA, also known generally as the Stimulus) provided for grants and tax incentives worth $400 million to the industry, which added 144 geothermal energy plants in fourteen states at the beginning of 2010. ARRA measures benefited the development of all renewable energy sources; it included a Treasury Department grant program for renewable energy developers, increased funding for research and development, and a three-year extension of the production tax credit for many renewable energy facilities.

It has been predicted that by 2070, 60 percent of all global energy will come from renewable energy sources. The World Bank, the World Solar Decade, and the World Solar Summit have designated $2 billion for projects focused on renewable energy resources and the environment.

Alice Myers

Further Reading

Craddock, David. *Renewable Energy Made Easy: Free Energy from Solar, Wind, Hydropower, and Other Alternative Energy Sources.* Ocala, Fla.: Atlantic, 2008.

Da Rosa, Aldo Vieira. *Fundamentals of Renewable Energy Processes.* 2d ed. Boston: Elsevier Academic Press, 2009.

Langwith, Jacqueline, ed. *Renewable Energy.* Detroit: Greenhaven Press, 2009.

MacKay, David J. C. *Sustainable Energy—Without the Hot Air.* Cambridge, England: UIT Cambridge, 2009.

Nelson, Vaughn. *Wind Energy: Renewable Energy and the Environment.* Boca Raton, Fla.: CRC Press, 2009.

Pimentel, David, ed. *Biofuels, Solar, and Wind as Renewable Energy Systems: Benefits and Risks.* New York: Springer, 2008.

Renewable resources

CATEGORIES: Resources and resource management; energy and energy use

DEFINITION: Natural resources that are capable of replenishing themselves for future use

SIGNIFICANCE: Nonrenewable resources such as coal, oil, gas, and mineral deposits regenerate themselves too slowly to keep up with human demand; once consumed, they are gone. By contrast, sustainably managed renewable resources can meet current needs and still provide for generations to come. Misuse or overuse, however, can tax renewable resources beyond their ability to recover.

The term "renewable resources" is often used interchangeably with "renewable energy." However, water, soil, wildlife, forests, plants, and wetlands are also types of renewable resources. Renewable energy sources, such as wind energy and hydroelectricity, are mainly derived from solar energy in one form or another. Direct solar radiation is usually converted into heat, which can be used for such purposes as heating homes or water. Solar water heating has been used in the southern United States since at least the early twentieth century. In mild climates such as southern Florida, it can easily furnish all the hot water requirements of a typical home. It has also been widely used in tropical countries throughout the world. As of 2008 solar photovoltaic systems and wind had become the fastest-growing renewable energy sectors in the United States.

TYPES OF SOLAR ENERGY

Passive solar heating, at its most basic, is the heating of a building by solar radiation that enters the building through south-facing windows (north-facing in the Southern Hemisphere). A properly designed passive solar home must have enough interior heat capacity, usually in the form of concrete floors or walls, to be able to keep the house from overheating on a sunny day and to store excess heat for release at night. In many parts of North America and Europe, passive solar homes have proved to be economical, because the passive system is part of the house itself (its windows, walls, and floors) and thus adds little or no extra cost. "Passive solar" can also refer to solar water-heating systems that involve no moving parts and consume no electricity. Using local water pressure, cold water flows into a collector, where solar energy heats it; the heated water, which rises to the top of the collector, then flows to a storage tank.

Active solar heating, by contrast, uses air or liquid solar collectors that convert solar radiation into thermal energy, which is stored and distributed using a mechanical system (fans or pumps). Active systems are more complex, cost more, and are more resource-intensive; however, they offer greater efficiency and can be used to retrofit an existing building. Two common types of active solar systems are used to heat water for household use: closed loop, in which a solar collector heats an antifreeze solution which in turn heats a water tank containing potable water; and open loop, a simpler, less expensive scheme in which potable water is routed through the solar collector to be heated before flowing into the tank.

Direct solar radiation can also be used to produce electricity. Concentrated solar power systems employ an array of mirrors that reflect sunlight onto a collector, where the solar heat is stored or converted into mechanical energy. In 2007 the capacity of concentrated solar power plants in the United States reached 419 megawatts. Ocean thermal conversion, a concept that has been partially tested, generates electricity using the difference in temperature between the warm, solar-heated upper portions of the ocean and the colder water farther down. No complete ocean thermal conversion plant has yet been built.

Photovoltaic or solar cells are semiconductor devices that generate electricity directly from solar (or other electromagnetic) radiation. Originally developed for artificial satellites after World War II, photovoltaic cells work well and are used to power everything from solar calculators, radios, battery rechargers, and patio lights to electric fences, traffic signal controls, field-deployed scientific monitoring equipment, and corrosion prevention systems on metal bridges. However, their price has kept them from gaining widespread use for generating electricity in homes.

OTHER RENEWABLE RESOURCES

A less direct type of renewable solar energy is hydroelectricity—electricity generated by water turbines that are turned by water flowing down a river or dropping from a dammed water reservoir. The kinetic energy of the moving water is derived from the gravitational potential energy of water at greater heights, and that energy is ultimately derived from solar radiation that evaporated the water from the oceans, allowing it to rain down in the mountains. An older form of water power was the waterwheel used by millers until well into the nineteenth century. Ocean energy in the form of tidal movement, wave action, and marine currents is another source of hydropower that is gaining increasing attention. Because of the great expense of harnessing tidal energy, the tidal power plant that has operated at the mouth of the Rance River in France since 1966 has remained the only major facility of its kind. Smaller commercial tidal power plants operate in Canada, Russia, and China, however, and by 2010 several experimental facilities for producing tide- or wave-generated power were online or under construction around the globe.

Wind energy is also a renewable solar energy resource, because it is the uneven heating of the earth's land and water areas by the sun that causes winds. Wind has long been used as an energy source: It powered the sailing ships that explored the globe, and it powered the windmills used in Asia and Europe since the Middle Ages to grind grain and pump water. Since the 1920's wind turbines have been used to generate electricity in rural areas of the United States. In 2008 the generation capacity of the world's wind power facilities reached 120.8 gigawatts.

Geothermal energy is the heat energy produced beneath the earth's surface by the decay of naturally occurring radioactive elements. According to the U.S. Geological Survey, if only 1 percent of the thermal energy contained within the uppermost 10 kilometers (6.2 miles) of the planet's crust could be harnessed, it would provide five hundred times the energy represented by the world's known oil and gas reserves. While present everywhere beneath the earth's surface, geothermal energy is commercially exploitable primarily in areas of active or geologically young volcanoes. The western United States accounts for most of the world's installed geothermal electricity capacity and generation.

Biomass is often defined as the total mass of living organisms in an ecosystem, including both plants and animals, but the term is also used for nonliving biological materials, such as wood from dead trees. The energy stored in biomass is solar energy that has been stored by photosynthesis. Biomass is an important resource not only for human life, because all human food is biomass in one form or another, but also for society in general because biomass materials can be used as a source of energy and organic chemical compounds, including therapeutic drugs. In 2008 biomass accounted for roughly 45 percent of the total renewable electricity generation (excluding hydropower) in the United States.

Biomass energy resources include solid, liquid, and gaseous fuels. The solid fuels include wood (the major energy resource used in the United States until about 1880) and agricultural wastes such as corn stover (the leaves and stalks left behind after a corn harvest) and sugarcane bagasse (the pulp remaining after juice extraction). These are increasingly being used for industrial electric power generation and home heating. Liquid biomass fuels include methanol and ethanol, both of which can be used in motor vehicle engines. The major gaseous biomass fuel is methane, the main constituent of the fossil fuel called

natural gas; methane is generated by the anaerobic (oxygen-starved) decomposition of manure and other organic materials.

Laurent Hodges
Updated by Karen N. Kähler

FURTHER READING

Graziani, Mauro, and Paolo Fornasiero, eds. *Renewable Resources and Renewable Energy: A Global Challenge*. Boca Raton, Fla.: CRC Press, 2007.

Kelly, Regina Anne. *Energy Supply and Renewable Resources*. New York: Checkmark Books, 2008.

National Renewable Energy Laboratory. *2008 Renewable Energy Data Book*. Golden, Colo.: U.S. Dept. of Energy, Office of Energy Efficiency and Renewable Energy, 2009.

National Research Council. *Electricity from Renewable Resources: Status, Prospects, and Impediments*. Washington, D.C.: National Academies Press, 2010.

Pimentel, David, ed. *Biofuels, Solar, and Wind as Renewable Energy Systems: Benefits and Risks*. New York: Springer, 2008.

Sharpe, Grant William, John C. Hendee, and Wenonah F. Sharpe. *Introduction to Forests and Renewable Resources*. 7th ed. Long Grove, Ill.: Waveland Press, 2009.

Wengenmayr, Roland, and Thomas Bührke, eds. *Renewable Energy: Sustainable Energy Concepts for the Future*. Weinheim, Germany: Wiley-VCH, 2008.

Young, Anthony. *Land Resources: Now and for the Future*. New York: Cambridge University Press, 2000.

Resource Conservation and Recovery Act

CATEGORIES: Treaties, laws, and court cases; waste and waste management; resources and resource management

THE LAW: U.S. federal legislation concerning the protection of human health and the environment from hazardous wastes

DATE: Enacted on October 21, 1976

SIGNIFICANCE: The Resource Conservation and Recovery Act aims to protect the environment by prohibiting the open dumping of wastes on land and by requiring federal agencies to establish programs to reduce the amounts of waste materials generated. The act also addresses the conservation of resources by requiring the recovery or recycling of certain kinds of waste materials.

As human industries and technologies have advanced, increasing numbers of materials have been deposited into the air and land that are dangers to human health. Many consumer products—including electronic devices and batteries—contain harmful components that can leach into the soil and contaminate it if these items are not disposed of safely. Gases and soot emitted from factories can pollute the air and cause difficult breathing as well as permanent damage to lungs. Radioactive materials used in nuclear plants or in hospitals can have deleterious effects if not handled properly.

During the 1970's, the U.S. Congress became aware that the disposal of solid and hazardous wastes in and on land without careful planning and management can present a danger to human health and the environment. The Resource Conservation and Recovery Act of 1976 (RCRA) was one result of this awareness. RCRA authorizes environmental agencies to order the cleanup of contaminated sites and promotes improvement in management techniques for solid and hazardous wastes. The law mandates that such wastes be handled by competent authorities from the time the wastes are generated until the time of their disposal, or "from cradle to grave."

Disposal of Solid and Hazardous Wastes

The Solid Waste Disposal Act was promulgated in 1965 by President Lyndon B. Johnson, who created the Office of Solid Waste within the U.S. Public Health Service. In 1970, the U.S. Environmental Protection Agency (EPA) took over responsibility for solid waste management. RCRA updated this law and made it clear that taking care of trash is a matter of public health. RCRA defines solid waste as any garbage, refuse, or sludge from a wastewater treatment plant, water-supply plant, or air-pollution-control facility. The law does not include household waste, but it does include waste generated by dry cleaners, auto repair shops, hospitals, exterminators, photo-processing centers, chemical manufacturers, electroplating companies, and petroleum refineries, as well as any other businesses that generate solid waste.

Those who handle solid waste must have an RCRA site identification number if they handle 100 kilograms (220 pounds) per month or accumulate more than 1,000 kilograms (2,200 pounds) of dangerous waste at any one time. Owners and operators of these sites must report each year on their waste management activities. Public participation in reporting is encouraged, and anyone can bring a suit in a federal district court to report anyone who is violating the act.

Hazardous waste is a specific type of solid waste, defined in RCRA as anything that is ignitable (burns readily), corrosive, reactive (explosive), or toxic. Hazardous wastes take many physical forms and may be solid, semisolid, or liquid. These wastes can be damaging to the eyes, the skin, and the tissue under the skin, and they may be poisonous when ingested or inhaled. When hazardous wastes are improperly treated, stored, transported, or disposed of, or otherwise mismanaged, they can pose a substantial hazard to the environment. Before the passage of RCRA, some thought that U.S. law allowed the use of hazardous wastes as fertilizer. Hazardous wastes were sometimes mixed with other fertilizing materials to lessen the wastes' potency, and the resulting mixes were thought to be safe for growing crops. RCRA expressly ended this method of disposal.

Characteristics of Hazardous Waste

The Environmental Protection Agency provides the following explanations of the characteristics that define wastes as hazardous under the Resource Conservation and Recovery Act.

- **Ignitability:** Ignitable wastes create fires under certain conditions or are spontaneously combustible, or have a flash point less than 60 degrees Centigrade (140 degrees Fahrenheit).

- **Corrosivity:** Corrosive wastes are acids or bases (pH less than or equal to 2 or greater than or equal to 12.5) that are capable of corroding metal containers, such as storage tanks, drums, and barrels.

- **Reactivity:** Reactive wastes are unstable under "normal" conditions. They can cause explosions, toxic fumes, gases, or vapors when mixed with water.

- **Toxicity:** Toxic wastes are harmful or fatal when ingested or absorbed. When toxic wastes are disposed of on land, contaminated liquid may drain (leach) from the waste and pollute groundwater. Toxicity is defined through a laboratory procedure called the toxicity characteristic leaching procedure.

REGULATORY ASPECTS OF THE LAW

RCRA regulates commercial businesses as well as federal, state, and local government facilities that generate, transport, transfer, treat, store, recycle, or dispose of hazardous wastes. Owners and operators of municipal solid waste landfills must keep track of these wastes from the moment they are generated until their ultimate disposal or destruction. Generators of toxic substances must maintain thorough records and must clearly label and use appropriate containers for the wastes they generate.

RCRA requires all waste treatment, storage, and disposal facilities to meet certain standards for the location, design, and construction of the facilities and for their operating methods and practices. Groundwater monitoring is required on an ongoing basis, and the act also calls for federal or state inspection of all treatment, storage, and disposal facilities at least every two years. Failure to comply with these regulations carries a penalty of a fine of $25,000 per day of noncompliance, one year in prison, or both.

Winifred O. Whelan

FURTHER READING

Blewett, Stephen, with Mary Embree. *What's in the Air: Natural and Man-Made Air Pollution.* Ventura, Calif.: Seaview, 1998.

Gano, Lila. *Hazardous Waste.* San Diego, Calif.: Lucent Books, 1991.

Harris, Glenn, and Leah Nelson. "Revisiting a Hazardous Waste Site Twenty-five Years Later." *Journal of Evvironmental Health* 69, no. 9 (2007): 36-43.

Leone, Bruno, ed. *Garbage and Waste.* San Diego, Calif.: Greenhaven Press, 1997.

Rizzo, Christopher. "RCRA's 'Imminent and Substantial Endangerment' Citizen Suit Turns Twenty-five." *Natural Resources and Environment* 23, no. 2 (2008): 50-51.

Wiseman, Joseph F. "Solid Waste Program Benefits Community in More Ways than One." *Public Works* 131 (2000): 46-52.

Resource depletion

CATEGORY: Resources and resource management

DEFINITION: Consumption of a resource faster than new supplies of that resource can be found or faster than it can naturally be replenished

SIGNIFICANCE: With the global population approaching 7 billion people during the early twenty-first century, the demand for higher living standards worldwide has accelerated resource depletion. In addition, modern technology has become dependent on a large number of scarce metal resources with rapidly dwindling known reserves.

Throughout history, humans have exploited resources until the resources have been used up. The discovery of the Americas by Europeans at the end of the fifteenth century began an unprecedented and unsustainable harvesting of natural resources that persisted for five centuries. During this period, vast stands of virgin timber were cut and large numbers of animals were slaughtered for pelts, trophies, and food. For centuries, human beings found new sources of various commodities when they had depleted known existing sources. European countries depended on obtaining supplies of scarce resources from African and Asian colonies during the Industrial Revolution, for example; this access to cheap raw materials waned rapidly after World War II, however.

Worldwide population growth in the nineteenth and twentieth centuries spurred waves of immigrants to the Western Hemisphere and accelerated resource consumption around the world. Demand for higher standards of living worldwide, along with technological advances and the availability of cheap energy, accelerated resource exploitation.

By the early twenty-first century, the developed countries, with their increasing reliance on high technology, had become vulnerable to exploitative limits on specific metals needed to maintain and expand their current standards of living. Certain commodities, such as clean drinking water, had come to be viewed as basic rights of citizens, with needs to be met by governments. (In many emerging countries, clean drinking water had yet to be achieved.) Access to readily available sources of cheap natural gas, fuel oil, gasoline, and electricity were also viewed as necessities, and costs of energy were subsidized by governments in both developed and developing countries.

SUPPLY AND DEMAND

When the cost of a commodity drops below its production price, exploitation of that resource ceases, unless a government or organization subsidizes continued production costs. Resource exploitation has always been labor-intensive. The advent of mechanization in the nineteenth century began reducing labor costs, and the availability of cheap energy from fossil fuels allowed greater exploitation of ever-dwindling resources to be profitable.

At times in history, resource exploitation has responded to paradigm shifts. When the cost of production, in nonmonetary value, exceeds what a society deems acceptable, a resource may no longer be exploited, or limits may be set on how much of the resource may be taken over a specified time period. The nonmonetary values of certain resources became increasingly important during the twentieth century, after developed countries had achieved relatively high standards of living. World exploitation of carbon-based fossil fuels may be significantly reduced over the course of the twenty-first century, as global consensus builds that greenhouse gas emissions pose a significant risk to future generations.

After World War II speculation began regarding how long diminishing supplies of essential minerals, metals, petroleum, and other nonrenewable sources of energy would last. By the beginning of the twenty-first century, many poor nations had begun to use their reserves of useful minerals to improve their standards of living by encouraging infrastructure investment rather than exporting raw materials to developed countries. Some of these useful minerals are limited in supply and are also needed by developed nations to maintain certain technologies equated with high standards of living. Future gains in living standards may be limited by real scarcity, or by nations deliberately denying access to raw materials.

PLANT AND ANIMAL RESOURCES

Although plants and animals are usually considered renewable resources, individual species of plants and animals can be consumed or otherwise destroyed faster than they can be naturally replaced. Lumbering practices of the past, such as clear-cutting, have permanently destroyed natural environments worldwide. When all the trees in an area of forest are cut down, the wildlife habitat is also destroyed, and soil erosion follows rapidly. When rivers become laden with sediment from eroded soil, riverine ecosystems are destroyed, and fishing industries are eliminated. The depletion of forest resources is accompanied by the depletion of the resources of adjacent ecosystems.

The growth in the numbers of bird and animal species considered to be endangered, along with the increasing numbers of species extinctions, shows that animal populations are often depleted. Attempts to place limits on fish catches have generally proved ineffective worldwide. It has been estimated that 75 percent of the earth's fish stocks are either fully exploited or overexploited. Overfishing for cod off the North American coast near Newfoundland depleted this resource; in 1992, no cod appeared at the start of the season.

Public concerns about endangered animal species often focus on "iconic" animals, such as elephants. Slaughtered for their ivory tusks prior to the international ban on the ivory trade signed by more than one hundred nations in 1990, only an estimated ten thousand African bush elephants remained in 2010, as poaching continued in spite of the ban.

FOSSIL FUELS

The high standard of living in developed countries has been achieved in large part because of the cheap cost of energy in the twentieth century. During the late twentieth century, periods of artificial scarcity of petroleum caused global political concerns. Coal, natural gas, and oil were readily available worldwide, however, and production costs remained small for these fossil fuels. The International Energy Agency (IEA) has estimated that petroleum production will peak in 2020. Some estimates suggest that proven oil reserves may last until 2060; the exploitation of as-yet unproven and prospective reserves and unconventional sources could extend supplies considerably. New techniques for drilling and oil recovery continue to increase oil production from older oil fields. (Large oil fields may produce more than 50 billion barrels of oil over their exploitable lifetimes. Estimated reserves increase after a field has been in production for a while.)

Known coal reserves are expected to last into the twenty-second century, but supplies of petroleum and natural gas will be exhausted sooner if rates of consumption do not decrease. Because the burning of cheap fossil fuels has led to increased concentrations of greenhouse gases in the atmosphere, limits to carbon consumption may be set by governments and by international agreements at some future time. (Developing countries argued at the United Nations Climate Change Conference in Copenhagen, Denmark, in late 2009 that they should not be required to limit their "carbon footprint.")

Eventually, biofuels may replace petroleum. Ethanol, which is most often derived from corn, has been determined to be a costly alternative to gasoline in the United States, but biodiesel continues to be investigated. "Sidestream products" from biofuels production have considerable value.

Some developed countries have opted to construct nuclear reactors to supply the energy they need. The member nations of the Organization for Economic Cooperation and Development (OECD) produce about 300 gigawatts of energy from nuclear reactors, enough to meet about 25 percent of these nations' demand for electricity. France and Sweden are among the nations that obtain more than half their electricity from nuclear power plants.

Elements Essential to High Technology

Most modern electronic devices, including computers and cell phones, use an array of scarce metals, including lithium, tantalum, indium, platinum, and rare earth elements. Demand for these scarce metals has accelerated along with increasing demand for green technologies, and shortages may limit the production of clean energy.

Indium and gallium are essential components in light-emitting diodes (LEDs) and flat-screen displays, and in the construction of solar panels. Commercially obtained as by-products of zinc mining, both metals are thought to have limited reserves; it is estimated that about 6,000 tons of indium exist on the earth, and about 1 million tons of gallium. Unless more deposits are found or alternatives to these metals are developed, the ability to produce solar panels will be limited.

The developed countries need lithium for lightweight car batteries if electric vehicles are to become viable in the long term. The largest known supply of lithium (more than 73 million tons) is in Bolivia, which has resisted exporting raw materials to Japan, the United States and Europe, preferring to attract infrastructure investment so that Bolivia can exploit the lithium itself. Lithium mines are in operation in Chile and Argentina, and much smaller deposits have been found in Tibet and Canada; exploration for the metal is ongoing.

Tantalum is an element necessary for the high-resistance capacitors used in cell phones, personal computers, and automobile electronics. It is mined in Australia, Brazil, Ethiopia, Mozambique, Rwanda, and the Democratic Republic of the Congo. It has been alleged that the mining of tantalum ore (columbite-tantalite, or coltan) in the Congo endangers elephants, lowland gorillas, and other wildlife, and provides funds for the ongoing civil war there. Tantalum ore deposits are also known to exist in Saudi Arabia and Egypt. Estimates of known tantalum reserves are in the region of 40 million kilograms (44,000 tons); in 2009 about 25 percent of the tantalum being used was obtained through recycling.

Rare earth elements are used for catalysts, ceramics, magnets, electronics, and in the chemical industry. Exploitable rare earth deposits (largely from the mineral monazite) are known to exist in the United States, Canada, Brazil, Australia, India, South Africa, Russia, Vietnam, and China. By the early twenty-first century, about 95 percent of commercially available rare earth elements were derived from China. On September 1, 2009, China set a limit on the export of rare earths at 35,000 tons per year for the next five years. This limit was set to encourage foreign companies to produce high-technology items in China.

Anita Baker-Blocker

Further Reading

Chiras, Daniel D., and John P. Reganold. *Natural Resource Conservation: Management for a Sustainable Future.* 10th ed. Upper Saddle River, N.J.: Benjamin Cummings/Pearson, 2010.

Cohen, David. "Earth Audit. " *New Scientist*, May 26, 2007, 34-41.

Edwards, Andres R. *The Sustainability Revolution: Portrait of a Paradigm Shift.* Gabriola Island, B.C.: New Society, 2005.

Larmer, Brook, and Randy Olson. "The Real Price of Gold." *National Geographic*, January, 2009, 34-61.

McKinney, Michael L., Robert M. Schoch, and Logan Yonavjak. "People and Natural Resources." In *Environmental Science: Systems and Solutions.* 4th ed. Sudbury, Mass.: Jones and Bartlett, 2007.

Managi, Shunsuke. *Technological Change and Environmental Policy: A Study of Depletion in the Oil and Gas Industry.* Northampton, Mass.: Edward Elgar, 2007.

Runge, Ian C. *Mining Economics and Strategy.* Littleton, Colo.: Society for Mining, Metallurgy, and Exploration, 1998.

SL-1 reactor accident

CATEGORIES: Disasters; nuclear power and radiation

THE EVENT: Destruction of the SL-1 nuclear reactor, a test reactor at the Idaho National Engineering Laboratory

DATE: January 3, 1961

SIGNIFICANCE: The accident involving the SL-1 reactor was the first nuclear reactor accident in the United States that resulted in fatalities. As a result of this incident, new design criteria were developed to ensure that a complete reactor shutdown could be accomplished safely.

In February, 1954, the U.S. secretary of defense authorized the U.S. Army to develop small nuclear reactors to provide electrical power and heat for military facilities in remote locations, such as Distant Early Warning (DEW) Line radar sites in Alaska and Greenland. A prototype, the Stationary Low-Power Reactor Number One (SL-1), began operation on August 11, 1958, at the National Reactor Testing Station in the desert west of Idaho Falls, Idaho. This small reactor was designed to operate at a maximum power of 3 megawatts, to produce electricity and steam heat for the crews and equipment at DEW Line radar sites or other military installations.

Combustion Engineering, the contractor that operated SL-1 for the Army, shut the reactor down on December 23, 1960, for the Christmas holiday. As part of the shutdown procedure, the control rod, which determined the rate of reaction in the core, was fully inserted and disconnected from its drive mechanism. A three-man crew arrived at the reactor site on the evening of January 3, 1961, to reconnect the drive mechanism for the main control rod in preparation for restarting the reactor. This required them to move the control rod out about 10 centimeters (4 inches). For reasons that were never determined, the crew instead moved the rod out about 51 centimeters (20 inches), resulting in an extreme power surge, with the reactor producing an estimated 20,000 megawatts. Within a few milliseconds the core overheated and the resulting steam explosion propelled the control rod upward and disrupted the reactor core. All three of the crew, the only people near the reactor, were killed.

Because the Army was intending to operate reactors like SL-1 in remote locations, the reactor had been built to be small and lightweight; it had no con-tainment structure like the ones on commercial power reactors. The reactor was housed in a steel cylinder with walls 0.63 centimeter (0.25 inch) thick, which trapped most of the radioactivity released in the explosion. Some radioactive iodine escaped, and monitoring downwind indicated that its radioactivity reached fifty times background levels near the plant. Because of the remote location of the SL-1 reactor no humans outside the test site were adversely affected.

Radioactivity inside the reactor structure was so high that each member of the rescue team, wearing whole-body protective clothing, was permitted to enter the site only once for a period of one minute to assess the situation and recover the victims. Because of its high radioactivity the reactor was buried on-site.

An investigation of the accident found that the direct cause was the improper withdrawal of the main control rod, but the investigators also concluded that the design of the SL-1 reactor was poor, because a single rod controlled 80 percent of the activity in the core. As a result, new design criteria were put in place requiring that a complete reactor shutdown could be accomplished with the most reactive control rod in its full out position. Nonetheless, the SL-1 accident demonstrated the general safety of the water-moderated reactor design, since even this severe accident resulted in dispersal of the nuclear core, shutting down the reaction, rather than a more serious nuclear meltdown.

George J. Flynn

FURTHER READING

McKeown, William. *Idaho Falls: The Untold Story of America's First Nuclear Accident.* Toronto: ECW Press, 2003.

Stacy, Susan M. *Proving the Principle: A History of the Idaho National Engineering and Environmental Laboratory, 1949-1999.* Washington, D.C.: Government Printing Office, 2000.

Tucker, Todd. *Atomic America: How a Deadly Explosion and a Feared Admiral Changed the Course of Nuclear History.* New York: Free Press, 2009.

Smart grids

CATEGORY: Energy and energy use

DEFINITION: Power grids that efficiently connect users with electrical power produced by a variety of sources

SIGNIFICANCE: Rebuilding the current power grid with smart-grid technology would provide the opportunity to make the delivery of electricity to consumers more efficient. Smart grids are also versatile enough to use different types of power sources, so their proliferation would encourage growth in the development of renewable energy sources such as solar and wind power.

The basic design of the current power grid in the United States and the design of many of its components go back to decisions made during the 1890's and the early twentieth century. The grid was originally constructed with power lines radiating outward from power plants to consumers and with interconnections so that if a generator went offline another could pick up the load. The U.S. grid has become a complex of some 482,800 kilometers (300,000 miles) of transmission lines connecting more than 9,200 power generators producing 1 million megawatts of power for American factories and homes. It is estimated that 9 percent of the energy fed into the grid is lost in transmission. A smart grid is more efficient and communicates with customers; it has the ability to shift load to off-peak hours and is versatile enough to accept power from a range of sources.

Generators may produce direct current (DC), which flows in one direction only, or alternating current (AC), which alternates its direction sixty times each second (in the United States). Almost from the first, it was decided to use AC because it can easily be transformed to high voltage and low current, and this reduces transmission losses. If power from another AC generator is to be added to the grid, it must have exactly the same frequency (60 hertz or cycles per second) and the same phase. It must rise and fall in exact lockstep with the power already on the grid; otherwise, power from the generator will cancel some of the power already on the grid, and it will be wasted. A smart grid has interfaces that exactly match the power from generators to the power already on the grid. As increasing numbers of electricity users install their own small windmill generators and solar cells, some have begun to produce sufficient power that they can

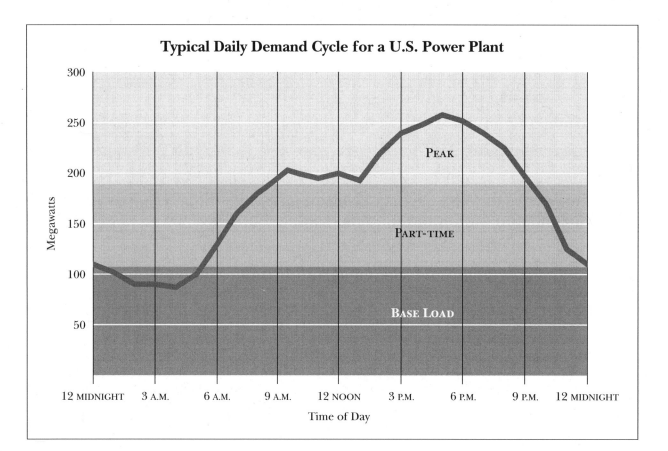

Typical Daily Demand Cycle for a U.S. Power Plant

sell what they do not use to the grid. Solar cells require an interface that converts DC to AC of the proper frequency and phase so that it can be added to the grid.

The amount of power used over the course of a day is not constant; rather, there are times of peak load, when more users—such as factories or home owners and businesses running air conditioners—are drawing power from the grid. Newer generators are usually more efficient and less polluting than older generators, so these generators are always in use. Power companies run their least efficient generators only during peak load periods, and this electricity costs more to produce. Smart power meters inform consumers of changing power costs so that they may shift their usage to off-peak hours if they wish. This not only saves the consumers money but also allows the power companies to use only their more efficient generators if enough load is shifted.

High-voltage DC (HVDC) lines can transmit power with less loss than AC lines, so for transmission lines over 400 miles (650 kilometers) long, DC may be used. Alternating current is first transformed up to as much as 800 kilovolts and then converted to DC. At the destination power station the DC is converted back to AC, and the voltage is reduced to typical substation voltage (2.4 to 33 kilovolts). Superconducting wire would be even more efficient, and trial smart grid projects involving such wire have been undertaken, such as Long Island's Project Hydra.

Charles W. Rogers

FURTHER READING

Blume, Stephen W. *Electric Power System Basics for the Nonelectrical Professional.* Hoboken, N.J.: Wiley-IEEE, 2007.

Bowman, Ron. *The Green Guide to Power: Thinking Outside the Grid.* Charleston, S.C.: BookSurge, 2008.

Fox-Penner, Peter. *Smart Power: Climate Change, the Smart Grid, and the Future of Electric Utilities.* Washington, D.C.: Island Press, 2010.

Solar automobile racing

CATEGORY: Energy and energy use

DEFINITION: Competitions in which drivers travel specified distances in vehicles powered by the sun's energy

SIGNIFICANCE: Races featuring solar automobiles demonstrate the potential of solar energy to provide sustainable transportation. Solar car races motivate engineers and scientists to refine vehicle and energy technologies utilizing solar power. Several manufacturers have appropriated innovative features and designs developed for those competitions to use in the vehicles they produce.

In 1982 Hans Tholstrup departed from Sydney, Australia, in a solar-energy-powered automobile. He traveled west, covering 4,052 kilometers (2,518 miles) in twenty days, averaging 23 kilometers (14.3 miles) per hour, to reach Perth. Inspired by that experience, Tholstrup envisioned a transcontinental competition in Australia to promote solar vehicle technology research. The detrimental impact of fossil-fuel emissions on the environment concerned Tholstrup, who emphasized that solar cars do not produce such damaging emissions. He established the World Solar Challenge (WSC), with the debut race occurring in 1987.

The first WSC started in Darwin in northern Australia, following the Stuart Highway 3,000 kilometers (1,864 miles) south to Adelaide. Tholstrup stressed that participants' vehicles had to rely completely on solar power. According to the rules, the cars could race from 8:00 A.M. to 5:00 P.M. daily, and the first vehicle to reach the finish line would be named the winner. The drivers endured extremely hot temperatures, windstorms, and other difficulties. A solar automobile developed by General Motors, the Sunraycer, won the race, averaging 66.9 kilometers per hour (41.6 miles per hour).

Solar cars raced in the WSC in 1990, 1993, and 1996 along the same route, before the South Australian government purchased the competition from Tholstrup; since that time the race has been held every two years. The WSC remains the most important solar automobile racing contest in the world, but solar automobile racing has gone on to attract diverse participants and sponsors, and other races are held worldwide, including the North American Solar Challenge. In 2009 the WSC became part of the Global Green Challenge, an event that encompasses both the WSC competition and the Eco Challenge, a competition for "environmentally friendly production and experimental vehicles."

A solar car is typically constructed with light carbon fiber composite materials, such as Kevlar, that form a wide surface area, approximately 6 square meters (65 square feet), on which are mounted solar cells, typically made from silicon, which convert solar energy into electricity; this energy is stored in lithium batteries, which power electric motors that power the vehicle. Competitors in solar races strive to reduce the weight and drag of their vehicles and improve the vehicles' aerodynamics. Many invest in relatively costly materials, such as gallium arsenide, for their solar cells to maximize the amount of solar energy converted into electricity; for example, solar cells made from gallium arsenide can convert 26 percent of solar energy into electricity, compared with 20 percent for solar cells made from silicon. Solar cars can move very quickly; racers in the WSC often exceed South Australia's speed limit of 110 kilometers (68 miles) per hour.

The strategies used by solar car racing teams include computer modeling to simulate races. Some teams use weather balloons to assess cloudiness on race routes. Racers often position mirrors on their solar cars to direct sunlight to the solar cells. Competitors also place microprocessors on batteries and utilize wireless communications between the solar cars and their support teams so the teams can remotely set the solar cars' speeds after interpreting data.

Many automobile makers have been impressed by the technologies developed by solar automobile racing competitors, some of which may be employed to enhance the energy efficiency and reduce the carbon emissions of other vehicles. As a result of advances made in solar automobile racing, for example, some manufacturers have incorporated tires with reduced rolling resistance, batteries that store more energy for greater durations, and improved aerodynamics in mainstream vehicles.

Elizabeth D. Schafer

FURTHER READING

Barry, Courtney. "Racing: Here They Come, as Fast as the Sun Will Carry Them." *The New York Times*, October 22, 2003, G34.

Excell, Jon. "Lighting the Way." *The Engineer*, April 6, 2009, 22-25.

Roche, David M., et al. *Speed of Light: The 1996 World Solar Challenge.* Sydney: Photovoltaics Special Research Centre, University of New South Wales, 1997.

Thacher, Eric F. *A Solar Car Primer.* Hauppauge, N.Y.: Nova Science, 2005.

Upson, Sandra. "Across the Outback on Photons Alone." *IEEE Spectrum* 45, no. 2 (February, 2008): 50-55, 59-60.

Zorpette, Glenn. "Sun Kings Cross the Outback." *IEEE Spectrum* 39, no. 2 (February, 2002): 41-46.

Solar energy

CATEGORY: Energy and energy use

DEFINITION: Conversion of energy from the sun into thermal or electrical energy

SIGNIFICANCE: Diminishing supplies of fossil fuels and the pollution problems that result from their combustion have made renewable resources such as solar energy increasingly important. While creating solar cells and solar power facilities is energy- and resource-intensive, once in operation solar power plants provide low-carbon, low-pollution energy.

The sun was essentially humankind's only source of energy before the Industrial Revolution. In its broadest definition, solar energy is remarkably diverse and takes many forms. Hydropower, which is derived from the kinetic energy of moving water, is possible because water evaporated from the oceans by solar radiation subsequently falls in mountainous areas and flows to lower elevations. Wind energy results from the uneven solar heating of the planet's surface. Biomass contains solar energy that has been stored by photosynthesis, as do fossil fuels. Defined more narrowly, viable solar energy technologies include active and passive systems that make use of the sun's heat energy and photovoltaic cells that convert the sun's energy into electricity.

According to the National Renewable Energy Laboratory (NREL), each day 46,700 quadrillion British thermal units (quads) of energy fall on the coterminous United States alone—substantially more than the 101.527 quads the nation consumed in peak year 2007, and more than one hundred times the total world consumption for the year 2006. This energy is available to anyone who is able to collect, transform, and store it.

Between 2000 and 2009 solar energy generation in the United States nearly quadrupled, rapidly increasing from 909 million kilowatt-hours at the beginning of the decade to almost 3.6 billion kilowatt-hours by its end. Between 2001 and 2009 U.S. venture capital and private equity investment in solar technology companies surged from $5 million to more than $1 billion. While solar energy has become an increasingly important source of power in the United States, by 2009 solar accounted for only 0.1 percent of the nation's total energy production and consumption, trailing behind biomass, geothermal, and wind.

By the end of the first decade of the twenty-first century, solar and wind energy had become the world's fastest-growing energy technologies. The total solar energy installed capacities in 2009 among the world's top users of the technology were 9,677 megawatts in Germany, 3,595 megawatts in Spain, 2,628 megawatts in Japan, 2,108 megawatts in the United States, and 1,158 megawatts in Italy.

Solar energy is both a centralized and a decentralized technology. There are many different methods for collecting and converting solar energy, from small-scale home installations to massive commercial power facilities. Research into solar power technologies is carried out by major corporations and universities and by small start-up companies. The NREL coordinates much of this research. Solar energy technologies can be divided into three categories: solar thermal energy, concentrating solar power, and photovoltaic solar power.

Solar Thermal Energy

The use of solar energy for heating and cooling is based on the simple fact that when an object absorbs sunlight it gets hot. The heat energy may be used in several ways: to provide space heating and cooling, to drive engines, or to heat water or other fluids. If this is accomplished by nothing other than appropriately designed and situated buildings and without moving parts, it is termed passive solar technology. Passive solar architecture was introduced about two thousand years ago by the Greeks and is a common feature in traditional Islamic architecture.

The simplest passive method of solar heating used in the Northern Hemisphere involves situating a building so that its windows face south and its long axis runs east-west (in the Southern Hemisphere, the windows must face north). During the winter the sun is low in the sky and provides heating to the windows. In the summer, when the sun is high in the sky, most of the radiation falls on the roof. The building's windows and walls are constructed to minimize heat transfer by conduction, convection, and radiation. Sufficient interior heat capacity, generally in the form of concrete walls or floors, keeps the building from overheating during the day while storing excess heat for release during the night. Double-paned windows with a layer of air between the sheets of glass are effective for preventing conduction and convection. Glass is transparent to visible and infrared radiation, so sunlight enters and infrared radiation exits through the windows. During daylight hours more energy comes in than goes out, and at night drapes or blinds can be closed to reduce energy loss. Specialized coatings can be applied to the windows to enhance their ability to reflect infrared radiation back into the interior.

Some buildings are designed so that the sun's heat creates convection currents, which draw cool air into the buildings through ducts that are underground or

Comparison of Two Types of Solar Energy Collectors

Solar Photovoltaic Collector	Solar Thermal Collector
Converts solar energy directly into electricity for immediate use.	Collects heat from solar energy for conversion into electricity.
Electricity can be converted into heat for thermal use.	Heat is used directly.
Solar radiation of only a very small range of energy can be utilized.	Radiation of a wide range of energy can be used.
Requires additional storage devices that are costly and inefficient.	Some have built-in storage devices that are relatively inexpensive and efficient.
Ideal for micropower and small appliances.	Unsuitable for micropower and small appliances.

north-facing (south-facing for the Southern Hemisphere) while hot air is vented to the outside. Traditional Islamic architecture frequently uses chimneys to vent this hot air. The Trombe wall, invented by French designer Félix Trombe during the 1970's, is a modern version of this feature. Well-designed passive solar buildings are economical to heat and cool because little or no additional thermal regulation is needed.

The term "passive solar" is also sometimes used to refer to solar water-heating systems that have no moving parts and operate without the use of electricity. In such a system, cold water flows under local water pressure into a collector, where it is heated by solar energy. The heated water rises and flows from there into a storage tank.

One small-scale passive application of solar heat that has the potential to have significant environmental impacts is the solar cooker. Low-cost passive solar cookers made from cardboard and reflective foil have been distributed in developing countries, particularly among refugee populations living in temporary settlements, as an alternative to cooking over open fires. Widely used, solar cooking can save tons of firewood every year, thereby reducing deforestation and desertification. The use of solar cookers also cuts back on the number of open cooking fires, which generate unhealthful levels of smoke and particulate matter when they burn within poorly ventilated structures. Solar cookers also offer the added advantage of costing nothing to operate.

Active solar heating involves heating a working substance, usually a liquid, and pumping it to where the heat is needed. Depending on the system used, the temperature increases of the fluid may be a few degrees or as much as a few thousand degrees. Such a system generally has tubes that are painted black or are in thermal contact with a metal sheet that is painted black. Fluid that is circulated through the tubes is heated, then sent to a heat exchanger, where the heat energy is used directly or stored for future use. The technology is fairly simple, but the initial installation costs of such systems continue to be a stumbling block for most home owners in the United States—particularly given that the average American changes residence every five to seven years, a time span too short to allow recoupment of the investment made on many residential solar installations. An advantage to active solar heating systems is that they can be installed in existing buildings.

CONCENTRATING SOLAR POWER

Concentrating solar power (CSP) technology uses direct solar radiation to produce electricity on a commercial scale. It is best suited to locations with direct sunlight, clear skies, and dry air, which is why CSP facilities tend to be located in desert areas. In a CSP system, an array of reflectors or lenses concentrates sunlight onto a collector, producing temperatures as high as 3,000 degrees Celsius (5,432 degrees Fahrenheit). There the heat may be retained in a storage system containing molten salts or some other fluid, or it may be converted into mechanical energy. Sun-tracking systems orient the reflectors or lenses to take best advantage of the available sunlight.

The most common solar concentrator design, and the one that has enjoyed the most commercial success, is the parabolic trough, a long array of curved mirrors that concentrates sunlight on receiver tubes that parallel each mirror along its focal line. Inside the tubes is a liquid medium, which is heated by the sunlight. The liquid is conveyed to a central collector, where it heats water to produce steam that drives an electric turbine. Another design, the linear Fresnel reflector system, involves a receiver tube positioned above several mirrors. This allows the mirrors to track the sun more effectively. Yet another design is the parabolic dish, which concentrates the sun's energy on a central thermal receiver. Such a system is often combined with a Stirling engine. Fluid heated in the receiver is transferred to the engine, where the heat moves pistons to create mechanical power. This in turn powers a generator or alternator to produce electricity. A fourth design, the central receiver, involves a large field of flat mirrors that focuses sunlight on a central location, typically a tower with a generator at its base. Heated fluid within the tower produces steam, which drives the generator below.

CSP systems can also be used in conjunction with photovoltaic cells, a technology known as concentrating photovoltaic (CPV). CPV systems used lenses or mirrors to focus sunlight onto high-efficiency solar cells.

In 2009 the United States led the world in CSP installed capacity, followed by Spain. The capacity of U.S. CSP plants reached 431 megawatts that year. States leading the nation in CSP installed capacity were California, Nevada, Hawaii, and Arizona. Nine commercial parabolic trough facilities have been operating in California's Mojave Desert since the 1980's. World CSP capacity began a rapid increase in 2007, but by 2009 CSP still accounted for less than 0.1 percent of the world's total installed capacity.

PHOTOVOLTAIC SOLAR POWER

Photovoltaic solar cells, first developed in 1954 by scientists at the Bell Telephone Laboratories, are solid-state devices that convert sunlight into electricity. The earliest solar cells were made using single-crystal silicon wafers. Silicon is an important type of element known as a semiconductor, which has properties between those of conductors and insulators.

Electric conduction in silicon results from the movement of negative charges (electrons) and positive charges (holes). One way to cause this movement is to add arsenic or phosphorus atoms—which have five outer-shell electrons—to the pure silicon, creating a semiconductor that has excess negative charge (n type). The addition of boron atoms with three outer-shell electrons creates a p-type semiconductor. Electric conduction occurs when p- and n-type slices are placed in close contact.

The simplest solar cell is a p-n junction sandwiched between two conductors. One of the tricks to fabricating efficient solar cells centers on the design of the top conductor. It should be large enough to capture the electrons but not so large that it blocks sunlight from passing into the center of the sandwich. Sunlight enters the top of the cell and excites electrons in the n-type layer, causing them to jump to the p-type layer, where they are captured and carried away to do work in the external circuit.

The earliest solar cells converted sunlight to electricity with about 1 percent efficiency and were expensive to produce, but since the 1950's photovoltaic technology has become substantially more efficient as well as less costly. Improvements have been made in crystalline silicon solar cells, and amorphous silicon (a-Si) solar cells have emerged. Although a-Si solar cells are less efficient than crystalline silicon cells, thin-film a-Si cells are comparatively inexpensive to manufacture, and their efficiency is boosted when they are stacked atop one another to create a multilayered structure. While silicon continues to be important for solar cell production, use of other materials such as cadmium telluride, cadmium sulfide, gallium arsenide, gallium phosphide, and copper indium gallium selenide has grown.

The efficiency of silicon cells depends, to a great extent, on the purity of the silicon. Working in vacuum and zero gravity, scientists can prepare exceptionally pure silicon. Transporting the materials into orbit and the finished product back down to earth, however, would substantially increase production costs. An alternative proposal would leave the finished product in space, where the sun shines every day of the year. Although it is technically possible to build enormous solar cells in space and beam the energy down to the planet's surface in the form of microwave or laser energy, the concept is a controversial one. An orbiting solar power station would be very expensive to construct and maintain, and the technical challenges of successfully beaming energy from earth orbit to the planet's surface are considerable. The U.S. National Aeronautics and Space Administration (NASA) initiated the Space Solar Power Exploratory Research and Technology program in 1999 to investigate the possibility of space-based solar power, but two years later it abandoned the program. Japan's space agency, however, has announced plans to develop and deploy such a system and have it in operation by 2030.

Photovoltaics have been used extensively in space to power almost all satellites, and the range of earth-bound consumer products with built-in photovoltaic cells is continually expanding. Such cells are used to power radios, calculators, battery rechargers, outdoor lights, and electric fences. One of the advantages of photovoltaics is that they are modular: Individual units can be combined to produce outputs covering a wide voltage range. The technology is also transportable: Units can be set up wherever there is enough sunlight. Photovoltaics are used to power traffic signal controls, roadside signage, scientific instrumentation, anticorrosion systems on bridges, and experimental cars and aircraft.

In 2009 the capacity of photovoltaic power plants in the United States reached 1,677 megawatts. CSP accounted for most of the nation's solar capacity until 2005, when photovoltaics surpassed it. Between 2008 and 2009 cumulative solar photovoltaic capacity in the United States grew nearly 52 percent. In 2009 California led the nation in photovoltaic installed capacity, followed by New Jersey, Colorado, Arizona, Florida, Nevada, New York, Hawaii, Connecticut, and Massachusetts.

The solar cell manufacturing industry experienced major growth in the early twenty-first century, and in 2008 world photovoltaic capacity began to rise. In 2009 photovoltaics accounted for 0.4 percent of the world's total installed capacity and 0.1 percent of total worldwide renewable electricity generation.

Germany was the world leader in cumulative photovoltaic installed capacity that year, followed by Spain, Japan, the United States, and Italy.

Grace A. Banks
Updated by Karen N. Kähler

FURTHER READING

Cassedy, Edward S. "Solar Energy Sources." In *Prospects for Sustainable Energy: A Critical Assessment.* New York: Cambridge University Press, 2000.

Foster, Robert, Majid Ghassemi, and Alma Cota. *Solar Energy: Renewable Energy and the Environment.* Boca Raton, Fla.: CRC Press, 2010.

Kalogirou, Soteris. *Solar Energy Engineering: Processes and Systems.* Burlington, Mass.: Academic Press, 2009.

Naff, Clay Farris, ed. *Solar Power.* Detroit: Greenhaven Press, 2007.

National Renewable Energy Laboratory. *2009 Renewable Energy Data Book.* Golden, Colo.: U.S. Dept. of Energy, Office of Energy Efficiency and Renewable Energy, 2010.

National Research Council. *Electricity from Renewable Resources: Status, Prospects, and Impediments.* Washington, D.C.: National Academies Press, 2010.

O'Keefe, Philip, et al. *The Future of Energy Use.* 2d ed. Sterling, Va.: Earthscan, 2010.

Pimentel, David, ed. *Biofuels, Solar, and Wind as Renewable Energy Systems: Benefits and Risks.* New York: Springer, 2008.

Solar One

CATEGORY: Energy and energy use

IDENTIFICATION: The first solar power tower system

DATES: Operated from 1982 to 1988

SIGNIFICANCE: The Solar One facility proved that power towers work efficiently to produce utility-scale power from sunlight.

Solar One, a pilot plant built as a large-scale test of the tower system of generating power using solar energy, was built in the early 1980's near Barstow, California, by Southern California Edison, with the support of Sandia Labs, the U.S. Department of Energy, the Los Angeles Department of Water and Power, and the California Energy Commission. Rated at ten megawatts of power, Solar One could efficiently and cost-effectively store energy, making it unique among solar technologies. Solar One operated successfully from 1982 to 1988.

A solar power tower operates by focusing a field of thousands of mirrors (heliostats) onto a receiver located at the top of a centrally located tower. The receiver collects the sun's heat in a heat-transfer liquid. This liquid is used to generate steam for a conventional steam turbine, which then produces electricity at the base of the tower. The mirrors of Solar One reflected and focused sunlight onto a central tower that was nearly 100 meters (328 feet) tall. The tower's absorber panels, which were painted black, absorbed 88 to 96 percent of the incident light. In order to capture sunlight from the south, the field of mirrors was oriented mostly toward the north. Solar energy was focused onto six panels to preheat the water that traveled to eighteen superheat panels.

After leaving the superheat panels, the water was at 510 degrees Celsius (950 degrees Fahrenheit). The hot water was sent either to turbines, where it generated electricity at 35 percent efficiency, or to a heat exchanger, where it heated oil that was sent to a thermal storage tank and circulated through crushed granite. The stored heat could be drawn back from the tank through the heat exchanger to produce steam for the turbine. In addition, the thermal storage allowed a buffer system for periods of cloudiness so that the plant could keep operating through changes in weather conditions.

Solar One proved that the heat-transfer liquid cycle is reliable, that the system could meet expectations, and that thermal storage is cost-effective. Furthermore, the power tower system with energy storage showed a unique advantage over other solar power systems because it could supply power to the local electrical utility company during peak periods. In Southern California, these periods occur on hot, sunny afternoons and into the evenings during the summer, when needs are high for air-conditioning of homes and workplaces and power production is most valuable to the power company.

Based on what they learned through the operation of Solar One, which used water and steam as the heat-transfer liquid, solar engineers determined that power towers operate more efficiently using molten salt. The salt also has the further advantage of providing a direct, practical way to store heat. The concept of storing energy in molten salt and decoupling solar energy collection from electricity production formed the basis for Solar Two, which operated from 1996 to 1999. The construction of Solar Two involved the conversion of Solar One from its water and steam system to a molten salt system. After Solar Two was decommissioned, the tower remained as a local landmark in the California desert until it was torn down in 2009. Construction on a third solar power tower plant, named Solar Tres, began in 2007 near Seville, Spain; the plant became operational in 2009.

Alvin K. Benson

FURTHER READING

Cassedy, Edward S. "Solar Energy Sources." In *Prospects for Sustainable Energy: A Critical Assessment.* New York: Cambridge University Press, 2000.

Gordon, Jeffrey, ed. *Solar Energy: The State of the Art.* London: James & James, 2001.

Miller, G. Tyler, Jr., and Scott Spoolman. "Energy Efficiency and Renewable Energy." In *Living in the Environment: Principles, Connections, and Solutions.* 16th ed. Belmont, Calif.: Brooks/Cole, 2009.

Naff, Clay Farris, ed. *Solar Power.* Detroit: Greenhaven Press, 2007.

Solar water heaters

CATEGORY: Energy and energy use

DEFINITION: Devices that heat water by using absorption of solar energy either exclusively or primarily

SIGNIFICANCE: Heating water by absorption of solar energy does not require any electricity or burning of fossil fuels, thus solar water heaters have extremely low environmental impacts. Even solar water heaters that use electric pumps to circulate water use far less electricity than water heaters that heat water using electricity.

Heating with sunlight is the easiest and most cost-effective method of utilizing solar energy, and humans have heated water using the sun since ancient times. The biggest drawback to solar water heating, however, has been that the sun heats most effectively during the middle of the day, and hot water is often needed in the evenings. A further difficulty is that if the heated water is not properly insulated from the environment, it will cool off on cold days. These problems, however, are fairly easily overcome by well-designed solar water heaters. Well-insulated systems can keep water warmed during the day and hot through the night and can permit water to be heated even when the outdoor temperature is quite cold.

A more difficult problem for solar water heaters to overcome is that they do not work well on cloudy days. They also do not work as effectively at very high latitudes in the winter, when there are few hours of sunlight during the day. Even in summer at high latitudes, the sun is at a low angle in the sky, reducing the effectiveness of solar water heaters. Many solar water-heating systems thus include gas- or electricity-powered backups.

TYPES

The simplest form of solar water heater is the integral collector system (ICS), which is basically a tank, often painted black, placed where the sun can shine on it during the day. This is the least effective system and is often used as a preheater for a conventional gas or electric water heater.

The most commonly installed type of solar water heater is the flat-plate collector, which consists of a series of pipes with fluid flowing through a large flat box, often insulated and with a transparent window through which the sun can heat the interior of the box and the pipes. The biggest drawback to simple ICS systems is that the warming tanks have a large volume compared with the surface area being heated. Flat-plate collectors overcome this difficulty by creating surface areas to be heated that are far larger than those of the storage tanks. In warm climates where temperatures almost never reach freezing, water can be circulated directly through the collector to be heated and then collected in an insulated storage tank that operates much like a conventional water heater. In locations where there is a risk for a freeze, a fluid resistant to freezing (such as water mixed with some sort of antifreeze) circulates in the collector and then through a set of pipes either inside the storage tank or in another tank near the storage tank. The second set of pipes in this indirect system acts as a heat exchanger to warm the water. In many systems, the storage tank has heating elements and serves as a backup heater if necessary.

In very cold climates an evacuated-tube solar collector may be used. The evacuated-tube collector is very similar to the flat-plate collector, except that the pipes in the collector are replaced by double-walled glass tubes. The space between the tubes is a vacuum, thus the loss of heat through conduction in the tubes

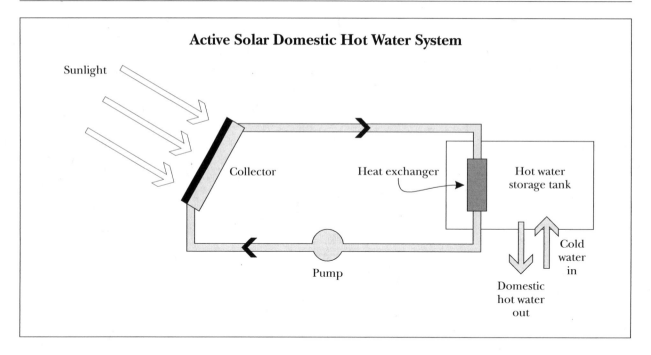

Active Solar Domestic Hot Water System

is limited, much as heat loss is limited in a vacuum Thermos bottle. Evacuated-tube systems can be either direct or indirect.

Both flat-plate and evacuated-tube collectors can be constructed as either active or passive systems. An active system uses a pump to circulate the fluid through the collectors; it is thus not a zero-energy-use system, as it requires a small amount of electricity to run the circulation pump. A passive system, in contrast, does not require any electricity. Instead, the heated fluid rises to a heat exchanger in a storage tank located above the collector. In most solar water heater installations, however, the collector is placed on a building's roof, so placement of the storage tank at a greater height than the collector is impractical. Active systems are thus more common than passive systems.

Costs of Installation and Operation

Because solar water heaters involve more plumbing than conventional systems, they are more expensive to install than conventional water heaters. The biggest cost of a conventional water heater is the tank, and a solar water heater also requires a tank in addition to other expensive components. Solar water heaters thus cost considerably more than conventional systems in terms of both parts and installation. A further reason for the high cost of solar water heaters is their comparative rarity compared with conventional water heaters. Relatively few plumbers and builders have had much experience with solar water heaters, so specialists who charge more for their services are often needed to install the systems.

ICS heaters are the least expensive solar water heaters, but they are also the least efficient. Evacuated-tube heaters are often so expensive that they are not practical except in commercial installations. Thus the flat-plate collector is the type of solar water heater most commonly used in residential systems.

Solar water heaters are much less expensive to operate than conventional water heaters, but it can still take many years for a system to save a home owner enough to cover the cost of the initial investment in the equipment. The high up-front cost is a significant deterrent to many people considering installing such systems.

Raymond D. Benge, Jr.

Further Reading

Galloway, Terry R. *Solar House: A Guide for the Solar Designer.* Burlington, Mass.: Architectural Press, 2004.

Laughton, Chris. *Solar Domestic Water Heating.* Sterling, Va.: Earthscan, 2010.

National Renewable Energy Laboratory. *Heat Your Water with the Sun.* Washington, D.C.: Government Printing Office, 2003.

Ramlow, Bob. *Solar Water Heating.* Gabriola Island, B.C.: New Society, 2006.

Strip and surface mining

CATEGORY: Resources and resource management

DEFINITION: Mining methods in which rock and soil are removed to enable extraction of the substance being mined

SIGNIFICANCE: Surface-mining methods make possible the extraction of minerals and coal from narrow seams that could not feasibly be mined using underground techniques. These methods, however, cause many different forms of damage to the environment, radically changing landscapes, blocking streams, destroying habitats, and polluting waterways.

Humans have long scraped away the surface of the land to get at the minerals and other materials underneath. For centuries this type of mining created scars on the landscape but rarely did major harm to the environment. In the twentieth century, however, surface mines became much larger and began to cause lasting environmental degradation. In some cases surface mining is the only feasible way to extract very narrow seams of coal or minerals. In addition, surface mining tends to be less hazardous for miners than underground mining and requires fewer and often less skilled workers, reducing costs. Massive surface mining is a characteristic of modern industrial society.

OPEN-PIT MINING

Minerals have long been mined using underground tunnels, but it is often more feasible to remove the dirt and rocks covering mineral deposits (the overburden) to get at them. In some cases the ore grade is so low that extensive treatment with crushers and chemicals (such as the cyanide leach process used with gold) is required. Open-pit mines are gradually expanded and deepened over time. The sides of such a mine are cut in a spiral, with benches ringing the sides so that trucks can access the material at the bottom of the pit. As the mine is deepened, seepage often becomes a problem, requiring pumping or other

The Bingham Canyon Mine, located in Utah, is the largest human-made excavation in the world. (©Gary Whitton/iStockphoto)

forms of water control to keep the mine from filling with water.

Shallow open-pit mines (often called quarries) are used to extract granite, limestone, gypsum, and clay. Some gemstones, such as diamonds, are mined in open pits such as was done in Kimberly, South Africa. Copper, nickel, iron ore, gold, and uranium are some of the minerals mined in this fashion. One of the largest open-pit mines in the world, the Hull-Rust-Mahoning Mine in Hibbing, Minnesota, has been in operation since 1895. This iron mine is 4.8 kilometers (3 miles) long, 3.2 kilometers (2 miles) wide, and 163 meters (535 feet) deep.

Starting during the early twentieth century, large open-pit copper mines began to be opened in the American West. One of the earliest was the Bingham Canyon Mine in Utah, which has been in operation since 1906. The pit of this mine covers 770 hectares (1,900 acres) and is 1.2 kilometers (0.75 miles) deep and 4 kilometers (2.5 miles) wide. By the early twenty-first century the mine had produced more than 17 million tons of copper, 190 million ounces of silver, 23 million ounces of gold, and 850 million pounds of molybdenum.

Bingham Canyon Mine is the largest human-made excavation in the world, but other copper mines are also quite large, such as the Chuquicamata in Chile, the Nchanga mines in Zambia, and the Grasberg mine in Indonesia. Although copper is a major product of these mines, some also produce other minerals, such as gold and silver. Indeed, the Grasberg mine is the largest gold mine and the third-largest copper mine (behind Chuquicamata and Bingham Canyon) in the world. Other open-pit mines, such as Kumtor in Kyrgyzstan, produce gold and uranium. Massive open-pit mines are also found in Russia, Australia, Canada, Peru, Mongolia, and Namibia. Some of these mines exist in environmentally fragile surroundings; Kumtor, for instance, is more than 4,000 meters (14,000 feet) above sea level on a high plateau, and Grasberg is located on a mountaintop near rare equatorial glaciers and in a region subject to earthquakes that produce large landslides.

Open-pit mining produces several environmental hazards. The overburden removed at an open-pit mine, which often contains hazardous chemicals, must be placed nearby. As the mine expands, it consumes nearby land. The Berkeley Pit, for example, consumed several neighborhoods in Butte, Montana. In addition, the processing of the material

taken from an open-pit mine often involves treating it with acid, which leads to extensive runoff. The acidic runoff, dissolved copper, and other materials from processing at the Grasberg mine, for example, wash into two rivers that are the water sources for several communities, and some of it ultimately reaches the ocean, a situation that will continue long after the mine is closed.

When mining ceases at an open-pit mine, the pit often becomes flooded, producing a large lake that is highly acidic. The Berkeley Pit in Montana provides an example of this process. The mine opened in 1955 and closed in 1982. Since 1982 water has filled the mine to within 46 meters (150 feet) of the natural groundwater level. The water contains several heavy metals, such as arsenic and cadmium, and is highly acidic (a pH of 2.5). A water diversion project has been established to keep the acidic water in the Berkeley Pit from entering the water supplies of Butte and surrounding communities. The U.S. Environmental Protection Agency has listed the Berkeley Pit as a site that requires massive cleanup efforts under the provisions of the Comprehensive Environmental Response, Compensation, and Liability Act of 1980, commonly known as Superfund.

STRIP MINING

The process of mining shallow deposits of coal and tar sands often involves the removal of the overburden. In the most common form of strip mining, the overburden is removed and placed in the excavation left by the previous strip. Contour mining involves removing land along the contour of the land and usually produces terraces on a mountainside. Massive pieces of equipment are used in strip mining, such as draglines, which remove the surface layer, and earthmovers, often two stories tall, which move the surface or coal.

Coal is strip-mined around the world. In the United States strip mining is used to remove surface coal seams in all parts of the country. The largest U.S. strip mines are found in the Powder River basin in northeast Wyoming and southeastern Montana. Unlike coal in other parts of the country, such as West Virginia, the Powder River coal lies close to the surface. The Powder River coal deposits are some of the largest in the world, and by 1988 Wyoming was producing more coal than any other U.S. state.

As energy companies seek out new sources of oil, oil-impregnated sands, known as oil sands or tar sands, are increasingly seen as sources of oil. Rising oil prices have made it cost-effective to, in essence, mine oil. One of the largest deposits of tar sands in the world is found in the Athabasca River basin in Alberta, Canada. In addition to endangering a fragile environment, the strip mining of these tar sands requires large amounts of energy to "crack" the oil and remove it from the sand.

MOUNTAINTOP REMOVAL

A variant on surface mining for coal that has come to be adopted in parts of West Virginia, Kentucky, and southern Ohio is mountaintop removal, a mining method in which explosives are used on mountain-sides to remove the overburden, which is then pushed into adjoining valleys. This approach allows miners to reach deeper into the earth than does conventional strip mining. In some cases not only are whole mountains removed but also the remaining earth is excavated.

Mountaintop removal drastically changes landscapes as whole mountains are destroyed and valleys are filled with overburden. Streams are often buried in the process, and sometimes large lakes are created in what remains of the valleys; the water in such lakes is highly acidic and contains heavy metals. Critics of mountaintop removal point out that the plant and animal species that live in mountain valleys, some of which are quite rare, are endangered by this mining method. In parts of West Virginia and Kentucky the environment has been changed permanently as mountains have been leveled by mining. In the Appalachia region mountaintop removal has damaged the water sources of several communities. In addition, the explosions that are part of this kind of mining can be dangerous to local people and structures, and the sulfur compounds in the dust created by the explosions poses a health hazard.

The Surface Mining Control and Reclamation Act of 1977 requires that the owners of any surface-mined land in the United States restore the land after mining operations have ceased, but with mountaintop removal this is not completely possible, as large flat areas of land are created where mountains once existed. The reclamation of some of these areas has taken the form of the creation of golf courses or industrial sites.

Material Handled at U.S. Mines, by Type
(million metric tons)

	SURFACE MINING			UNDERGROUND MINING		
	CRUDE ORE	WASTE	TOTAL	CRUDE ORE	WASTE	TOTAL
2002	3,880	1,460	5,330	123	3	126
2003	3,930	1,430	5,360	121	1	122
2004	4,190	1,470	5,650	153	2	155
2005	4,300	1,420	5,720	156	2	158
2006	4,450	1,320	5,760	144	3	147

Source: Data from U.S. Geological Survey, *Minerals Yearbook, 2006.*
Note: Because data are rounded, they may not exactly total to figures shown.

MINING AND INDUSTRIAL PROGRESS

Access to coal and to minerals such as copper and gold is essential for modern industrial society. Achieving this access cheaply is also an important ingredient for economic development. In some cases access helps to reduce environmental problems, such as the strip mining of the Powder River basin's low-sulfur coal to replace high-sulfur coal and reduce emissions of sulfur dioxide into the atmosphere. Some surface-mining approaches seem to be the only economically feasible way of acquiring certain minerals or energy sources that are essential to industrial society.

Nonetheless, an important drawback to surface mining is the extensive environmental degradation that often occurs during the mining process and after mines have ceased operations. In addition to the environmental damage posed by mining itself, many sites where deposits of desirable minerals or coal are located are heavily timbered and must be cleared before mining can begin; such deforestation destroys plant and animal habitats, contributes to global warming, and leads to soil erosion. Mining companies often opt for the cheapest approaches to resource extraction, even though these approaches may produce higher levels of environmental harm than other approaches.

Some countries have placed extensive regulations on surface mining of all kinds, with the aim of limiting the environmental damage such mining can do, whereas regulations in other nations are minimal. In the United States, the Surface Mining Control and Reclamation Act requires that owners of surface mine sites reclaim the land at least to some degree when mining has ended. Other laws limit the damage that mining operations are allowed to do to streams and endangered species. Debates are ongoing, however, regarding how effective these laws have been, especially after the presidential administration of George W. Bush weakened the application of some of the laws.

The societal dilemma posed by surface mining is that such mining is essential for economic progress yet often results in environmental harm. Further, the costs of this harm are not always shared equitably—industrialized nations frequently profit from surface mining that is conducted in developing countries, which often bear most of the costs of the environmental damage.

John M. Theilmann

FURTHER READING

Goodell, Jeff. *Big Coal: The Dirty Secret Behind America's Energy Future.* New York: Houghton Mifflin, 2006.

LeCain, Timothy J. *Mass Destruction: The Men and Giant Mines That Wired America and Scarred the Planet.* New Brunswick, N.J.: Rutgers University Press, 2009.

Lynch, Martin. *Mining in World History.* London: Reaktion Books, 2002.

McQuaid, John. "Mining the Mountains." *Smithsonian,* January, 2009, 74-85.

Montrie, Chad. *To Save the Land and People: A History of Opposition to Surface Coal Mining in Appalachia.* Chapel Hill: University of North Carolina Press, 2003.

Power, Thomas Michael. *Lost Landscapes and Failed Economies: The Search for a Value of Place.* Washington, D.C.: Island Press, 1996.

Shnayerson, Michael. *Coal River.* New York: Farrar, Straus and Giroux, 2008.

Superphénix

CATEGORIES: Nuclear power and radiation; energy and energy use

IDENTIFICATION: A fast-breeder nuclear reactor located near Lyon, France

DATES: Operated from December, 1985, to December, 1996

SIGNIFICANCE: The technological problems that arose during the years that the Superphénix nuclear reactor was in operation, as well as the finan-

cial consequences of those problems, contributed to a loss of confidence in the development of commercial fast-breeder reactors in other nations.

After twelve years of construction, the Superphénix nuclear reactor, a 1,240-megawatt fast breeder, went into operation in Creys-Malville in the Lyon area of France in December, 1985. Breeder reactors maximize the production of new fuel by using surplus neutrons not required to sustain the fission chain reaction to produce more fissionable fuels, such as plutonium. However, the Superphénix breeder was continually plagued by accidents and incidents during the years it was in use, and it operated at full power for a total of only 278 days. The reactor's cooling system, which used liquid sodium, repeatedly suffered costly shutdowns because of leaks. In addition, low uranium prices undercut the value of the plutonium fuel produced by Superphénix.

In 1994 it was decided that Superphénix would be converted from a breeder into a burner of plutonium and that the facility would be used only as a research tool. Consequently, on July 11, 1994, the license under which the facility operated was changed to reflect the fact that Superphénix was no longer a power reactor; it was licensed to operate as a research reactor for the demonstration of burning nuclear waste in breeder reactors. Superphénix was closed temporarily in December, 1996, for repair, maintenance, and reconstruction, with the plan to restart it in June, 1997. Based on procedural grounds, however, the reactor license was canceled in February, 1997. On June 6, Europeans Against Superphénix, a confederation of 250 environmental and antinuclear groups, demanded that Superphénix be shut down permanently. Subsequently, on June 19 newly elected French prime minister Lionel Jospin announced in his general policy statement to the parliament that operations at the Superphénix breeder reactor would be discontinued for economic reasons. Running Superphénix had cost France billions of dollars, and the nation had gained only approximately six months of electricity in return. The final announcement of the closure of Superphénix came on February 2, 1998. Many of the residents of Creys-Malville protested the shutdown; the facility had provided some thirteen hundred jobs in a town of twelve thousand people.

The dismantling of Superphénix was scheduled to begin in 2005 and was predicted to cost about $1.76

billion. However, since France's huge nuclear power industry generates 80 percent of the country's power, many groups lobbied for the Superphénix facility to remain standing. The closure of Superphénix made necessary a review and revision of the French breeder and plutonium recycling programs. The shutdown struck a serious blow to the French breeder program and raised questions about breeder programs in other countries, particularly Japan, India, and Russia.

Alvin K. Benson

FURTHER READING

Garwin, Richard L., and Georges Charpak. *Megawatts and Megatons: The Future of Nuclear Power and Nuclear Weapons.* Chicago: University of Chicago Press, 2001.

Murray, Raymond L. *Nuclear Energy: An Introduction to the Concepts, Systems, and Applications of Nuclear Processes.* 6th ed. Burlington, Vt.: Butterworth-Heinemann/Elsevier, 2009.

Synthetic fuels

CATEGORY: Energy and energy use

DEFINITION: Solid, liquid, or gaseous sources of energy that do not occur naturally

SIGNIFICANCE: Given the finite nature of the world's stores of natural petroleum, the development of economically viable, environmentally safe, and renewable synthetic fuels is important for human survival.

Synthetic fuels are normally produced from abundantly occurring natural resources such as coal, tar sands, oil shale, and biomass. One of the main objectives in the production of a synthetic fuel is to eliminate sulfur and nitrogen from the fuel compound, thereby creating an environmentally clean energy source. Oxides of nitrogen and sulfur dioxide are among the most undesirable of common air pollutants. Sulfur dioxide is one of the major causes of acid rain, which is created when sulfur dioxide combines with water vapor in the atmosphere to form sulfuric acid. Similarly, oxides of nitrogen produce nitric acid. These acids fall back to earth in rain and are detrimental to aquatic life as well as botanical life. Synthetic fuel manufacturers thus strive to eliminate these pollutants, as well as others such as carbon monoxide, hydrocarbons, particulates, and photochemical oxidants, from the fuel supply.

PRINCIPLES OF SYNTHETIC FUEL MANUFACTURE

The manufacture of liquid and gaseous synthetic fuels normally involves transforming naturally occurring carbonaceous raw material through a suitable conversion process. The techniques employed include hydrogenation, devolatilization, decomposition, and fermentation. The principal aim in the manufacture of synthetic fuel is to achieve a low carbon-to-hydrogen atomic mass ratio, or a high hydrogen-to-carbon atomic ratio, whenever possible. This results in a clean-burning fuel that releases by-products that are harmless to the environment. For example, pure methane (CH_4), with a molecular weight of 16, has a high hydrogen-to-carbon ratio of 4:1. Methane gas is a common component that is absorbed into coal. The method used to release the gas involves fracturing the coal and exposing it to low pressures. Coal-bed methane is one of the cleanest-burning fossil fuels; the by-products of burning it are simply carbon dioxide and water. Synthetically generated substitute natural gas is more than 90 percent methane. Natural gas (of which methane is the chief constituent) has a hydrogen-to-carbon ratio of approximately 3.4:1, which is also quite high. The ratios for liquefied petroleum gas and for naphtha lie between 2:1 and 3:1. (In comparison, the ratios for gasoline and fuel oil are less than 2:1. Bituminous coal has one of the lowest values, with ratio of much less than 1:1.)

COAL GASIFICATION AND LIQUEFACTION

Although coal is among the most abundant natural energy sources, it is also among the dirtiest. The composition of this solid fossil fuel is a major disadvantage; it consists of about 70 percent carbon and about 5 percent hydrogen, translating to a highly undesirable carbon-to-hydrogen mass ratio of 14:1. Coal-burning power-generating stations thus spew out large quantities of gases that are harmful to the environment. Despite the use of such emission-reducing devices as electrostatic precipitators, the levels of pollutants emitted by coal-burning plants remain high. Techniques such as coal gasification and coal liquefaction yield synthetic fuels that are safer for the environment.

The process of coal gasification involves making coal react with steam at very high temperatures (in the range of 1,000 degrees Celsius, or 1,832 degrees

Fahrenheit). This process produces synthetic gas. Three types of synthetic gas are in common use. Low-calorific-value gas (also called producer gas) is used in turbines. Medium-calorific-value gas (also called power gas) is used as a fuel gas by various industries. High-calorific-value gas (also called pipeline gas) is a very good substitute for natural gas and is well suited to economical pipeline transportation. Pipeline gas contains more than 90 percent methane; as a result, it has a high hydrogen-to-carbon ratio.

The process of coal liquefaction is employed to generate a liquid fuel with a high hydrogen-to-carbon ratio; it is also used to obtain low-sulfur fuel oil. Several methods are employed to accomplish coal liquefaction, including direct catalytic hydrogenation, indirect catalytic hydrogenation, pyrolysis, and solvent extraction. All of these methods produce fuels that are much safer for the environment than the original coal.

Tar Sands and Oil Shale

Naturally occurring tar sands contain grains of sand, water, and bitumen. Bitumen, a member of the petroleum family, is a high-viscosity crude hydrocarbon. A method known as hot water extraction is used to procure bitumen from tar sands. The bitumen is subsequently upgraded to synthetic crude oil in refineries. Synthetic crude oil (also called syncrude) is similar to petroleum and can be obtained through coal liquefaction as well as from tar sands and oil shale.

Large deposits of tar sands are found in Alberta, Canada; the United States has huge reserves of oil shale in Utah, Wyoming, and Colorado. Oil shale is probably the most abundant form of hydrocarbon on earth. Oil shale is a sedimentary rock that contains kerogen, which is not a member of the petroleum family. A popular method known as retorting is used to produce oil from shale. The process involves the method of pyrolysis, which reduces the carbon content in the raw hydrocarbon through distillation. Because the process is costly, however, the production of shale oil has not provided an economically feasible alternative to petroleum.

Biomass Fuels and Gasohol

Like oil and coal, biomass is derived from plant life. Oil and coal, however, are considered nonrenewable resources, as it takes vast periods of time for geologic processes to produce these materials naturally. Be-cause biomass consists of any material that is derived from plant life, it is produced in far shorter spans—one hundred years or less—and is thus considered renewable. Wood is the most versatile biomass resource; farm and agricultural wastes, municipal wastes, and animal wastes are also considered to be biomass. Biomass can be processed into fuel using a variety of methods. Fermentation, for example, yields ethanol, or ethyl alcohol (sometimes called grain alcohol). Other methods include combustion, gasification, and pyrolysis.

Gasohol is a mixture of gasoline and small quantities of ethanol. The mixture burns cleaner than conventional gasoline; however, it can cause damage to plastic and rubber materials used in automobile engines. In the United States, therefore, the Environmental Protection Agency (EPA) permits the addition of only 10 percent ethanol by volume to gasoline to create gasohol. Methanol, or methyl alcohol (also called wood alcohol), can also be combined with conventional gasoline to produce cleaner fuel; however, the EPA limits the amount of methane in such mixtures to 3 percent.

Other Fuels

A nonpolluting rocket fuel based on alcohol and hydrogen peroxide has been developed by U.S. Navy research engineers at China Lake, California. This nontoxic homogeneous miscible fuel (NHMF) can be modified and used to drive turbines, which in turn drive alternators that produce electricity. Further developments based on what has been learned about this fuel may permit its use in automobiles. During World War II, moreover, Germany produced synthetic fuels in large quantities to meet its energy demands, employing coal gasification and also creating diesel oil and aviation kerosene using a reconstitution process; this process is still in use in many places.

Although the present abundance of natural petroleum limits the economic competitiveness of most synthetic fuels, the finite nature of the world's oil supply virtually ensures that synthetic fuels will become increasingly important energy sources. The U.S. Department of Energy and governmental agencies in many other countries thus provide funding to encourage research into the creation of economically viable, environmentally safe, and renewable synthetic fuels.

Mysore Narayanan

FURTHER READING

Deutch, John M., and Richard K. Lester. "Synthetic Fuels." In *Making Technology Work: Applications in Energy and the Environment.* New York: Cambridge University Press, 2004.

Lorenzetti, Maureen Shields. *Alternative Motor Fuels: A Nontechnical Guide.* Tulsa, Okla: PennWell, 1996.

Manahan, Stanley E. "Adequate, Sustainable Energy: Key to Sustainability." In *Environmental Science and Technology: A Sustainable Approach to Green Science and Technology.* 2d ed. Boca Raton, Fla.: CRC Press, 2007.

Miller, G. Tyler, Jr., and Scott Spoolman. "Nonrenewable Energy." In *Living in the Environment: Principles, Connections, and Solutions.* 16th ed. Belmont, Calif.: Brooks/Cole, 2009.

Speight, James G. *Synthetic Fuels Handbook: Properties, Process, and Performance.* New York: McGraw-Hill, 2008.

Tennessee Valley Authority

CATEGORIES: Organizations and agencies; energy and energy use

IDENTIFICATION: A federal corporation authorized to generate, transmit, and sell electric power through municipal distributors and rural electric cooperatives

DATE: Established in 1933

SIGNIFICANCE: The Tennessee Valley Authority's building of twenty-nine dams on the Tennessee River brought many improvements to the river basin while at the same time making unprecedented alterations to the natural environment.

Established by the Tennessee Valley Authority Act of 1933, the Tennessee Valley Authority (TVA) was, by 1945, the largest electrical utility in the United States. In addition to its original hydroelectric capability, the TVA later also invested in solar thermal-electric, nuclear, and other kinds of power plants, giving it the capacity by 2010 to produce 164 billion kilowatt-hours of electricity annually and provide electric power to some nine million customers.

The Tennessee River stretches for 1,049 kilometers (652 miles) and drains most of the state of Tennessee and parts of six other states. The TVA provided for the maximum development of the Tennessee River basin in what has been referred to as the most comprehensive environmental program in history. In addition to providing inexpensive and abundant electric power, the TVA undertook dam building to control the floods that periodically devastated the basin and to increase the navigation potential of the Tennessee River. With its system of locks and dams, the river is now navigable from Knoxville, Tennessee, to its junction with the Ohio River at Paducah, Kentucky. Other goals of the TVA were to encourage good conservation practices, to institute agricultural programs, to improve air and water quality, to attract industry and commerce, and to increase resource development, all of which would generally improve the quality of life for the residents of the region. During World War II and throughout the Cold War era, the TVA provided the energy for aluminum processing factories and uranium enrichment facilities.

To accomplish its purposes, the TVA built a total of twenty-nine dams on the Tennessee River and its tributaries; the largest is Kentucky Dam, and the highest, at 146 meters (480 feet), is Fontana Dam. The TVA dams are of two types: high dams with large reservoir capacities, which were constructed on the tributaries to provide flood protection and electric power generation, and low, broad dams on the Tennessee River designed to control navigation. To construct the first sixteen TVA dams between 1933 and 1944, the federal government purchased or condemned 445,000 hectares (1.1 million acres) of land and moved fourteen thousand families.

Donald J. Thompson

FURTHER READING

Andrews, Richard N. L. *Managing the Environment, Managing Ourselves: A History of American Environmental Policy.* 2d ed. New Haven, Conn.: Yale University Press, 2006.

Billington, David P., and Donald C. Jackson. *Big Dams of the New Deal Era: A Confluence of Engineering and Politics.* Norman: University of Oklahoma Press, 2006.

Black, Brian. "Referendum on Planning: Imaging River Conservation in the 1938 TVA Hearings." In *FDR and the Environment,* edited by David Woolner and Henry L. Henderson. New York: Palgrave Macmillan, 2005.

Three Mile Island nuclear accident

CATEGORIES: Disasters; nuclear power and radiation

THE EVENT: Malfunction at the Metropolitan Edison nuclear power plant at Three Mile Island on the Susquehanna River near Harrisburg, Pennsylvania

DATE: March 28, 1979

SIGNIFICANCE: The accident at Three Mile Island exposed serious weaknesses in U.S. nuclear power plant operations, as well as in government oversight of the nuclear power industry, and prompted reforms intended to prevent such accidents in the future.

Metropolitan Edison's nuclear power plant at Three Mile Island (TMI) was designed with two pressurized water reactors, units 1 and 2, that generated electric power by boiling water into steam that spun the blades of a turbine generator. The heat to convert water to steam was produced by fission of uranium in the reactors' cores. These were submerged in water and encapsulated in a containment building 12 meters (40 feet high), with walls of steel 20 centimeters (8 inches) thick. Because the radioactive coolant water was under pressure, it could be superheated to 302 degrees Celsius (575 degrees Fahrenheit) without boiling. When it reached that temperature, it was pumped to a steam generator, where, in a secondary system and under less pressure, it heated cooler water to steam, which spun turbine blades and propelled a generator. The steam then passed through a condenser, where it changed back to water and began the circuit back to the steam generator.

THE ACCIDENT

At 4:00 A.M. on Wednesday, March 28, a valve in the system inexplicably closed, interrupting the water supply to the steam system. The main water pumps automatically shut down, which decreased the steam pressure and shut down the steam turbine a few seconds later. This interrupted the transfer of heat from the reactor cooling system, where the pressure began to rise. A pressurizer relief valve opened, which reduced some of the pressure but also allowed radioactive water and steam to drain into a tank designed to hold excess water. The valve should have shut off after thirteen seconds; however, it remained open for more than two hours, during which time the primary coolant water continued to drain.

Less than one minute later, emergency backup pumps automatically engaged to maintain the water supply in the secondary system. No water was actually added, however, because two valves that controlled the flow had been closed for routine maintenance two days earlier. (Nuclear Regulatory Commission rules required that a plant be shut down if these valves remained closed for more than seventy-two hours.) Instead, two minutes into the crisis, as the temperature continued to rise and steam pressure declined, the emergency core coolant system began to operate, adding water to the reactor core.

There were no meters to measure the depth of water in the reactor core, but the technicians believed that sufficient water was present. To prevent the pressure in the primary cooling system from rising too high, they turned off one emergency pump and a few minutes later reduced the other one to half speed. This would have been proper procedure if the system had indeed been filled with water. In fact, the reactor core was not covered with water, and temperatures continued to rise.

At eight and one-half minutes into the crisis, technicians opened valves to fill the secondary system with water and draw heat away from the primary system. With the relief valve stuck open, however, the primary cooling water was still draining into the excess water tank, which overflowed and spilled its radioactive contents onto the containment building's floor. This activated suction pumps, which removed the water to a tank in the nearby auxiliary building. This tank too overflowed, and at 4:38 A.M., radioactive gases began to be released into the atmosphere.

By this time, the fuel rods in the reactor, which should have been covered with water, had become exposed. With no cooling system in operation, temperatures had continued to rise, leading to a partial melting of reactor fuel; the zirconium shields around the rods reacted with the steam and released radioactive debris and hydrogen, which collected in the containment building. At 6:50 A.M., a general emergency was declared.

Early Wednesday afternoon, some of the hydrogen in the containment building exploded. Hydrogen continued to be created by the exposed fuel rods, giving rise to fears that the hydrogen bubble at the top of the reactor building could self-ignite and result in a meltdown. Controlled and uncontrolled radiation leaks from the plant continued through March 28 and 29. Lack of information, poor communication among

Three Mile Island, Pennsylvania

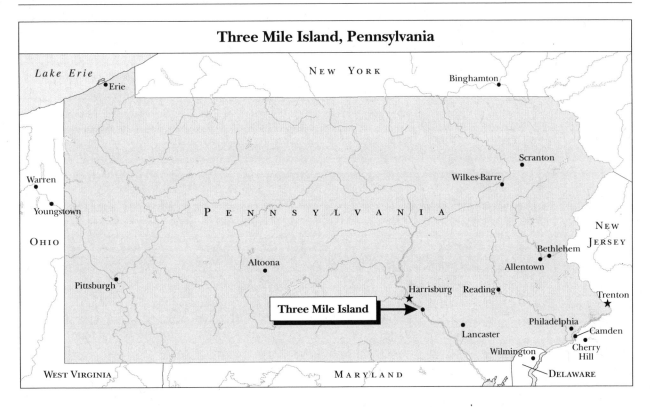

the numerous agencies involved, and some degree of sensationalist news reporting fueled mounting public alarm. On Friday, March 30, Governor Richard Thornburgh ordered an evacuation of pregnant women and small children living within five miles of the facility. Administrators considered ordering a general evacuation but feared that doing so might set off a panic and result in more injuries than it would prevent. Finally, on Sunday, April 1, when President Jimmy Carter visited the facility, it was announced that the hydrogen bubble had shrunk and no longer posed a danger.

Effects

The Three Mile Island accident exposed weaknesses in U.S. nuclear power plant design, management, and operation; in U.S. emergency preparedness; and in the workings of the Nuclear Regulatory Commission (NRC). The matter was investigated by a presidential commission and congressional committees and internally in the nuclear industry. An immediate response to the event was the closing of seven reactors similar to those at TMI and a delay in restarting others that had been shut down for maintenance. The NRC, which was eventually completely restructured, placed a temporary moratorium on the licensing of all new nuclear reactors; several reactor projects were canceled outright. Other countries reassessed their nuclear industries; Japan closed one reactor and postponed restarting nine others. In addition, the event mobilized the campaign of opponents to nuclear power worldwide. Longer-term results included changes to the design and operation of all nuclear power plants in the United States.

The TMI accident prompted widespread reconsideration of nuclear power and a reassessment of its relatively low economic cost in light of its risks, which were tragically demonstrated by the 1986 nuclear disaster at Chernobyl. Perhaps the most lasting effect of the TMI crisis was on the general public's faith in industry and government representatives. The actions of Metropolitan Edison and government officials during the crisis made it clear that their first priority had been not the health and safety of the public but rather the safeguarding of their own and the plant's reputations. Projections about the potential results of a nuclear disaster and uncertainty about the long-term health effects of radiation contributed to growing public mistrust and increasing militancy on the part of opponents of the nuclear industry.

John R. Tate

FURTHER READING

Cantelon, Philip L., and Robert C. Williams. *Crisis Contained: The Department of Energy at Three Mile Island.* Carbondale: Southern Illinois University Press, 1982.

Del Tredici, Robert. *The People of Three Mile Island.* San Francisco: Sierra Club Books, 1980.

Gray, Mike, and Ira Rosen. *The Warning: Accident at Three Mile Island.* New York: W. W. Norton, 2003.

Osif, Bonnie A., Anthony J. Baratta, and Thomas W. Conkling. *TMI Twenty-five Years Later: The Three Mile Island Nuclear Power Plant Accident and Its Impact.* University Park: Pennsylvania State University Press, 2004.

Walker, J. Samuel. *Three Mile Island: A Nuclear Crisis in Historical Perspective.* Berkeley: University of California Press, 2004.

Tidal energy

CATEGORY: Energy and energy use

DEFINITION: Power generated during the rise and fall of the tides

SIGNIFICANCE: The energy generated during the rise and fall of the tides may be cleanly and safely converted into electrical power, but large-scale tidal power installations can have severe consequences for the environment, including decimation of fisheries; destruction of the feeding grounds of migrating birds; damage to shellfish populations; interference with ship travel, port facilities, and recreational boating; and disruption of the tidal cycle over a wide area.

Tidal power projects can be important sources of local electricity generation because they produce energy that is free, clean, and renewable; they produce neither air pollution nor thermal pollution, and they do not consume exhaustible natural resources. Only a limited number of places in the world offer the potential for such power installations, however, because a vertical tidal rise of 5 meters (16.4 feet) or more is required. Installations must also be near major population centers so that transmission requirements are minimized, and a natural bay or river estuary is required to store a large amount of water with a minimum of expense for dam construction. The seawater impounded behind the dam at high tide produces a hydrostatic head so that electricity is generated as the water passes through the dam's turbines when sea level falls. If the turbines in the dam are reversible, power can be generated on both incoming and outgoing tides.

Tidal power plants have been constructed on the Rance River near St. Malo, France (240 megawatts of power), on the Annapolis River in Nova Scotia, Canada (20 megawatts), on the Yalu River in the People's Republic of China (3.2 megawatts), in Kislaya Guba, Russia (1.7 megawatts), and on Strangford Lough in Northern Ireland (1.2 megawatts). In the first decades of the twenty-first century, South Korea began construction of a plant on Sihwa Lake (254 megawatts) and planned to build several more around the country. The Rance River plant, which has been in continuous operation since November, 1966, was for many years the world's largest tidal power installation. It bridges the estuary with a dam nearly 0.8 kilometer (0.5 mile) long and provides power for 300,000 people.

The environmental impacts of the Rance River dam have generally been limited to the modification of fish species distributions, the disappearance of some sandbanks, and the creation of high-speed currents near the sluices and the powerhouse. Tidal patterns have also changed, with the maximum average rise reduced from about 13.4 meters to 12.8 meters (44 feet to 42 feet) and a corresponding increase in the height of the mean low-tide level.

The environmental impacts of the smaller Annapolis River plant in Nova Scotia, which became operational in 1984, reportedly have included the generation of silt, which destroyed clam beds in the basin behind the dam, and increased erosion of the river's banks. The Nova Scotia Power Corporation reached a settlement with one nearby landowner whose house suffered a cracked foundation and shifted toward the river as a result of erosion.

Several tidal power projects were proposed for the United States during the early and mid-twentieth century but were never built because of environmental concerns. A proposed tidal power plant on the upper Saint John River in Maine was halted, for example, because damming the river would have destroyed a unique stand of a rare wildflower. The flower was later found growing elsewhere. Objections cited for other projects included possible effects on historic and archaeological sites, as well as presumed economic and social impacts on Native American communities such as the Passamaquoddy.

Shortly after the dramatic jump in world oil prices during the 1970's, the Tidal Power Corporation, a venture owned by the Nova Scotia government, proposed building a major tidal power project in the Bay of Fundy, which lies between Nova Scotia and New Brunswick in eastern Canada. This plant would have been the world's largest tidal power installation, producing 4,560 megawatts of power—nearly twenty times the output of the Rance River plant and more than three times the output of Hoover Dam on the Colorado River in the United States. A major feature of the project was to be a dam 8.5 kilometers (5.3 miles) long across the Bay of Fundy, which has the largest tidal range in the world, averaging more than 15 meters (50 feet). The enormous scope of the project forced scientists to pay close attention to its anticipated environmental consequences, and these appeared to be so severe that the project was never begun.

Disrupted bird migrations were predicted after the dam's completion because of the submersion of tidal mudflats where large numbers of semipalmated sandpipers and other shorebirds annually gorge on mud shrimp before beginning their fall migrations to wintering grounds in South America and the Caribbean. Damage to fish stocks was also predicted because of repeated passage of the fish through the dam's turbines as the tides rose and fell. Particularly affected would have been the American shad, a member of the herring family, which migrates to the Bay of Fundy each year from as far away as Florida in order to fatten itself on mysid shrimp living on the tidal mudflats. Oceanographers also used computer modeling to show that dam construction would alter tidal patterns over a broad area, resulting in tidal levels 10 percent higher and lower as far south as Cape Cod, Massachusetts, 400 kilometers (250 miles) away. They predicted that these tidal changes would flood coastal lands and threaten roads, bridges, waterfront homes, water wells, sewage systems, salt marsh areas, harbors, and docking areas along the entire coast.

Donald W. Lovejoy

FURTHER READING

Charlier, R. H., and C. W. Finkl. *Ocean Energy: Tide and Tidal Power.* London: Springer, 2009.

Cruz, João, ed. *Ocean Wave Energy: Current Status and Future Perspectives.* New York: Springer, 2008.

Hardisty, Jack. *The Analysis of Tidal Stream Power.* New York: John Wiley & Sons, 2009.

McKinney, Michael L., Robert M. Schoch, and Logan Yonavjak. *Environmental Science: Systems and Solutions.* 4th ed. Sudbury, Mass.: Jones and Bartlett, 2007.

Peppas, Lynne. *Ocean, Tidal, and Wave Energy: Power from the Sea.* New York: Crabtree, 2008.

Trans-Alaska Pipeline

CATEGORY: Energy and energy use

IDENTIFICATION: Pipeline built to transport oil across Alaska from Prudhoe Bay to Valdez

DATE: Completed in July, 1977

SIGNIFICANCE: The plan to construct an oil pipeline across Alaska presented many technical challenges that exemplify the potential conflicts between supplying energy for human needs and protecting the environment.

In December, 1967, oil was first discovered during test drilling at Prudhoe Bay on the North Slope of Alaska. It soon became evident that this was the largest petroleum field in the United States. However, transporting the oil from Prudhoe Bay to a port at Valdez, on the southern coast of Alaska, would require the construction of a pipeline that would traverse 1,000 kilometers (620 miles) of federal land. The U.S. Geological Survey (USGS) was assigned the task of conducting an environmental impact assessment for the proposed project.

After an exhaustive investigation, the federal agency recommended against construction on the trans-Alaska route. Its objections were technical, geological, and ecological. The route crossed difficult terrain in an Arctic region where local environmental damage could be severe and long lasting. The geological hazards included active earthquake fault zones in southern Alaska, mountains (the Brooks Range in the north and the Alaska Range in the south), thirty rivers (many of which flood periodically), and unstable soil and permafrost (permanently frozen soil). Construction, subsequent pipeline operation, and potential accidental rupture or spillage would disturb the ground, water, fragile vegetation, and wildlife, including migratory routes of land species such as caribou.

In addition, transporting the oil southward from Valdez would require oil tankers to face the hazards of

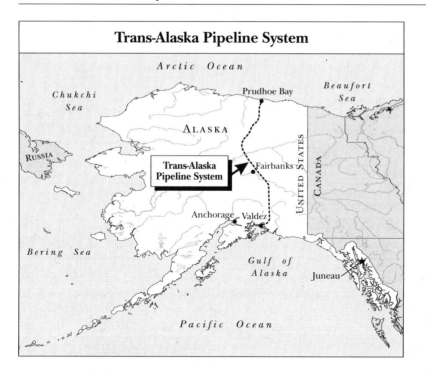

Trans-Alaska Pipeline System

pipeline can deliver oil at a rate of 1.6 million barrels per day. The oil revenues for Alaska from state taxes have enabled the state to abolish its personal income tax and to distribute substantial annual cash dividends to all state residents.

Because the Arctic ecology, with its fragile plant and animal life and slow recovery, is particularly susceptible to damage from pipeline breaks and crude oil leaks, efforts were made during construction and have been made in subsequent pipeline monitoring to minimize any spillage. Despite these attempts, some incidents have occurred, a few caused by acts of vandalism. In June, 1981, a valve ruptured and spilled some 5,000 barrels of oil onto the soil. Corrosion in feeder pipelines caused a spill of some 6,000 barrels of oil in March, 2006. By far the greatest environmental and ecological damage related to the pipeline, however, although not caused by it directly, occurred in March, 1989, when the *Exxon Valdez* supertanker, loaded with more than 1.2 million barrels of crude oil from the pipeline, ran aground in Prince William Sound and spilled more than 240,000 barrels (10 million U.S. gallons) of oil into the water. This was one of the worst environmental disasters in the history of the United States, not only for the extent of the contamination and its impact on wildlife and fishing but also because of the remote location and Arctic climate, which made cleanup and reclamation particularly difficult.

Robert S. Carmichael

docking in the Arctic and the possibility of spills and pollution. The USGS favored a longer inland pipeline route through Canada to refineries in Chicago, Illinois. Others, however, wanted to keep the construction and its economic benefits within Alaska and within U.S. territory. The USGS recommendation was overruled, and the U.S. Congress exempted the pipeline project from the law requiring a favorable environmental impact statement before work could begin.

Construction on the pipeline, which was projected to cost $900 million, was started in April, 1974, by a consortium of eight major oil companies named the Alyeska Pipeline Company. By the time the pipeline was completed in July, 1977, costs had reached nearly $8 billion, making it the most expensive privately financed construction project in history. Part of the overrun was caused by redesign and construction techniques adopted to minimize environmental impact.

The pipeline, which is 1.2 meters (4 feet) in diameter, extends 1,300 kilometers (800 miles) from Prudhoe Bay across Alaska to Valdez Arm, an inlet off Prince William Sound on the Pacific coast. The terminus of the pipeline is across the inlet from the town of Valdez. The first supertanker was filled with oil from the pipeline at Valdez in August, 1977—almost ten years after the North Slope discovery was made. The

FURTHER READING

Coates, Peter A. *The Trans-Alaska Pipeline Controversy: Technology, Conservation, and the Frontier.* Bethlehem, Pa.: Lehigh University Press, 1991.

McBeath, Jerry. "Oil Transportation Infrastructure: The Trans-Alaska Pipeline System and the Challenge of Environmental Change." In *Smart Growth and Climate Change: Regional Development, Infrastructure, and Adaptation*, edited by Matthias Ruth. Northampton, Mass.: Edward Elgar, 2006.

Ross, Ken. *Environmental Conflict in Alaska.* Boulder: University Press of Colorado, 2000.

Trans-Siberian Pipeline

CATEGORY: Energy and energy use

IDENTIFICATION: Pipeline built to carry natural gas from the Siberian Urengoy gas field to Western Europe

DATE: Completed in 1984

SIGNIFICANCE: The building of the Trans-Siberian Pipeline through formerly pristine and fragile ecosystems resulted in serious environmental damage to those systems, and environmentalists continue to be concerned regarding the quality of the ongoing maintenance of the pipeline system.

After World War II, Europe became increasingly dependent on the oil-producing countries of the Middle East for its fuel needs. However, the Arab-Israeli conflicts of 1973 alarmed European countries and prompted them to seek other sources of energy. One alternative was to utilize larger amounts of natural gas; the use of this form of fuel more than doubled during the late 1970's. Natural gas is cheaper than oil or coal, but transporting it requires enormous initial investments of capital and technology because pipelines are the only practical means of conveyance. In such pipelines, the natural gas is moved along the pipes in liquid form by the use of strategically located compressing stations.

In 1980 West German chancellor Helmut Schmidt, after a visit to Moscow, announced a plan for the Soviets to build a Euro-Siberian gas pipeline. It would start at Urengoy, east of the Ural Mountains and near the Arctic Circle, and extend westward to West Germany, France, and Italy. Objections to building the pipeline came largely from Europe's North Atlantic Treaty Organization (NATO) ally, the United States. It was feared that if an armed conflict were to break out, the Soviets would have an undue advantage over the Western Europeans.

The plan called for a 5,790-kilometer (3,600-mile) pipeline, four times the length of the controversial Trans-Alaska Pipeline, which had just been completed. Several small cities were built to accommodate the construction workers. Preparations for extraction and construction of the pipeline, which began in the early 1980's, required technical assistance, materials, and personnel provided by the potential European customer nations. In addition to West Germany, the largest purchaser, other countries were Austria, Belgium, France, Italy, the Netherlands, and Switzerland. Construction of the pipeline began in 1982 and was completed in 1984, with a finished length of 4,500 kilometers (2,800 miles). Despite the demise of the Soviet Union in 1991, the pipeline has operated for the most part without adverse economic or political consequences.

Although successful as a political and commercial venture, the Trans-Siberian Pipeline deserves attention because of its environmental impact. The resource-rich region of Siberia includes vast areas of tundra, taiga, and other fragile ecosystems, many of them in relatively pristine condition. As a result of the extraction process, the building of roads, and related activities, significant damage occurred to the environment that will require centuries for nature to correct. Many of these environmental concerns were compounded by the collapse of the Soviet Union and the resulting economic chaos. Given the new Russian republic's need of cash and weak environmental laws, some observers expressed concern that the pipeline would not be properly maintained, thus creating the potential for considerable environmental damage. Several sections of the Trans-Siberian Pipeline have burst over its years of operation, including a major oil seepage that occurred near the port of Archangel in 1994. In 2007 two explosions occurred at different places along the pipeline.

Thomas E. Hemmerly

FURTHER READING

Miller, G. Tyler, Jr., and Scott Spoolman. "Nonrenewable Energy." In *Living in the Environment: Principles, Connections, and Solutions.* 16th ed. Belmont, Calif.: Brooks/Cole, 2009.

Tusiani, Michael D., and Gordon Shearer. *LNG: A Nontechnical Guide.* Tulsa, Okla.: PennWell Books, 2007.

Wind energy

CATEGORY: Energy and energy use

DEFINITION: Energy harnessed from moving air to produce mechanical or electrical power

SIGNIFICANCE: Wind energy is one of several non-polluting, renewable types of energy that are considered potential candidates to replace fossil fuels, which are finite in supply and produce by-products that are harmful to the environment. It has been predicted that wind and solar industries will be significant sources of new manufacturing jobs in the twenty-first century.

Human harnessing of wind energy goes back thousands of years. Historically, people used sails to harness wind energy to propel ships long before the invention of the steam engine. Wind energy has also long been used to drive windmills to grind grain, pump water for irrigation, and keep lands from being flooded with seawater. At the dawn of the twentieth century, however, as fossil fuels became cheap and widely accessible and as the usage and applications of electricity became widespread, windmills began to be neglected except by a few interested researchers and users.

Rapid increases in the prices of fossil fuels during the 1970's brought a resurgence of interest in wind energy as an alternative source of power. This led to the progressive evolution of windmills into wind turbines—wind-driven machines connected to electrical generators to produce electricity. By the beginning of the twenty-first century, the combination of practical experience, advances in technology, and scientific research had led to the sophisticated wind turbines that dot the landscapes of many countries, including Germany, Denmark, the Netherlands, South Africa, and the United States.

How Wind Turbines Work

A turbine is a machine that converts the energy that is stored in a moving fluid (such as air, water, or steam) into another form of energy (such as electricity or mechanical work). Wind turbines catch energy from the wind by using blades that are shaped like propellers. The blades are attached to a shaft and are tilted in such a way that the force of the wind on them attempts to lift each blade. The lift is only partially complete, because the shaft begins to turn before the blade rises very high above its original station. This lift effect holds true for each blade, and it is repeated over and over again. The net result is that the shaft rotates continuously as long as the speed of the wind remains above a certain threshold. The assembly consisting of the blades and the shaft to which they are attached is part of what is called the rotor.

During the early days, windmills had six or more blades. It is now known that, by carefully shaping the blades, one can use fewer of them and capture much more energy than windmills did. Thus, in modern times, turbines are equipped with only two or three blades. The wind turbine assembly is mounted onto a tall tower. As a general rule, the taller the tower, the better. This is because the higher above the ground the turbine is located, the less the wind that reaches it is disturbed or reduced by what is on the ground and by surrounding objects such as trees and buildings.

Applications and Systems

Wind energy applications can be divided into three types: stand-alone wind turbines, distributed energy systems, and turbines that are connected to utility power grids. Stand-alone systems are generally used by home owners and by small business owners—such as ranchers, farmers, and owners of small retail stores—seeking to reduce the size of their electric bills. Others use them for communications and for pumping water. Distributed energy systems are various small power generation technologies that can be grouped and combined for the purpose of improving or expanding the operation and delivery of electrical energy.

For wind turbines to be connected to a local power grid, large numbers of them, generating many megawatts of power, are needed to make the required costs of construction, operation, and maintenance worthwhile. Such arrangements are called wind farms or wind plants. Several providers of electrical power, in the United States and other nations, use wind farms to supply power to their customers.

Benefits

Research by the American Wind Energy Association indicates that two main categories of benefits are associated with the adoption of wind energy: First, the production of electricity using wind energy reduces environmental risks while enhancing health benefits; and second, the installation of wind farms spurs economic development in the areas, usually rural, where they are located.

The generation of electricity using wind energy produces little air pollution. It is estimated that extensive use of this technology could reduce total U.S. emissions of carbon dioxide, a greenhouse gas associated with global warming, by one-third. This corresponds to a reduction of 4 percent at the world level. Survey data show that forty-six of fifty states in the United States have wind resources that could be developed; thus the potential for growth in this area is very great. For example, if ten of the windiest states in the United

States were to develop 10 percent of their wind energy potential, the result would offset the carbon dioxide emissions from all U.S. power plants that burn coal.

The American Wind Energy Association estimated in 2010 that every megawatt of electrical power produced from wind energy generated $1 million in economic development. The association found that when wind energy is adopted by rural communities, local farmers and other landowners receive steady income through the lease of their land and the payment of royalties. Furthermore, the advent of wind energy operations brings new jobs to the communities where they are located. Some of these jobs are directly related to the installation and maintenance of wind turbines, whereas others come from road and building construction and from the transportation, hospitality, and services needed as the local economy changes.

Josué Njock Libii

FURTHER READING

Burton, Tony, et al. *Wind Energy Handbook.* New York: John Wiley & Sons, 2001.

Eggleston, David M., and Forrest S. Stoddard. *Wind Turbine Engineering Design.* New York: Van Nostrand Reinhold, 1987.

Gipe, Paul. *Wind Power: Renewable Energy for Home, Farm, and Business.* 2d ed. White River Junction, Vt.: Charles Green, 2004.

Hansen, Martin O. L. *Aerodynamics of Wind Turbines.* 2d ed. Sterling, Va.: Earthscan, 2008.

McKinney, Michael L., Robert M. Schoch, and Logan Yonavjak. "Renewable and Alternative Energy Sources." In *Environmental Science: Systems and Solutions.* 4th ed. Sudbury, Mass.: Jones and Bartlett, 2007.

BIBLIOGRAPHY

Ayres, Robert U., and Ed Ayres. *Crossing the Energy Divide: Moving from Fossil Fuel Dependence to a Clean-Energy Future.* Upper Saddle River, N.J.: Wharton School Publishing, 2010.

Elliott, David. *Energy, Society, and Environment.* 2d ed. New York: Routledge, 2003.

International Energy Agency. *Key World Energy Statistics 2010.* Paris: Author, 2010.

Kutz, Myer, and Ali Elkamel, eds. *Environmentally Conscious Fossil Energy Production.* Hoboken, N.J.: John Wiley & Sons, 2010.

McCully, Patrick. *Silenced Rivers: The Ecology and Politics of Large Dams.* Enlarged and updated ed. London: Zed Books, 2001.

McLean-Conner, Penni. *Energy Efficiency: Principles and Practices.* Tulsa, Okla.: PennWell, 2009.

Murray, Raymond L. *Nuclear Energy: An Introduction to the Concepts, Systems, and Applications of Nuclear Processes.* 6th ed. Burlington, Vt.: Butterworth-Heinemann/Elsevier, 2009.

National Research Council. *Electricity from Renewable Resources: Status, Prospects, and Impediments.* Washington, D.C.: National Academies Press, 2010.

Nivola, Pietro S. *The Long and Winding Road: Automotive Fuel Economy and American Politics.* Washington, D.C.: Brookings Institution Press, 2009.

O'Keefe, Philip, et al. *The Future of Energy Use.* 2d ed. Sterling, Va.: Earthscan, 2010.

Sandalow, David. *Freedom from Oil: How the Next President Can End the United States' Oil Addiction.* Columbus, Ohio: McGraw-Hill Professional, 2008.

Twidell, John, and Anthony D. Weir. *Renewable Energy Resources.* 2d ed. London: Taylor & Francis, 2006.

CATEGORY INDEX

INDEX